Subjects
AND Narratives
IN Archaeology

Subjects
AND Narratives
IN Archaeology

EDITED BY
Ruth M. Van Dyke
AND *Reinhard Bernbeck*

UNIVERSITY PRESS OF COLORADO
Boulder

© 2015 by University Press of Colorado

Published by University Press of Colorado
5589 Arapahoe Avenue, Suite 206C
Boulder, Colorado 80303

All rights reserved
Printed in the United States of America

 The University Press of Colorado is a proud member of
Association of American University Presses.

The University Press of Colorado is a cooperative publishing enterprise supported, in part,
by Adams State University, Colorado State University, Fort Lewis College, Metropolitan
State University of Denver, Regis University, University of Colorado, University of Northern
Colorado, Utah State University, and Western State Colorado University.

∞ This paper meets the requirements of the ANSI/NISO Z39.48-1992 (Permanence of Paper).

ISBN: 978-1-60732-387-7 (pbk.)
ISBN: 978-1-60732-381-5 (ebook)

Multimedia materials related to this book can be found at http://www.upcolorado.com
/component/k2/item/2712-subjects-and-narratives-in-archaeology-media.

Library of Congress Cataloging-in-Publication Data

Subjects and narratives in archaeology / edited by Ruth M. Van Dyke & Reinhard Bernbeck.
    pages cm
  Includes bibliographical references.
  ISBN 978-1-60732-387-7 (pbk. : alkaline paper) — ISBN 978-1-60732-381-5 (ebook)
  1. Archaeology—Methodology. 2. Archaeology—Philosophy. 3. Archaeology—Moral
and ethical aspects. 4. Representation (Philosophy) 5. Subject (Philosophy) 6. Narration
(Rhetoric) 7. Imagination. 8. Archaeology and art. 9. Multimedia systems. 10. Publications. I.
Van Dyke, Ruth M. II. Bernbeck, Reinhard, 1958-
  CC75.S787 2015
  930.1—dc23

                    2014029011

Cover illustration by Phillip Tuwaletstiwa

Subjects
AND Narratives
IN Archaeology

*Alternative Narratives and
the Ethics of Representation*
An Introduction

RUTH M. VAN DYKE AND
REINHARD BERNBECK

Traditionally, archaeologists have constructed arguments through expository texts supported with images.
However, there is an increasing clamor for and interest
in alternative forms of archaeological narratives, involving writing fiction, making films, constructing hypertexts, and creating media that transcend the traditional
limitations of expository prose and the linearity of language. Visual art, fiction, creative nonfiction, film, and
drama have much to offer archaeological interpretation
and analysis, as many critics since the 1990s have made
clear (e.g., Joyce 2002; Pluciennik 1999).

Despite the hegemony of third-person expository
texts in archaeological scholarship, archaeologists
have long experimented with representational forms
that transcend these boundaries, producing novels (e.g.,
Bandelier 1971 [1916]; Carmean 2010; King 1983; Nelson
1999, 2004), vignettes (e.g., Deetz 1977, 1993; Edmonds
1999; Flannery 1976; Mithen 2003; Spector 1991,
1993; Yamin 1998, 2008), plays (e.g., Gibb 1998, 1999;
Praetzellis and Praetzellis 1998; Praetzellis, Ziesing,
and Praetzellis 1997), performance art (e.g., Cochrane
and Russell 2008; Pearson and Shanks 2001; Vilches
2007), paintings (e.g., Jameson 2003), musical com-
positions (e.g., Bullard and Bryant 1999), films (e.g.,
Archaeology Channel 2013; Avikunthak 2001), photography (e.g., Shanks 1997; Webmoor 2005), virtual
realities (e.g., Archaeology Southwest 2011; Witmore
2005), hypertexts (e.g., Joyce, Guyer, and Joyce 2000;
Joyce and Tringham 2007), and websites (e.g., Ashley,

DOI: 10.5876/9781607323815.c001

Tringham, and Perlingieri 2011; Metamedia 2010; Tringham and Ashley 2012).

The authors in this book seek to move beyond the customary limits of archaeological prose and representation. We explore narrative forms that range from creative nonfiction and drama through hypermedia and visual art. At the same time, however, we recognize that alternative formats pose a host of methodological and ethical challenges. While exploring new and not so new forms, the authors in this volume discuss bounds and delineate the connections between empirical data and archaeological imagination. We must tread carefully as we attempt to imagine—but not speak for—the people who populate our imagined pasts. This volume offers not just an array of ideas on and attempts at creatively employing narrative forms. It also provides reflections on the complexities and the ethical issues involved in constructing these narratives.

A BRIEF SURVEY OF THE ISSUES

This book is both a critique and an experiment. Authors discuss the goals, advantages, and difficulties of alternative forms of archaeological representation. Chapters in the volume are illustrated and enhanced by such media as paintings, sound files, dialogues, and links to online databases, videos, and PowerPoint presentations. Electronic publishing makes it possible to incorporate a range of media into written texts. This volume as a whole also represents an experimental attempt to engage with issues of representation in a hybrid format. A traditional hard-copy version will contain the text, black-and-white static images, and printed links to online material. The electronic "book" contains the text, images, and multimedia files so the work comes in two different forms. It is fitting to produce a volume on experimental narrative forms in a format that is itself an experimental step beyond the boundaries of traditional publishing.

Most of us agree that there are a plethora of good reasons to engage in alternative modes of archaeological representation. Public outreach is perhaps the most commonly cited reason for archaeologists to construct alternative narratives. Fiction, creative nonfiction, drama, visual arts, and other forms of storytelling can powerfully convey ideas to non-specialists who are interested in archaeology but are put off by the dry and jargon-laden technical writing style we archaeologists frequently employ. There is a shared sense among most of the authors in this volume that it is better for archaeologists to attempt to transcend traditional formal styles than to leave it to journalists and novelists to do (see also Kircher 2012: 87–110).

Of course, we as archaeologists spend years honing our skills at technical, expository writing. In the process, mentors and gatekeepers discourage us from practicing the art of constructing metaphors or from developing an aesthetic sense for speech. We are disciplined into an objective, descriptive style to the point of self-censorship at the level of language use. We would need active de-conditioning and retraining in creative nonfiction, fiction, or other forms of literary and artistic expression to improve our capabilities of representation. With this goal in mind, our colleague Brian Fagan (2006) has written a book coaching archaeologists about how to write readably and accessibly for wide audiences. However, Gilead (this volume) is justified in his concern that most archaeologists lack not only the training but possibly also the talent to be good creative nonfiction writers. There are plenty of bad novels written by archaeologists to attest to the difficulties of venturing into an unfamiliar genre. Thomas (this volume) discusses how unexpectedly difficult it is to create imagined narratives; he bemoans that he cannot "be the servant of contemporary literature, the archaeological record, and critical theory all at once." If public outreach is the goal, should we then leave the storytelling to professional storytellers? After all, Bernbeck (2005) analyzed novels by well-known, non-archaeologist authors on the ancient Near East and concluded that some of them are extremely powerful. Thomas, in contrast, is disturbed by the lurid plotlines and lack of accuracy in non-archaeologist-authored novels (e.g., Auel 1980).

No one experiences life as a linear, written, expository narrative; why should we be confined to presenting it as such? We use the artistic as well as the analytical parts of our brains when interpreting the past. Experimental narratives and multimedia projects have the power to take us out of the two-dimensional world of data and into the multidimensional world of sensory life (Day 2013). It is easier to invoke not only the sights but also the sounds, tastes, smells, and tactility of the past using a range of media and imagined dialogues. However, these multi-sensorial attempts, realized in famous exhibitions such as the York Castle Museum in the United Kingdom, have been castigated as producing a false sense of authenticity by implying entry into a past reality (Walsh 1992: 110–15). "Felt history" is not the same as past reality.

If the creation of authenticity is at the core of some chapters, others use art to convey a new and distinctly non-authentic sense of aspects of the past. Contributions by Phillip and Judy Tuwaletstiwa and by Doug Bailey and Melanie Simpkin blur the boundaries between science and art, opening up alternative, artistic spaces through which to contemplate the past. Bailey and Simpkin (this volume) argue that we need to transcend disciplinary boundaries to help us understand the human condition.

The socio-political context of such ideas, however, needs to be taken into account. In our times, standard academic discourse loses its power, since scientific truth claims are increasingly challenged in non-academic circles and public media. The contestation of concepts such as biological evolution and global warming shows this erosion of the power of scientific knowledge most glaringly. If we give up standard forms of academic, "dry" representation in the course of processes of representational change, we need to take stock of what we gain and what we may lose. This volume is part of a larger discourse on exactly that subject.

Public outreach, authenticity, and art are not the only reasons for archaeologists to explore alternative forms of interpretation. Experimental narratives enable us to think differently and talk differently about the past among ourselves—they benefit our work in all kinds of interesting ways. Many of the authors in this volume view experimental narratives as analytical tools that provide us as professionals with new ways of thinking about, not just representing, the past (see especially Bailey and Simpkin, Gibb, Nelson, Praetzellis and Praetzellis, and Van Dyke in this volume). Experiments in writing and in alternative representations more generally are not just means to convey the "content" to a fast-changing, media-savvy audience. Perhaps one of the most important points of our volume is that the same means of alternative writing and media very often have the effect of leading to new insights because such unusual forms require a knowledge of the past whose details and structures are often unavailable. Therefore, such representations can work in concert with, rather than as an alternative to, more traditional empirical modes of investigation (Edmonds 1999; Gibb 2000). Form is content, and for this reason we should embrace aesthetic and playful forms of representation; play is an important aspect of generalized human learning and innovation (Praetzellis and Praetzellis, this volume). Art and stories "to think with" can challenge traditional understandings and expand them. For example, using the format of a first-person singular narrative as a paper assignment in college courses is an excellent way to produce a critique of chronocentrism. The suggestion that Harappans had breakfast and similar ideas is just as unlikely às Kathleen Kenyon's (1957) contention that the "Neolithic housewife" in Jericho needed hard floors to clean them adequately.

What do archaeologists learn when they venture out into these alternative spaces? As an archaeologist tries to imagine a series of events from the vantage point of specific human individuals in the past, he or she must make a host of decisions, bringing into sharp relief the lacunae in our interpretations and showing us what we know well, which ideas need work, and what areas we have completely failed to think about (Thomas, this volume; Van Dyke 2013). Hermeneutic interplay among scales can help archaeologists address larger analytical questions. For example, Tringham (this volume) is ultimately interested in why and how Neolithic households in western Asia and southern Europe were involved in various and different trajectories toward urbanism and centralized authority.

These attempts at understanding the past are criticized by others (Bernbeck, this volume) because they necessarily involve a relationship with past peoples that is one-sided. We can use our fantasies to produce imagined past individuals and motivations for their actions, but real past people can't reply by doing the same with us. Were we to take this reproach seriously and seek remedial strategies, the obvious first step would be *not* to imagine a past Other but rather to imagine how, for example, the last Inka Atahualpa would feel after reading all of what has been written about him before starting any further hermeneutic experiments (see Gottowik 1998: 71–72).

The Internet and Related Issues

Archaeological scholarship involves deductive, inductive, and (one might argue) abductive reasoning; none of these happen in isolation from one another. Rather, investigations are hermeneutic attempts to construct present meanings from partial evidence of past practices and meanings, which are themselves multivocal and partial. Our imaginations are constantly in play as we navigate among these various kinds of fragments (Shanks 2012). Thus, it is not surprising that the archaeologists in this volume are interested in creative, nonlinear ways to nest and connect commentaries, data, and interpretations. For example, each page of the Talmud consists of two parts—the Mishnah, or the core text, and the Gemarah, a polyphonic commentary that explains and expands on the Mishnah. The Gemarah can in turn be surrounded by additional commentaries and references added over the course of a thousand years or more (Gilead, this volume). Midrash is a technique for fleshing out the interstices in Talmudic stories (Praetzellis and Praetzellis, this volume). Interestingly, both of these resemble non-electronic forms of hypertext.

The web has been employed to good avail in the work of Michael Shanks, Rosemary Joyce, Ruth Tringham, and others who have created multidimensional websites. Here, viewers/readers browse in free play, charting their own pathways through interrelated concepts and voices (Joyce and Tringham 2007; Lopiparo and Joyce 2003; Metamedia 2010; Webmoor 2005). For example, Joyce and colleagues' (2000) nonlinear, web-published *Sister Stories* incorporates Nahuatl voices through the writings of Bernardino de Sahagún, a sixteenth-century Spanish cleric who created the Florentine Codex by compiling the words of male elites at Tenochtitlán. Shanks's Metamedia website (http://metamedia.stanford.edu) is home to interrelated projects that question the ways archaeological knowledge is constructed, represented, and disseminated. Ruth Tringham's Chimera Web, focused on excavations at the Neolithic site of Opovo, was an early experiment in online narratives (Joyce and Tringham 2007; Tringham et al. 1992; Wolle and Tringham 2000). Tringham's subsequent project, Last House on the Hill, was based on a Berkeley team's excavation of one house at Çatalhöyük (Ashley, Tringham, and Perlingieri 2011). The Last House project involved a printed monograph and an online digital database with maps, drawings, photographs, and video connected with narratives about analysis and interpretation.

Archaeological materials are fragmentary, as are the uses we make of them, as are all human understandings of the world. Tringham (this volume) describes her current efforts to move beyond hypertext into a platform that supports the endless recombination of fragments of narratives and data. For Tringham, infinitely recombinant fragments are an appropriate way to represent and share archaeological work with colleagues and the public. Archaeology involves "the cutting and reassembling of fragments of meanings, images, things, quotations, and borrowings, to create new juxtapositions" (Shanks 1997: 84).

Hypermedia also lends itself well to tacking back and forth among different scales of analysis. Anthropologists—from practice theorists to environmental determinists—continue to debate the roles of individuals and collectives in causing, participating in, and dealing with long-term change (see Robb and Pauketat 2013). As archaeologists seek to understand change over time, we must grapple with the problem of scale. A gradual transition from, for example, hunting and gathering to farming may appear relatively straightforward in the archaeological record, but it would have looked very different from the perspective of the individuals living through it—if anyone was ever "living through it." Archaeologists are good at seeing long-term changes, but our perspective tends to flatten individuals and generations, even centuries, into homogeneous time periods (Bailey and Simpkin, this volume). Tringham argues that recombinant histories allow us to think about the past from the perspectives of past imagined individuals and to juxtapose those insights against broad archaeological contexts.

Yet ultimately, most of us want to weave our open-ended, fragmentary montages into some kind of larger picture, through which we can make sense of the longue durée (Praetzellis and Praetzellis, this volume). Therefore, projects such as Tringham's need to be seen in the context of a field of tension within historiography in general. First, keeping the past as unwieldy, refracted, and opaque as it is before any interpretation is done may simply counter the desire that is at the base of any historical and archaeological activities: to reduce the complexity of the past exactly to a story that is linear and that can be narrated, that can be said to be plausible if not approaching past "truths."

What if those who are confronted with the disparate fragments feel over-challenged by the task? Research about the attraction of the past in hypermedia and TV has confirmed that the simplified past is what non-specialist consumers are after. Pop-cultural and media-soaked archaeology can be described as fundamentally escapist (Kircher 2012: 35). Who, then, would tackle Tringham's extremely demanding construction out of fragments? Finally and perhaps most important, what are the consequences of a past that can be reassembled in myriad ways? Isn't a likely result the affirmation of the political status quo, exactly because one refrains from guidance about how to construct and interpret a story/history?

ETHICS AND NARRATIONS

Hypermedia foreground the constructed nature of archaeological interpretation, making the process of construction transparent. As visitors to hypermedia sites create their own courses of navigation, choosing from parallel and intersecting routes among texts, sounds, and images, they must make decisions about what to examine next. The traditional use of a library provides a good analogy for hypermedia use. Two important differences are the slower speed with which these processes happen in a "traditional" library and, equally important, the necessity to move and use the body to assemble one's own textual construction. Hypermedia remove the body even further from the construction of narratives.

Engagement with hypermedia can quietly seduce visitors into a state of critical self-awareness, as they realize they are actively engaged in the construction of meanings through the juxtaposition of the materials they choose to read and view. However, visitors are just as likely to enter into a state of "clicking coherence" (Schmitz 2006: 254–55) by integrating many zapped sites into their own life-world, a process they will have learned to pursue without need of advice. Putting out hypermedia snippets is a conscious effort by archaeologists to integrate themselves into these new ways of making sense of the world. But it is impossible to task the visitor to stay within the confines of one's own website, however complexly constructed that may be: won't they leave as soon as they find elements that do not conform with what they are pursuing in their own life-world?

Web-based environments can encourage collaborations and visitor contributions. Pluciennik discusses the role of archaeologists as facilitators of discussion in what he terms a demotic environment, "a proliferation of voices in which archaeologists are only one of many producing and consuming archaeologically relevant narratives and texts" (Pluciennik, this volume). Employing concepts derived from Bakhtin (1981; Todorov 1984: 49–56), Joyce (2002: 8–10) suggests that at least three voices are present in an archaeological (or any) text—the speaker/writer, the listener/reader, and the dialogic others—those who have used the words in the past, thereby imbuing them with meanings both speakers and listeners can understand. Bernbeck (2005, this volume) adds to this the narrator and elaborates on his or her role. The construction of archaeological texts thus entails dialogue not only between author and reader or narrator and reader but also between the narrator and other archaeologists past and present, between them and a diversity of peoples in the past.

Of course, this has implications for our "authority" as archaeologists. In the pages of the leading scholarly journals, authors appear as the credentialed and legitimate purveyors of value-neutral knowledge. This is the position Pluciennik calls *diktat* (this volume). Archaeological authority is not in question. Knowledge is presented as passively waiting for discovery by the specialist rather than actively constructed by the archaeologist (Joyce 2002; Pluciennik 1999; Shanks 1997; Thomas, this volume). When archaeologists—either deliberately, through polyphonic hypermedia, or, less obviously, through creative projects—give up the appearance of neutral, scientific objectivity, we weaken or abrogate our position as authoritative specialists. This leads us to the familiar conundrum of relativism—if we consider all voices as equally legitimate, by what rational or ethical criteria do archaeologists gainsay those who think aliens built the pyramids? It also leads to the question of which kinds of discourses allow the emergence of a critical voice and which ones do not.

One way out of this potential impasse is to recognize archaeology as a situated and political discourse and to accept our position as experts and advocates in the field. Pluciennik (this volume) distinguishes between archaeologists as one voice among many and archaeologists as facilitators, engaged in collaborative dialogues but advocating for the views we have developed. McGuire (2008: 82–91) argues that archaeological knowledge should be evaluated according to criteria that include *context* and *consequences*. *Context* requires archaeologists to be cognizant of our audiences, constituents, and stakeholders, including descendant communities, the public at large, and our disciplinary colleagues. *Consequences* ask us to consider the political impact of our work in the world: whose interests are served by a particular interpretation or analysis? Most of the authors in this volume contend that we have an ethical responsibility to the peoples of the past and that we should particularly be concerned with marginalized peoples and voices, whether past or present.

McGuire (ibid.) contends that two further notions of archaeological knowledge are *coherence* and *correspondence*. Interpretations of the past should *cohere*—that is, they should be logical and rational, and they should fit with existing social theory. The majority of the contributions to this book run counter to such a requirement, either because of a concern with the freedom of constructing multiple pasts (e.g., Tringham), because of a different ontological environment (e.g., Tuwaletstiwa 1997, 2007), or because of a generalized suspicion of coherence as ideological reductionism (Bernbeck). Finally, according to McGuire, archaeological knowledge should *correspond* to data—that is, interpretations should be supported by empirical observations. Clearly, when archaeologists write imagined narratives, we must ground them in empirical data (McCarthy 2003). Koselleck (1977: 45–46) maintains that sources have the "right to veto."

Pollock (this volume) claims that it is critical to be clear about what are data, what is derived directly from data, and what is an author's imagination. The problem with such requirements is that they restrain imagination so much as to make a story based on free associations impossible. However, if these bounds are blurred and readers think we are simply "making things up," we run the risk of losing credibility. Cultures of representation in modern worlds make a sharp distinction between reader-subjects "who are supposed to believe" when approaching a particular set of texts, such as those deriving from academic realms and those of state administration, as opposed to developing an attitude of a "subject supposed to suspend belief" when reading novels. It is possible for those who write novels to challenge this boundary, whereas it is much more dangerous to do so from the academic side.

How do readers know whether and how much of a creative project is "authentic" or true to empirical data? The authors in this volume address this issue in a variety of ways. Bernbeck suggests that we should carefully distinguish among terms of three kinds of writing: empiricist description, creative nonfiction, and fiction. Websites offer perhaps the clearest demarcation between data and invention, as the different kinds of information can be kept on separate pages, and readers can follow connections between them (Tringham, this volume). The Praetzellis have constructed reports consisting of three separate volumes— data, interpretation, and stories—and they provided a table that illustrates the linkages among the three (Praetzellis 1998). Other authors (Nelson, Thomas, Van Dyke, this volume) discuss data separately from the invention but ask readers to trust that their inventions are backed up by facts. However, the factual support is not a categorical matter but rather an issue of degrees. The difference between imaginative archaeological texts, such as Schmidt's (2012) account of Göbekli Tepe, and fictional ones that try to stick as much as possible to a factual base can be astonishingly small.

Gibb (this volume) is explicitly using invention to explore the interstices between data. The more experimental among us (Bailey and Simpkin, Tuwaletstiwa and Tuwaletstiwa, this volume) do not engage with the issue at all. Shanks (2012) does not see a problem with the difference between facticity and fiction because we archaeologists are using our imaginations all the time anyway. This may seem acceptable for an archaeology of Classical Antiquity (e.g., Shanks 1996), of European prehistory, or of the Old Testament (Dever 2005). But we quickly reach the limits of such freedoms of invention in a case such as an archaeology of Nazi extermination camps (Gilead, this volume). Even painstakingly researched fictional narratives that remain in the realm of the highly plausible, such as Jonathan Littell's (2009) *The Kindly Ones*, have been praised by some and sharply criticized by many others (Mendelsohn 2009) for the audacity of claiming that it is possible to render unspeakably horrible events, such as the mass killings at Babi Yar near Kiev, from the position of an invented first-person narrative of a perpetrator.

Alternative representations are mostly meant to humanize archaeology, to open up a space where past peoples—often marginalized peoples—can speak. But can they? Experimental forms can help illustrate differences among past peoples' experiences, roles, genders, ages, statuses, ethnicities, and occupations. However, are recognition of past subjects and respect for them achieved through the construction of "human faces" with sensory experience, emotion, and meaning, or is this merely one further way for archaeologists to appropriate and subjugate past peoples? If we imagine voices for subjects in other times and places, are we actually silencing them by placing our own words in their mouths (Bakhtin 1990: 27–36; Bernbeck, this volume)? If emotions and sensory experiences are already largely cultural constructs (e.g., Tarlow 2000; Thrift 2009), can we conceive of narrative forms that leave the imagination and experience of past subjects truly open?

It can be uncomfortable, at best, to put words in the mouths of long-dead subjects. Thomas (this volume) arbitrarily employed Finnish (non-Indo-European) place names to convey distance and difference. The task is easier for historical archaeologists who sometimes juxtapose their own words with those of their subjects, taken from journals, letters, or other literary sources (e.g., Beaudry 1998; Gibb, this volume; Praetzellis and Praetzellis, this volume;

Yamin 1998). But imagined narratives are unavoidably embedded in the archaeologist-writer's own experiences and worldviews. One solution may lie in making this as transparent as possible and engaging readers in a dialogue about the process of narrative construction. Another may consist of resisting the temptation of inserting invented subjects but still experimenting with narrative forms (Bernbeck, this volume).

All the authors in this volume agree that archaeologists have ethical responsibilities to the peoples of the past, although we differ about the best way to carry our responsibilities forward. We are not arguing that all archaeologists should attempt to construct alternative representations, but we think there should be more room in the discipline for this kind of creative experimentation to produce relations to past peoples that go beyond a simple, stale, and dehumanizing objectivation.

WHAT LIES AHEAD

Authors in this volume offer both direct and indirect critiques of traditional expository formats. Some (Pluciennik, Pollock) provide critical commentary. Other authors (Tuwaletstiwa and Tuwaletstiwa, Bailey and Simpkin) work with entirely experimental projects. Most (Tringham, Van Dyke, Thomas, Gibb, Gilead, Praetzellis and Praetzellis, Nelson, Bernbeck) offer a discussion of the ideas in play illustrated with experiments that include hypermedia, plays, fiction, or audio. In the pages and sections that follow, we have interwoven experimental chapters with those that veer more toward the expository.

Ruth Tringham's richly conceived work explores recombinant histories—mutable, reconfigurable bits of narratives and data. Tringham argues that the fragmentary nature of archaeological materials lends itself well to fragmentary narratives in which readers come face to face with past individuals or past moments in time. Like Bailey (this volume), who is frustrated with the reductive nature of archaeological time, Tringham seeks to unpack the archaeological record into many moments or micro-histories lived at a human scale. Her work challenges and eschews any kind of linear meta-narrative. Rather, recombinant histories are demotic (in Pluciennik's sense, this volume), leading to an infinite number of open-ended narratives and perspectives.

Tringham is one of the pioneers of web-based representations that involve multiple links among data and interpretive narratives. Websites have different paths that can be navigated by users, but Tringham wants to use new software to move beyond hypertext into a platform where fragments can be infinitely recombined. Thus, she is developing Dead Women Do Tell Tales, a website for recombinant histories drawn from two earlier projects. Tringham's chapter (this volume) contains a link to this project. Dead Women includes five micro-histories or narratives that revolve around the burial of a woman at Çatalhöyük. The people in these narratives include both imagined residents of the past and real contemporary archaeologists. The narratives are linked to or embedded within data and metadata that can be followed in many different directions. For example, a narrative about a basket is linked to empirical data about the basket, to a video of the excavation of the basket, and to a discussion of basketry analysis. These sites, in turn, lead to many other connections, so the reader becomes entangled, looping back and crossing paths with earlier links as well as other projects. Interestingly, Tringham describes this process with words such as "weaving" and "harvesting." Readers are drawn into a realization that they themselves are charting multidimensional connections among bits of data and interpretations. Part of the point is to foreground the role of the reader in the creation of knowledge. Tringham explicitly recognizes that one of the challenges is to suggest a way to clearly chart relationships between the imagined and the empirical parts of the entanglement. She provides a guide in the form of a table (e.g., Praetzellis et al. 1997:72) that links micro-histories to kinds of media, descriptions of sources, and data. This is similar to the one developed by Adrian and Mary Praetzellis who delineate the connections among data, interpretations, and imagined narratives.

Mark Pluciennik unpacks the issues of authority and ethics in archaeological narratives as the discipline moves from *diktat* (objective texts written by specialists) to the demotic (a proliferation of voices). Pluciennik identifies three possible positions for archaeological authors: specialists, participants, and facilitators. Traditionally, under diktat, archaeologists write as authoritative specialists presenting neutral, objective truths. This primary position has been amply critiqued by post-processualists who have pointed out that archaeological knowledge is situated and that archaeologists are but one voice among many. The second position follows Roland Barthes and deconstruction to consider archaeologists as merely one of many groups who have something to say about the past. But here, archaeologists have rescinded any claim to authority. A third position sees archaeologists as facilitators, engaged in collaborative dialogues that involve a plurality of voices but advocating for the views we have developed as specialists. Pluciennik sees archaeology as moving toward this third position. He argues that we have an ethical responsibility to represent the interests of past and marginalized peoples, but we cannot simply speak for them. We must make sure our data are intelligible and accessible, and we must empower the voices of others when possible. It is the archaeologist's responsibility to be cognizant of the political implications of her or his narratives.

Ruth Van Dyke contends that creative projects are "good to think with," bringing the limits of archaeological knowledge into sharp relief and raising new research questions. Hypermedia expand archaeological representation beyond the confines of the printed page, allowing us to explore multidimensional visual and aural relationships. Van Dyke shares her fellow authors' conviction that imagined narratives should be grounded in empirical data and that these connections should be as clear as possible. She provides a brief summary of the relevant material evidence from Chaco Canyon in northwest New Mexico. Van Dyke then presents two short experimental works incorporating visual and aural components. Both enable her to argue for specific phenomenological insights and to allow the reader/audience to experience aspects of Chaco that are not possible in a linear, text-based format. Van Dyke believes the benefits to such an approach outweigh the potential difficulties with claims to academic authority or ethical issues of relations with past others.

Phillip and Judy Tuwaletstiwa's contribution to the volume is an experiment melding art and narrative. Phillip is a Hopi geodeticist who has been working with Southwest archaeologists for many years. He collaborated with Anna Sofaer (1999) on the film *The Mystery of Chaco Canyon*. Sun, rain, and landscape are integral to Hopi (and all Pueblo) experiences of the world. Judy is an internationally renowned artist and writer who works in mixed media. She has had recent shows in Flagstaff, Santa Fe, and New York, and she has published two limited-edition books (Tuwaletstiwa 1997, 2007). Southwest desert light and landscape inspire her pieces, which often engage the senses in unexpected ways. Together, Judy and Phillip Tuwaletstiwa have created a dialogue between art and text, seeking to draw archaeological and artistic representation nearer to each other. They tack back and forth between art and text, between present and past, relying on agricultural rhythms as a link between ancient and contemporary protagonists.

For ancient as well as contemporary farmers raising corn on the high desert, water is of paramount importance. It is necessary for the crops to grow and for life to continue. Water sources such as springs and pools are seen as portals between upper and lower worlds. Much Pueblo ceremonialism revolves around bringing rain and ensuring the successful growth and harvest of corn. As the Tewa Pueblo anthropologist Alfonso Ortiz (1969) elegantly demonstrated, for Pueblo peoples, society, ritual, subsistence, and political relationships all exist within a nested, hierarchical, interrelated schema. The Pueblo is in the middle place—balanced between sky and underworld, in the center of the cardinal directions. Phillip and Judy Tuwaletstiwa's work communicates these ideas through the senses—visually, emotionally, poetically—without the use of an expository framework.

Mary and Adrian Praetzellis have gained notoriety for their "archaeologists as storytellers" sessions at professional meetings, beginning with the Society for Historical Archaeology in 1997. Their publicly funded historical archaeology projects have generated multi-volume reports, consisting of data, interpretations, and imagined stories. They have carefully considered the pedagogical and methodological issues involved in their storytelling, and they detail some of the issues here. In this volume, Mary and Adrian Praetzellis present a commentary within a play within a commentary. The characters in their "docudrama" are all real people—the archaeologists Jim Deetz, Stanley South, Bill Rathje, and Rosemary Joyce and the Jewish historian Flavius Josephus. Mary and Adrian Praetzellis use these characters' own published words to create a dialogue reflecting on the development of various kinds of narrative storytelling in archaeology.

They contend that there are archaeological data and facts, but each of us sees these facts imperfectly and partially through the lens of the present. It is the archaeologists' task to assemble these material bits into a whole picture. There might be multiple stories that fit with the evidence. However, archaeologists cannot write just any story, nor can we skip the interpretive step—stories do not stand in for analysis. Mary and Adrian Praetzellis choose their topics according to clarity, power, and use. Clarity is the quality of a site's data, or how clearly it represents a phenomenon. Power has to do with the ability of a story to create an emotional connection with the audience. A story is useful if it has something to teach us about past mistakes and successes. In Pluciennik's schema, the Praetzellis would see themselves as facilitators, advocating for perspectives that resonate with the data and that illuminate particularly compelling events or underrepresented voices from the past. Data must clearly evoke a story; the story must have emotional impact; and the story should have a political or pedagogical purpose, helping the audience learn from the mistakes and successes of the past. Like the Talmudic method of midrash, their stories fill the interstices between data points, fleshing out the details. Adrian and Mary Praetzellis write for archaeologists as well as for the larger public—they contend that creative, playful engagement with our data can help spark new insights and ideas. They delineate the connections among data, interpretations, and narratives by means of graphic guides that illustrate the relationships among these three sets of texts. They also keep data and fiction separate by incorporating explanatory introductions into their work and by using costumes and "silliness" in their dramas.

For James Gibb, playwriting is an analytical tool. Like all the authors in this volume, Gibb contends that imagination has a place in the construction of archaeological knowledge, but it should be used judiciously and appropriately. Playwriting helps Gibb gain insights where no direct archaeological or historical data exist. Through imagined dialogues, Gibb can experiment with different past actors' motives and characteristics. His goal is not to write a play but rather to perceive connections and relationships that might not otherwise be apparent. As a historical archaeologist, he works with texts and with sites. His characters are real historical personages in imagined dialogue with one another and with archaeologists.

Gibb illustrates his process with two brief dialogues set in the Maryland town of Port Tobacco. During the eighteenth century the local waterway was vital for commerce, yet no one intervened when the waterways silted up, destroying the tobacco-shipping industry. Geomorphology and archaeology document the process of sedimentation, but historical records are silent as to why nothing was done to ameliorate the problem. To illuminate this question, Gibb creates a dialogue between two historical personages whose personalities, class, financial situation, and ethnicity are known from documents but who wrote nothing directly about sedimentation. As Gibb imagines how Semple, a penurious Scottish warehouse owner, might have interacted with Hanson, an aristocratic tobacco farmer, it becomes clear how each man's short-term interests could have prevented the other from acting to avert a long-term disaster that affected both. Gibb's experimental scenario fits the existing archaeological and historical data, filling in the interstices and providing him with insights he could not have achieved by other means.

Jonathan Thomas argues that if archaeologists do not write engaging narratives for the public, others will and will do it poorly. Like the other authors in this volume, he contends that alternative narratives not only help communicate with the public, they can also challenge stereotypical views of the past and can spark archaeologists' creative insights. Just as Geertz advocated "thick description" for ethnographies, Thomas considers imagined narratives to be a kind of "thick description" for archaeologists, in which we derive meaning from critical dialogue with past materials. In his chapter in this volume, Thomas describes an experiment in which he wrote a series of fictional vignettes about Upper Paleolithic Venus figurines. He meant the vignettes to represent different interpretations for the figurines and to communicate how archaeological theories and approaches have changed over time. He employed a deconstructive method, creating fragmented texts within texts. Readers, however, had a hard time following along and found it difficult to separate the facts from the fiction. Thomas (this volume) then created a Rashomon-like sequence of narratives focused on one scene of Upper Paleolithic art through the imagined perspectives of three different viewers. He prefaces each with an explanatory description. This helps with clarity and fragmentation, but Thomas still found it discomfiting to create speech for subjects who lived at such a vast remove from our own place and time. He is concerned that he is making his imagined characters speak in a "hokey" or unbelievably contrived manner. It is not really possible, he concludes, to write for past peoples without projecting some degree of our present interpretations and understandings back into the past. The ethics of this procedure remain ambiguous for Thomas.

Like Judy and Phillip Tuwaletstiwa, Doug Bailey and Melanie Simpkin have created an experimental project that blurs the boundaries between archaeology and art. Bailey and Simpkin invite the reader to think about the disconnects between life as experienced in real time and the awkwardly condensed timescales employed by archaeologists. During fieldwork at a Neolithic site in Romania, Bailey became frustrated with the temporal coarseness of the archaeological past, notwithstanding archaeological rhetoric about agency and the individual. As an experiment, he set up a video camera on a street corner in the local village and filmed four twenty-minute segments across one day. The four videos capture the movements of people, animals, and weather as they unfold in real time. The electronic version of Bailey and Simpkin's chapter contains a link to the videos. To create a static, textual representation of their ideas, Bailey and Simpkin translated the activities from one of these twenty-minute film segments into the nontraditional notation system BMN, used by dance choreographers. They then created a twenty-page piece that appears similar to a chronological table or a musical score. Images, artifacts, and BMN symbols constitute the attributes or notes. This is "uncertain territory" for archaeologists and readers, who may be confused about how to proceed. Bailey and Simpkin assure us that there is no one correct way to experience the piece. Rather, readers are encouraged to flip back and forth across the pages and between the text and the videos. The authors' goal is to disrupt our traditional, linear perceptions and provoke us to think about patterns within the real pace of life.

Sarah Nelson's chapter is a self-reflexive look at her own process of creating archaeological fiction. She has written three novels set in ancient East Asia. All three use what Nelson terms "binocular vision," juxtaposing the imagined lives of contemporary archaeologists and past peoples. The reader follows a fictional archaeologist, Clara Alden, as she works at actual sites and uncovers real features and artifacts. Clara then has dreams in which she visits the past, where she exists as a yellow bird who interacts with imagined characters living in the times and places represented by the sites. *Spirit Bird Journey* takes place in Early Neolithic Korea, *Jade Dragon* is set in Late Neolithic China, and *The Jade Phoenix* revolves around the historical figure of a Shang Dynasty monarch. Nelson writes for archaeologists as well as for the public. She seeks to humanize the past for a wide audience, but she also seeks to explore issues such as gender and power, using specific archaeological artifacts—bronzes and oracle bones, for example—as her starting points. Nelson's narratives are fictional, but they are congruent with empirical archaeological data. These stories relate to archaeological data in a metonymic way. In this chapter, she discusses the key artifacts that inspired her stories, explaining how each led her to develop the narrative in a particular direction. In her novels, Nelson attempts to flag for the reader which aspects of her work are empirical and which are imaginary through the voice of her protagonist, Clara Alden. "The voice of the fictional archaeologist explains what has been discovered in sites and written in documents and which events . . . are created from . . . artifacts but have no other basis in the archaeological record" (Nelson, this volume). Nelson's/Clara's authority as an archaeologist is assumed and uncomplicated. For her, appropriating the voices of past peoples serves to improve communication with the public, and creative analytical tools provide justification for an approach that is decidedly obscuring boundaries between fact and fiction.

Isaac Gilead writes from the perspective of his work excavating at the Holocaust extermination centers of Bełżec and Sobibór in eastern Poland (Gilead 2009). At Bełżec, Sobibór, Treblinka, and Chełmno, Nazis gassed 1.7 million Jews in 1942–43. The Holocaust attracts great public interest, with controversial perspectives as to how and even whether these events can be represented in art and literature. Literary accounts of the Shoah have been classified as nonfiction because the events portrayed really happened, despite the inclusion of fictional specifics. In such a case, it is still important to distinguish between survivors of the horrors who explicitly refuse the pretension of being able to talk objectively about their experiences and memories (e.g., Semprun 1994; Wiesel 1960) and those who use fictive elements as a way to represent something they themselves did not go through (Littell 2009; Spiegelman 1986). The realities of the Holocaust throw the ethics of multivocal representation into sharp relief, however. On a very basic level, if there are multiple perspectives on many versions of the past, how can we take care not to open the door to Holocaust deniers? Even any fictional approach to the monstrosity is in danger of doing grave injustice to the victims. Thus, it is extremely important for Gilead that archaeological writers make sure readers can separate the empirical from the imagined. He argues that archaeologists can invent narratives as long as they remain grounded in empirical data and as long as the links between fact and fiction remain clear.

Archaeological sites and artifacts have unique contributions to make to narratives about the Holocaust. We do not need them to corroborate eyewitness accounts of the exterminations, but they can powerfully evoke connections with the human beings who were victims and perpetrators in the camps. As an example, Gilead offers the thick description of a Lysol bottle found at Sobibór. In the late nineteenth and early twentieth centuries, Lysol was used not only as a disinfectant but also as a contraceptive. Gilead alludes to the possibility that the bottle belonged to a victim but refrains from speculating about her, leaving the reader to imagine who might have been concerned about contraception in the camp and why.

Concerns close to Gilead's underlie Reinhard Bernbeck's proposal for a kind of narrative that diverges from standard academic prose but avoids at the same time the imagination of scenarios, events, objects, and personal relations. Bernbeck thinks expository writing has an advantage over more open and creative styles: it remains a relatively faithful translation of visible things and features, as well as measurable distances between them, into language. However, the cost is regularly an almost complete reification of past subjects. To avoid both of these conundrums, Bernbeck recommends reliance on the principles of the *nouveau roman*, an avant-gardist style of narration developed by a small group of writers in France (e.g., Robbe-Grillet 1957). The nouveau roman minimizes flowery language and adjectives; writings in this vein abstain from an internal view of any protagonists and other subjects. Bernbeck argues that this set of artistic elements is congruent with the situation in which archaeologists find themselves when giving an account of the past and provides a short section of this type of prose for an archaeological example.

Recently, journalists, memoirists, and literary writers have been grappling with the issues of authority and authenticity. "Truth" can be multifaceted and situational, but the literary world has roundly castigated writers who have presented false memoirs, for example, as works of nonfiction. Sarah Pollock, a professor of creative nonfiction, comments on our volume's archaeological forays into experimental narratives. Pollock contends that authors have an ethical responsibility to clearly demarcate facts from fabrication. But to what extent can authors "fill in the blanks" when details of a factual occurrence are not known? Scientific artists, for example, must make decisions as to what colors to paint dinosaurs for museum displays. Pollock cites Bonnie Rough (2007: 66), who states, "Nonfiction writers imagine. Fiction writers invent." Imagination can and must be used responsibly to add details that fit with known empirical data. The problems arise when authors intentionally aim to deceive, by either misrepresenting or not clearly delineating empirical facts from fiction. Thus, Pollock insists that archaeologists must include clear signposts directing readers to the data that inform imagined narratives. All the authors in this volume are cognizant of the need to connect narratives with data, but in Pollock's assessment we do a variable job of making these relationships explicit, especially for a nonprofessional reader. Pollock also urges us to think about what we lose and what we gain through creative endeavors. We may create a more engaging, humanized past but at the cost of our scientific authority.

FUNDAMENTAL, UNRESOLVED ISSUES

The chapters in this book address three major disputed issues connected with narration in archaeology. First is the idea that the formal elements we mobilize to give an account of the past simultaneously participate in the shaping of content. Both alternative and standard forms of archaeological communication lead to media-specific emphases, silencing, repression, and foregrounding in the vast world we call past/history. Although it is problematic to try to separate issues of content and form, it would be equally false to pretend that all potential ways of narrating are equally suited for a rendering of past worlds. Archaeology should not mindlessly multiply the media at its disposal to narrate and present its results to increasingly heterogeneous publics. Such a Holtorfian "archaeology for sale" model of the discipline would tend to utilize critique only in a functionalized way of increasing output (Holtorf 2007). By contrast, we maintain that archaeology is fundamentally about a critical discourse of evaluation, sorting through a multiplicity of truth claims. This process is as much bound to forms of narration as to equalities of different voices and listeners, that is, to the principle of maximizing the potential of participation by all those interested in the past. It is here that Habermas's oft-criticized "ideal speech situation" (Habermas 1971:123–141) raises its head, even though this idea is not addressed in our volume.

A second issue is the role of imagination and "facts" versus "fiction." Any academic text includes fictional elements. Some of these elements are what one could call "purgative fiction": the exclusion and omission of some obvious presences, such as the close mix of contexts of discovery and the discovered, to produce a scenario that pretends to describe an objective past world that was never encountered by the author of a text. Other kinds are "combinatorial fictions": data sets are per se unrelated jumbles of single entries without any links. Erstwhile secretary of state Condolezza Rice's (in)famous phrase of "connecting the dots" describes an imaginative process that is supposed to lead to greater insights, if not approaching some "truth." Standard archaeological narratives "connect dots" to coherent stories by inventing the connections. This type of fiction is present in all writing about the past, no matter how much we formalize the process of combining and connecting through statistical methods, maps, and other means.

But does this recognition of the necessity of invention free us scholars and the larger public to make up elements of the past, and, if so, to what extent? Our volume does not provide a clear answer to this fundamental problem. If we believe German State Television ZDF, which exclaims that "historical documentaries are more 'in' than ever before, and people all over the world are hungry for facts. History, not hearsay! In depth but in tune with the times. History with heart and soul" (cited in Kircher 2012: 174), then there is a general thirst for facticity among the public. People want to be put in the position of the "subject supposed to believe" and have acquired the flexibility to switch from this state of subjectivity to one in which this same supposition is suspended. Is it necessary to keep the fact-fiction boundaries clear-cut, and, if so, what should the signposts be that mark them? Or is the obfuscation of this very boundary a matter of emancipation from positivism, naive realism, and other ills of a slowly vanishing modernity? As narrators of history, we cannot but position ourselves in this debate. Yet in archaeology, there is no sincere discussion of the problem. It is rather declared a matter of paradigmatic difference that is simply thought to be beyond discussion—to the detriment of the "discipline."

Finally, Spivak's (1988) famous essay with the provocative title "Can the Subaltern Speak?" is at the core of this volume. Several authors in our collection think our voice is the only one that can help past peoples defend a modicum of a standing in the present. For them, past peoples are not simply "the dead" but might share the right not to be functionalized for present (and future) purposes in an objectivizing way. Within this field, there is no consensus about our means to successfully integrate past subjects in present discourses. Another position on the Spivakian question is more concerned with the present and mobilizes stories to try to mitigate present injustices, for example, of gender or age, by appealing to past different worlds. Here, the past's ambivalence becomes a resource for pointing the way to a better future. Instead of utopian imaginations of a better world with their often devastating consequences, past alterities serve as sources for the production of more realistic and moderate expectations for a better future (Rüsen 1994: 48–68).

If this volume becomes part of an ongoing effort to reflect on, rethink, and evaluate the conditions of what we traditionally perceive to be archaeology's representational means, this may also lead to a rethinking of what and how we think. We would be more than satisfied with this result.

REFERENCES

Archaeology Channel. 2013. http://www.archaeologychannel.org, accessed February 20, 2013.

Archaeology Southwest. 2011. "Innovative Virtual Exhibit to Explore Chaco's Legacy." http://www.archaeologysouthwest.org/2011/08/04/innovative-virtual-exhibit-to -explore-chacos-legacy, accessed February 20, 2013.

Ashley, Michael, Ruth Tringham, and Cinzia Perlingieri. 2011. "Last House on the Hill: Digitally Remediating Data and Media for Preservation and Access." *Journal on Computing and Cultural Heritage* 5 (4). http://dx.doi.org/10.1145/2050096.2050098.

Auel, Jean M. 1980. *The Clan of the Cave Bear*. New York: Crown.

Avikunthak, Ashish, director. 2001. *Rummaging for Pasts: Excavating Sicily, Digging Bombay*. DVD available from the author at http://www.avikunthak.com.

Bakhtin, Mikhail M. 1981. *The Dialogic Imagination: Four Essays*. Ed. Michael Holquist. Trans. Caryl Emerson and Michael Holquist. Austin: University of Texas Press.

Bakhtin, Mikhail M. 1990. *Art and Answerability: Early Philosophical Essays*. Ed. Michael Holquist and Vadim Liapunov. Trans. Vadim Liapunov and Kenneth Brostrom. Austin: University of Texas Press.

Bandelier, Adolf F. 1971 [1916]. *The Delight Makers*. Orlando: Harcourt Brace/Harvest.

Beaudry, Mary C. 1998. "Farm Journal: First Person, Four Voices." *Historical Archaeology* 32: 20–33.

Bernbeck, Reinhard. 2005. "The Past as Fact and Fiction: From Historical Novels to Novel Histories." In *Archaeologies of the Middle East: Critical Perspectives*, ed. Susan Pollock and Reinhard Bernbeck, 97–122. Oxford, MA: Blackwell.

Bullard, Mary R., and Curtis Bryant. 1999. *Zabette: An Opera in Three Acts*. Performed at the Rialto Center for the Performing Arts, Atlanta, Georgia, April 29–30.

Carmean, Kelly. 2010. *Creekside: An Archaeological Novel*. Tuscaloosa: University of Alabama Press.

Cochrane, Andrew, and Ian Russell. 2008. "Archaeoclash: Manifesting Art and Archaeology." In *Archaeologies of Art: Papers from the Sixth World Archaeological Congress*. UCD Scholarcast Series 2, ed. Ian Russell. Transcript online at http://www.ucd.ie/scholarcast/transcripts/Archaeoclash.pdf, accessed December 27, 2008.

Day, Jo, ed. 2013. *Making Senses of the Past: Towards a Sensory Archaeology*. Proceedings of the 27th Annual Visiting Scholar Conference. Carbondale: Southern Illinois University.

Deetz, James. 1977. *Small Things Forgotten: The Archaeology of Early American Life*. Garden City, NJ: Anchor.

Deetz, James. 1993. *Flowerdew Hundred: The Archaeology of a Virginia Plantation, 1619–1864*. Charlottesville: University Press of Virginia.

Dever, William G. 2005. *Did God Have a Wife? Archaeology and Folk Religion in Ancient Israel*. Grand Rapids, MI: Eerdmans.

Edmonds, Mark. 1999. *Ancestral Geographies of the Neolithic: Landscape, Monuments, and Memory*. London: Routledge.

Fagan, Brian. 2006. *Writing Archaeology*. Walnut Creek, CA: Left Coast.

Flannery, Kent V. 1976. *The Early Mesoamerican Village*. New York: Academic Press.

Gibb, James. 1998. *London Shades: A Play in Three Acts*. Performed at the London Town Historic Site, Edgewater, MD, October 1998 and October 1999.

Gibb, James. 1999. *Revolutionary Spirits: A Play in Two Acts*. Performed at the London Town Historic Site, Edgewater, MD, April 1999.

Gibb, James. 2000. "Imaginary, but by No Means Unimaginable: Storytelling, Science, and Historical Archaeology." *Historical Archaeology* 34 (2): 1–6.

Gilead, Isaac, Yoram Haimi, and Wojciech Mazurek. 2009. "Excavating Nazi Extermination Centres." *Present Pasts* 1: 10–39.

Gottowik, Volker. 1998. "Der Andere als Leser: Zur indigenen Rezeption ethnographischer Texte." In *Figuren der/des Dritten. Erkundungen kultureller Zwischenräume*, ed. Claudia Breger and Tobias Döring, 65–86. Amsterdam: Editions Rodopi.

Habermas, Jürgen. 1971. "Vorbereitende Bemerkungen zu einer Theorie er kommunikativen Kompetenz." In *Theorie der Gesellschaft oder Sozialtechnologie*, ed. Jürgen Habermas und Niklas Luhmann, 101–141. Frankfurt: Suhrkamp.

Holtorf, Cornelius. 2007. *Archaeology Is a Brand! The Meaning of Archaeology in Contemporary Popular Culture*. Walnut Creek, CA: Left Coast.

Jameson, John H., Jr. 2003. "Art and Imagery as Tools for Public Interpretation and Education in Archaeology." In *Ancient Muses: Archaeology and the Arts*, ed. John H. Jameson Jr., John E. Ehrenhard, and Christine A. Finn, 57–64. Tuscaloosa: University of Alabama Press.

Joyce, Rosemary A. 2002. *The Languages of Archaeology*. Oxford, MA: Blackwell. http://dx.doi.org/10.1002/9780470693520.

Joyce, Rosemary A., Carolyn Guyer, and Michael Joyce. 2000. *Sister Stories*. New York: New York University Press.

Joyce, Rosemary A., and Ruth Tringham. 2007. "Feminist Adventures in Hypertext." *Journal of Archaeological Method and Theory* 14 (3): 328–58.

Kenyon, Kathleen M. 1957. *Digging up Jericho*. New York: Praeger.

King, Kathleen. 1983. *Cricket Sings: A Novel of Pre-Columbian Cahokia*. Athens: Ohio University Press.

Kircher, Marco. 2012. *Wa(h)re Archäologie. Die Medialisierung archäologischen Wissens im Spannungsfeld von Wissenschaft und Öffentlichkeit*. Bielefeld: transcript.

Koselleck, Reinhart. 1977. "Standortbindung und Zeitlichkeit: Ein Beitrag zur historiographischen Erschließung der gechichtlichen Welt." In *Objektivität und Parteilichkeit in der Geschichtswissenschaft*, ed. Reinhart Koselleck, Wolfgang J. Mommsen, and Jörn Rüsen, 17–46. Munich: dtv.

Littell, Jonathan. 2009. *The Kindly Ones*. Trans. Charlotte Mandell. New York: HarperCollins.

Lopiparo, Jeanne, and Rosemary A. Joyce. 2003. "Crafting Cosmos, Telling Sister Stories, and Exploring Archaeological Knowledge Graphically in Hypertext Environments." In *Ancient Muses: Archaeology and the Arts*, ed. John H. Jameson Jr., John E. Ehrenhard, and Christine A. Finn, 193–203. Tuscaloosa: University of Alabama Press.

McCarthy, John P. 2003. "More Than Just 'Telling the Story': Interpretive Narrative Archaeology." In *Ancient Muses: Archaeology and the Arts*, ed. John H. Jameson Jr., John E. Ehrenhard, and Christine A. Finn, 15–24. Tuscaloosa: University of Alabama Press.

McGuire, Randall H. 2008. *Archaeology as Political Action*. Berkeley: University of California Press.

Mendelsohn, Daniel. 2009. "Transgression: Review of Jonathan Littell, *The Kindly Ones*." *New York Review of Books* 56 (5) (March 26): 18–21. http://www.nybooks.com/articles/archives/2009/mar/26/transgression/?pagination=false, accessed February 20, 2013.

Metamedia: A Collaboratory at Stanford University. 2010. http://metamedia.stanford.edu, accessed March 15, 2010.

Mithen, Stephen. 2003. *After the Ice*. London: Weidenfeld and Nicolson.

Nelson, Sarah M. 1999. *Spirit Bird Journey*. Littleton, CO: RKLOG.

Nelson, Sarah M. 2004. *Jade Dragon*. Littleton, CO: RKLOG.

Ortiz, Alfonso. 1969. *The Tewa World: Space, Time, Being, and Becoming in a Pueblo Society*. Chicago: University of Chicago Press.

Pearson, Mike, and Michael Shanks. 2001. *Theatre/Archaeology*. London: Routledge.

Pluciennik, Mark. 1999. "Archaeological Narratives and Other Ways of Telling." *Current Anthropology* 40 (5): 653–78. http://dx.doi.org/10.1086/300085.

Praetzellis, Adrian, and Mary Praetzellis. 1998. "A Connecticut Merchant in Chinatown: A Play in One Act." *Historical Archaeology* 32 (1): 1–3.

Praetzellis, Adrian, Grace H. Ziesing, and Mary Praetzellis. 1997. *Tales of the Vasco*, vol. 5. Los Vaqueros Final Project Report. Rohnert Park, CA: Anthropological Studies Center, Sonoma State University Foundation.

Praetzellis, Mary, ed. 1998. "Archaeologists as Storytellers." Special issue of *Historical Archaeology* 32 (1).

Robb, John, and Tim Pauketat, eds. 2013. *Big Histories, Human Lives: Tackling Problems of Scale in Archaeology*. Santa Fe: School of Advanced Research Press.

Robbe-Grillet, Alain. 1957. *La Jalousie*. Paris: Éditions de Minuit.

Rough, Bonnie J. 2007. "Writing Lost Stories: When Bones Are All We Have." *Iron Horse Literary Review* (Spring).

Rüsen, Jörn. 1994. *Historische Orientierung*. Bonn, Germany: Böhlau.

Schmidt, Klaus. 2012. *Göbekli Tepe: A Stone Age Sanctuary in South-Eastern Anatolia*. Berlin: ex oriente.

Schmitz, Ulrich. 2006. "Schreiben und neue Medien." In *Didaktik der deutschen Sprache*, vol. 1, ed. Ursula Bredel, Hartmut Günther, Peter Klotz, Jakob Olssner, and Gesa Siebert-Ott, 249–60. Paderborn, Germany: Schnönigh.

Semprun, Jorge. 1994. *L'écriture ou la vie*. Paris: Éditions Gallimard.

Shanks, Michael. 1996. *Classical Archaeology of Greece: Experiences of the Discipline*. London: Routledge. http://dx.doi.org/10.4324/9780203171974.

Shanks, Michael. 1997. "Photography and Archaeology." In *The Cultural Life of Images: Visual Representation in Archaeology*, ed. Brian L. Molyneaux, 73–107. London: Routledge.

Shanks, Michael. 2012. *The Archaeological Imagination*. Walnut Creek, CA: Left Coast.

Sofaer, Anna. 1999. *The Mystery of Chaco Canyon*. Oley, PA: Bullfrog Films.

Spector, Janet. 1991. "What This Awl Means: Toward a Feminist Archaeology." In *Engendering Archaeology*, ed. Joan M. Gero and Margaret Conkey, 388–406. Oxford, MA: Blackwell.

Spector, Janet. 1993. *What This Awl Means: Feminist Archaeology at Wahpeton Dakota Village*. St. Paul: Minnesota Historical Society Press.

Spiegelman, Art. 1986. *Maus: A Survivor's Tale*. New York: Pantheon Books.

Spivak, Gayatri Chakravorti. 1988. "Can the Subaltern Speak?" In *Marxism and the Interpretation of Culture*, ed. Cary Nelson and Lawrence Grossberg, 271–315. Urbana: University of Illinois Press.

Tarlow, Sarah. 2000. "Emotion in Archaeology." *Current Anthropology* 41 (5): 713–46. http://dx.doi.org/10.1086/317404.

Thrift, Nigel. 2009. "Understanding the Affective Spaces of Political Performance." In *Emotion, Place and Culture*, ed. Mick Smith, Joyce Davidson, Laura Cameron, and Liz Bondi, 79–96. Aldershot, UK: Ashgate.

Todorov, Tzvetan. 1984. *Mikhail Bakhtin: The Dialogical Principle*. Trans. Wlad Godzich. Minneapolis: University of Minnesota Press.

Tringham, Ruth, and Michael Ashley. 2012. "Afterword: Last House on the Hill: The Digital Mirror of House Lives." In *House Lives: BACH Area Reports from Çatalhöyük, Turkey* (Çatalhöyük, vol. 7), ed. Ruth Tringham and Mirjana Stevanovic, 553–54. Archaeologica Monumenta 27. Los Angeles: Cotsen Institute of Archaeology Publications, UCLA.

Tringham, Ruth, Bogdan Brukner, Timothy Kaiser, Ksenija Borojevic, Ljubomir Bukvic, Peter Steli, Nerissa Russell, Mirjana Stevanovic, and Barbara Voytek. 1992. "Excavations at Opovo, 1985–1987: Socioeconomic Change in the Balkan Neolithic." *Journal of Field Archaeology* 19 (3): 351–86.

Tuwaletstiwa, Judy. 1997. *Canyon Poem*. Galisteo, NM: Galisteo.

Tuwaletstiwa, Judy. 2007. *Mapping Water*. New York: Radius Books.

Van Dyke, Ruth M. 2013. "Imagined Narratives: Sensuous Lives in Ancient Chaco." In *Making Senses of the Past: Toward a Sensory Archaeology*, ed. Jo Day, 390–408. Carbondale: Center for Archaeological Investigations, Southern Illinois University.

Vilches, Flora. 2007. "The Art of Archaeology: Mark Dion and His Dig Projects." *Journal of Social Archaeology* 7 (2): 199–223. http://dx.doi.org/10.1177/14696053 07077480.

Walsh, Kevin. 1992. *The Representation of the Past: Museums and Heritage in the Post-Modern World*. London: Routledge. http://dx.doi.org/10.4324/9780203320570.

Webmoor, Timothy. 2005. "Mediational Techniques and Conceptual Frameworks in Archaeology: A Model in 'Mapwork' at Teotihuacan, Mexico." *Journal of Social Archaeology* 5 (1): 52–84. http://dx.doi.org/10.1177/1469605305050143.

Wiesel, Elie. 1960. *Night*. New York: Hill and Wang.

Witmore, Christopher L. 2005. "Four Archaeological Engagements with Place: Mediating Bodily Experience through Peripatetic Video." *Visual Anthropology Review* 20 (2): 57–71. http://dx.doi.org/10.1525/var.2004.20.2.57.

Wolle, Anja, and Ruth Tringham. 2000. "Multiple Çatalhüyüks on the World Wide Web." In *Towards Reflexive Method in Archaeology: The Example at Çatalhüyük by*

Members of the Çatalhüyük Teams, ed. Ian Hodder, 207–18. Cambridge: McDonald Institute for Archaeological Research.

Yamin, Rebecca. 1998. "Lurid Tales and Homely Stories of New York's Notorious Five Points." *Historical Archaeology* 32 (1): 74–85.

Yamin, Rebecca. 2008. *Digging in the City of Brotherly Love: Stories from Philadelphia Archaeology*. New Haven: Yale University Press.

2

---

*Creating Narratives
of the Past as
Recombinant Histories*

RUTH TRINGHAM

There are narratives about history with beginnings and endings, and there are narratives with no beginning and no ending. Even as a ten-year old I was never happy with E. Nesbit's philosophy of writing: "There are some things I must tell before I begin to tell about the treasure-seeking, because I have read books myself, and I know how beastly it is when a story begins, 'Alas!' said Hildegarde with a deep sigh, 'we must look our last on this ancestral home'—and then some one else says something—and you don't know for pages and pages where the home is, or who Hildegarde is, or anything about it" (Nesbit 1899: 10).

WRITING FRAGMENTS

Chaos, entanglement, complexity, ambiguity are not popular, yet they are praised by those who have the patience to follow their intricacy. Is an entangled web worth it? I believe it is, if it creates a narrative that leads to further and deeper exploration and complexity of representation. Can we make complex narratives easier to grasp and engage with? Digital formats are much better for this than printed linear text; but, as Angela Piccini (2007) among others has remarked, they are not usually used to their full potential.

Kathleen Stewart starts her printed book *Ordinary Affects* by saying that the book "is an experiment, not a judgment. Committed not to the demystification and uncovered truths that support a well-known picture of

DOI: 10.5876/9781607323815.c002

the world, but rather to speculation, curiosity, and the concrete, it tries to provoke attention to the forces that come into view as habit or shock, resonance or impact. Something throws itself together in a moment as an event and a sensation; a something both animated and inhabitable" (Stewart 2007: 1). My vision of alternative narratives in this chapter comprises similarly entangled fragments of events, experiences, and sensations that are documented, remembered, or imagined in the past (from very distant to very recent).

Most of the narratives presented in this volume are fragments, but so they would have to be within the word count restrictions. For example, Nelson's fragments are extracted from what are conceived ultimately as longer coherent linear texts. Both Thomas's and Van Dyke's fragments are created as demonstrations of the different formats of narratives that address the same content and of the power of "alternative" formats that use creative imagination to narrate beyond a heavily empirically based text; I created such fragments myself in a previous work (Tringham 1994).

The fragmentary narratives I create in this current work may fulfill both of these aims, but my ultimate aim is neither the creation of a longer cohesive text nor the demonstration of the value of multiple genres in archaeological expression. Rather, the fragmentary (vignette) format is the *end product* of my creative efforts, as it is with Kathleen Stewart and "flash fiction" writers. The latter fragmentary style of writing[1] has developed in close association with changes in writing styles brought about by digital technology, as has the public diary or blog (Pratt 2009). I was very interested to read in this volume Gilead's comparison of the Talmud to a website in which commentary could be added to an online publication. I suppose Twitter would represent the ultimate in fragmentary writing!

However, the fragmentary style in which I create is inspired by another source of digital narratives. They emerge as a result of the filtering, guidance, and "scaffolding" (in this case mine, but it could be any database creator's) out of an archaeological database of media, text, and alphanumeric documentation as "database narratives," following the inspirational work of Lev Manovich (2001). Such narratives are by definition closely and explicitly linked to the empirical data and their media representation.

By definition also, such narratives are written at an intensely intimate scale. Together or as individual narratives they become "micro-histories" (an increasingly popular form of writing history) (Brown 2003: 10–12; Ginzburg 2012: 193–214; Szijártó 2002) or—a more obscure but no less significant concept— "recombinant histories" (Anderson 2011: 122). The agenda of my chapter is not to downplay the significance of Kathleen Stewart's (2007) wonderful printed volume or the printed bulk of micro-histories (Davis 1984; Ginzburg 1980; Ladurie 1997). Nor would I wish to deny the importance of the majority of chapters in this volume, which emphasize their alternative narratives as explicitly and "thickly" (apologies to Clifford Geertz) founded in the empirical details of archaeology and being "written" at the slow pace of the intimate scale of everyday life.

In this chapter I hope to demonstrate that the creation of narratives using the digital technology involved in constructing database narratives enables the combining and recombining of the fragments into a woven fabric or, to use a more "trendy" metaphor, a tangled fishing long-line, to create a complexity of history that more closely approaches reality. I believe, as do many authors in this volume, that writing about people and their multi-sensorial experience of places and events has a greater appeal to a broad set of audiences to engage in how we construct history. How much greater is that appeal when constructed in a tangled but content-rich framework akin to a multiplayer real-world online (or mobile) game (for thoughts of this nature I have also been greatly inspired by the many ideas in Wardrip-Fruin and Harrigan 2004).

EARLY NARRATIVES

Since my enlightenment in the late 1980s/early 1990s as to the importance of giving life histories and voices to people of the past and to expressing and celebrating the ambiguity of the archaeological construction of the past (Tringham 1991, 1994), I have been trying to achieve the twin ambitions of making the process of archaeological interpretation transparent to a broader public and, in doing so, legitimizing the use of imagined narratives about prehistoric people by making explicit their connection to the primary archaeological data. Without the support of Meg Conkey, Janet Spector, and Rosemary Joyce, I might have been discouraged from this endeavor in the resistant atmosphere of the early 1990s, as Sarah Nelson and others also note in this volume.

The construction of the Chimera Web in 1994–96 with content from the Opovo project (Serbia) (Tringham, Brukner, and Voytek 1992) was my first digital attempt in this direction (Wolle and Tringham 2000). I have described this process and the exhilaration of transferring narratives from printed to digital formats in a number of publications (Joyce and Tringham 2007). It was especially the open-endedness and democratization of the digital format that I found inspiring, in that it provided an opportunity to use data-centered imagination to present alternative viewpoints, interpretations, and scenarios that were more engaging to create and, I think, to "read" than the closed definitive narratives represented by the printed word.

The structure of the Chimera Web was based in George Landow's (1992) concept of hypertext—the ability to create nodes with links through which a user can navigate around documents, just as we do in Web 1.0 "pages." It was designed with a hypertext authoring program called Storyspace[2] that was used (and still is) to create standalone hypertext narratives, for example, Rosemary Joyce and colleagues' *Sister Stories* (Joyce, Guyer, and Joyce 2000; Lopiparo and Joyce 2003). I chose to build the Chimera Web as a standalone (not web-based) interactive hypermedia opus in the multimedia authoring application Macromedia Director (to incorporate a rich audiovisual content), which ultimately was a disastrous decision in terms of its sustainability.

The narratives of the burning of House 2 at Opovo are told through the voices of two female survivors, Baba and Yaya. They did not really exist, of course, but someone like them certainly did. These people are given fictional biographies and are placed on a multiscalar chronological chart at an appropriate point of Opovo's stratigraphy, associated with the biography of a house and household (Tringham 1994: figure 6). At different periods of their lives they embrace other Neolithic settlements of the region. Their narratives are fiction, but they are grounded in the archaeological data. The design ambitiously aimed to link the imagined narratives about why and how Neolithic people burned houses to a web of data about the Opovo archaeological project, the investigation of Neolithic house fires, modern arson investigations, the socio-politics of archaeology in the Balkans, and the basis of the project in archaeological method and theory as well as the excavation database. This crucial last step—integration with the database—proved elusive with the technology and expertise available to me at that time and until very recently.

DATABASE NARRATIVES AND HISTORY

A number of technical and theoretical developments have helped make these original ambitions a more feasible—and sustainable—reality. The concept of Database Narratives has had an important effect on thinking differently about the relationship of narratives (of whatever genre) to databases. At the same time, the enormous growth and consumer access to processing power, networking power, and storage capacity in the ethereal world of the Internet have transformed what mere mortals (as opposed to highly trained and specialized software engineers) can do to construct interfaces and databases that are openly accessible, downloadable, searchable, and updatable through an Internet browser.

Lev Manovich (2001: 221–26) took a rather different standpoint on hyperlinking from that of George Landow (1992) when he formulated his concept of the Database Narrative. He pointed out that the opposition of database and narrative is a symbiotic one. Databases have a data structure that contrasts with the algorithmic structure of a narrative. Interfaces with an obvious algorithmic narrative structure can be drawn out of a database, resulting in the creation of a complex, fluid, even ephemeral web of alternating interfaces/narratives (database narratives), as Manovich himself created in his Soft Cinema[3] and Steve Anderson created in Technologies of History[4] (see also Soar and Gagnon 2013).

Steve Anderson (2011: 122–27) directed the idea of database narratives toward the construction of narratives of history, what he called "digital histories" or "recombinant histories." He recognizes two directions in which historiography has embraced digital technology. On the one hand is the idea of amassing the "total" historical record of events through accessible networked interoperable databases, creating history that is as full and definitive as possible. On the other hand, "Digital technologies have . . . enabled strategies of randomization and recombination in historical construction resulting in a profusion of increasingly volatile counter-narratives and histories with multiple or uncertain endings" (ibid.: 125); in other words, recombinant histories. Both of these practices are legitimate pathways to creating narratives about the past.

Recombinant histories, however, rather than being narratives that describe an experience of the past, are "collections of infinitely retrievable fragments, situated within categories and organized to predetermined associations . . . by which the past may be conceived as fundamentally mutable and reconfigurable" (ibid.: 122). In thinking about how recombinant histories would in practice change the writing of history and the role of the historian, Anderson (who is interested in the potential of recombinant histories for artistic works, history-based games, and the exploration of popular culture and film) points out that "the database and search engine enable non-linear accessing and combining of information into forms that defy both literary and historical conventions. Works of history once understood to comprise an expanding field of collective historical knowledge are thereby repositioned as raw materials in infinitely reconfigurable patterns of revision, remixing and recontextualization" (ibid.: 125).

By now, it is probably clear that this concept of an endless combination of fragmentary narratives has been a guiding principle of my current construction of narratives about archaeology and prehistory. Although the majority of archaeological narratives are constructed as coherent linear narratives with a beginning, middle, and end that, moreover, focus ultimately on broad and long-term themes, I have argued elsewhere that archaeological data are in the first instance most appropriate for narratives that are nonlinear fragments and that are written at an intimate scale (Tringham 1994: 198).

In historiography, starting in the 1980s and currently flourishing, a trend toward writing "micro-histories" has focused on this scale of narrative and a very close reading of the documentary evidence, in contrast to the more traditional "history writ large" (Ginzburg 2012: 193–214). The historians' argument for writing at this microscale (seen most clearly in Szijártó 2002) is, first, that the narrative is more closely associated with primary documentation or "little facts," thus decreasing the degree of ambiguity. As I argue later, any interpretation is more clearly and closely sourced in empirical data; it enables the historian to come "face to face" with individual actors of the past, arguably closer to "reality" in the "Cinema Verité" sense of the word, providing a richer picture of the context as can be seen in the micro-histories and, as I have argued, as a strong aspect of the feminist practice of archaeology (Tringham 1994: 183–84). At the same time, micro-historical narratives, with their imagined extensions of the primary documents, enable readers to immerse themselves in the experience of the everyday of the past from many points of view (Davis 1984; Ladurie 1997). The challenge for the prehistoric archaeologist is how to create such attractive narratives when the only primary documents (in the historiographic sense) are those of the archaeologist-interpreter separated by thousands of years from original action. The rest of this chapter addresses that challenge, as, I believe, have all the other chapters in this volume.

An important critique of "micro-historical" narratives has been their tendency to become so absorbed in the particulars of the story that the broader historical context is ignored or poorly articulated (Lamoreaux 2006). The argument for multiscalarity is one with which archaeologists are quite familiar. I have long been delighted that the technology of hypertext and now Database Narratives enables the author to link to ever-expanding scales of interpretation and back again to the particular (Joyce and Tringham 2007). Lutz has pointed to a number of works in the micro-historical genre that have demonstrated the power of web-based narratives to present a multiscalar aspect to the work and is delighted, as am I, by the open-endedness of such narratives and their ability to juxtapose narrative with the source document (Lutz 2007). It is not surprising, therefore, that an increasing number of micro-historical works are written as online narratives.[5]

LAST HOUSE ON THE HILL ONLINE DATABASE

During the summers of 1997–2005, I directed a team from the University of California at Berkeley (BACH team) that carried out an archaeological project of excavation and analysis at the site of Çatalhöyük in central Turkey, a 9,000-year-old Neolithic settlement mound, as part of the overall Çatalhöyük Research Project. The project focused on the life history of a single house (Building 3). The printed monograph report of the BACH project, titled *Last House on the Hill* (Tringham and Stevanovic 2012), is mirrored by an online digital database with the same name (http://lasthouseonthehill.org) (Ashley, Tringham, and Perlingieri 2011).[6] The digital Last House on the Hill (LHotH) project, however, "does much more than provide a digital presentation framework for publishing *Last House on the Hill*. Its ambition, one which we have long wished to satisfy, is to embed, interweave, entangle and otherwise link the complete project database (including all media formats such as photographs, videos, maps, line drawings) with their interpretation and meaningful presentation in an open access, sharable platform. It is an open-ended data stream that can grow and—as long as it is well curated—can live for many decades" (Tringham and Ashley 2012: 554–54). Our greatest challenge has been how to enable the user to make sense of such a deluge of rich media, data, analysis, and interpretation; how to link the components meaningfully for a variety of publics, to ensure their long-term preservation through access and usage.

CREATING MEANINGFUL NARRATIVES AND RECOMBINANT HISTORIES

The ultimate aim of the LHotH database is to encourage both archaeologists and a broader public to be inspired by interpretive guides and other kinds of scaffolds or "outerfaces"[7] to explore our data and media in order to use them in creative and productive ways to think about both the past and the present. Anderson and Manovich structure their databases in various ways, using filters and other means to guide the creation of narrative interfaces.[8] In the same way, the LHotH database has been structured to make sense of the mass of archaeological documentation as the relationships among people, actions, tasks, and the contingencies of time and space, grouped together as events in archaeological (Neolithic) time or the more recent time of the BACH excavation project (figure 2.1). Narratives that represent these relationships can be drawn out of the database through the filter of the alternating perspectives or standpoints of people, places, things, and media, thus enabling the recontextualization and remixing of the content that resides in the database (figure 2.2).

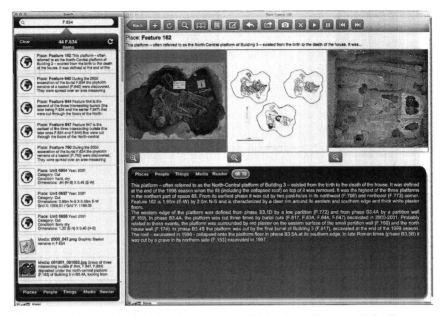

FIGURE 2.1. *Screenshot of the Last House on the Hill database, after a search for Feature 634, showing the presence of 44 directly related entities, and after the selection of the place Feature 162, which has 76 related entities*

An eBook/iPad version of the printed *Last House on the Hill* monograph could be one such narrative, but one that does not stray far from the conventions of linear "reading" of the printed monograph and what Bolter and Grusin (1999) refer to as "respectful remediation." In contrast, at UC Berkeley's Multimedia Authoring Center for Teaching in Anthropology (MACTiA), we have always encouraged in our students and colleagues a more "radical remediation" (ibid.) of the data and media of the BACH project in which an explorer of our data reuses and recontextualizes our excavation products to create in his or her own narrative an alternative interpretation or "reading" of the data, challenging the apparent authority of the "expert," even using such tools as irony and satire. We have already created some "remixes" of this kind, such as RAVE: Requiem for a "boneyard"; Dido's Lament; Remixing Dido's Lament (Tringham 2012b).[9]

But I believe we can go much further in using online database and web- (or mobile) based interface technology to radically and creatively remediate our archaeological data to explore the many possible trajectories and scenarios of the past. Unlike the original hypertext narratives (e.g., Joyce, Guyer, and Joyce

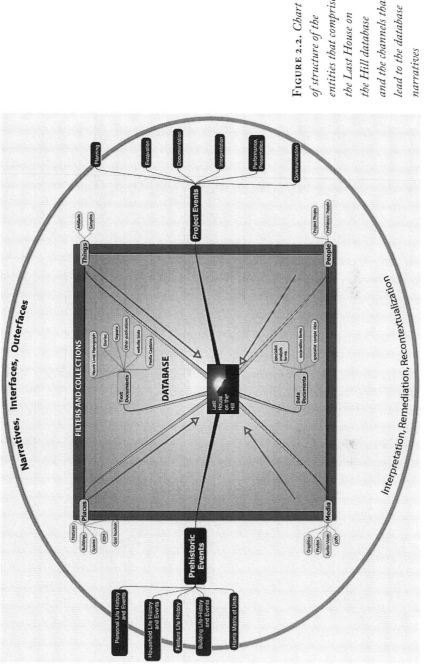

FIGURE 2.2. *Chart of structure of the entities that comprise the Last House on the Hill database and the channels that lead to the database narratives*

2000), in which the nodes are fixed but a path of navigation or juxtaposition can be followed allowing the narrative to be "read" differently each time the group of elements is visited, the data and media that provide the sources for database narratives are infinitely reconfigurable (albeit structured and scaffolded with filters), they are infinitely (within reason) expandable and updatable, and they can be "harvested" and related in a much more complex fashion.

DEAD WOMEN DO TELL TALES—THE BEGINNING

To demonstrate the potential of such a database narrative, I have gathered together a selection of fragments, some of which are entities harvested from the LHotH database, others from my creative imagination, into a preliminary set of micro-histories that themselves are fragments of a bigger (yes, probably endless) work—Dead Women Do Tell Tales (DWdTT). With this chapter, it is at the beginning of its construction. It is a "recombinant history," made up of fragments from the archaeological construction of Neolithic households in southeast Europe and Anatolia. Many of the fragments are drawn from the database of the Last House on the Hill (i.e., the BACH project at Çatalhöyük, Turkey). Others (not presented in this chapter) draw upon data and media from the archaeological projects of Opovo and Selevac, both in Serbia and both of which figured heavily in the hypermedia Chimera Web.

Dead Women Do Tell Tales harvests and then recombines these data fragments to think about a very big question: what is it in the Neolithic household–based foundation that leads to such a contrast in the trajectories of southeast Europe and Anatolia toward the establishment of centralized authority and urbanism in which the social reproductive role of the individual household is lost (Tringham 2000)? This very large question forms the background—and perhaps the ultimate aim—to the many micro-historical narrative fragments in DWdTT that, like Stewart's *Ordinary Affects*, are about everyday social practice, multi-sensorial experiences, and small events in the life histories of people, places, and things: "Ordinary affects are the surging capacities to affect and to be affected that give everyday life the quality of a continual motion of relations, scenes, contingencies, and emergences" (Stewart 2007: 2). Doug Bailey and Melanie Simpkin in this volume have a similar desire—but a different response to the challenge—to think about the slow rhythm and small time increments of the everyday.

There are, for example, seemingly contrasting ways in which the continuity of place is established—at Çatalhöyük, the dead are buried under the house floors, "open" sites like Opovo and Selevac, the houses are given a funeral pyre and the dead are nowhere to be seen; walls of old houses form the foundations for a new house, creating a settlement mound ("tell"), a new house is built next to an old house. How these contrasts play out in everyday life can be explored by following the imagined life-paths of the people who resided in these places. Such life-paths are full of ambiguity even with the support of archaeological data, so the narratives help explore alternative scenarios. How do the archaeologists in these places struggle in their research with this same ambiguity on a daily basis? The history thus created is multi-formatted, cumulative, never complete, rich in imaginative thinking, and hard (impossible?) to grasp as a definitive story.

The focus of the narratives in DWdTT is always on people—past and present residents (including archaeologists themselves) and visitors who created and continue to create places in the different locations embraced by the project. In the LHotH database, prehistoric people are associated with their final resting places (as in figure 2.1 for the character "Dido"), with the surviving places and things they experienced with all their senses as they went about their everyday lives, as well as with the life histories of themselves, their houses, and their villages. Archaeologists—who have life histories and experiences—are also related with these places (such as human remains specialist Lori Hager). Their first-person narratives in both prehistoric and present are of necessity the product of memory and thus sometimes seem to be nonlinear and incomplete, with elements of the bias, wistfulness, and secrecy that diaries and memories emote. The skill for the reader, as when listening to any stories, is to "read" between the lines and "read" from multiple sources.

The complexity of this task is exacerbated by the fact that the prehistoric "voices" so far have only one source—my imagination. I am in agreement with Michael Shanks (2012) that we need to be aware that our imaginations are in play throughout the archaeological process. I believe we need to be aware as much as is feasible of its sources and how we are articulating between past and present imagining (Ashley 2012). The sources for my imagination are multiple but come from many years of fieldwork in the countryside of southeast Europe and Anatolia, as well as broad reading of ethnographies and histories. I am not aware of explicitly modeling any of the characters in DWdTT on people from my experience, but I am sure that I do.

The creation of both character and plot is more like the process described by Beveridge (1974: 53) in his *Art of Scientific Investigation,* quoting from Dewey (1933): "First comes awareness of some difficulty or problem which provides the stimulus [RT: in our case a combination of empirical evidence, such as "Dido's" injuries of healed broken ribs and dislocated hip, or burning a house deliberately at high temperatures, that needs explanation]. This is followed by a suggested solution springing into the conscious mind." Even so, as with any writer of creative fiction, I know I cannot avoid something of my modern worldview embedding itself in the prehistoric "voice." Mark Pluciennik in this volume has covered for me the implications of my author-ity in doing this; I choose his third option—to make this fact transparent and be ready to enter into a dialogue with my readers, including those who may be offended by my focus on death as well as life. These products of creative imagination at this point in the development of Dead Women Do Tell Tales are expressed as responses 9,000 years ago of an informant, not to an ethnographer but more likely to a curious traveler, who has ended up at Çatalhöyük by accident, rather like Ibn Fadlan, the hero of Michael Crichton's *Eaters of the Dead* (Crichton 1977). I am sure that this will change during further development of Dead Women Do Tell Tales. The "modern" voices are based in diaries, video, and publications of archaeologists and visitors harvested from the LHotH database.

For the purposes of this demonstration of DWdTT, I am focusing on five micro-histories or database narratives drawn out of entities and their relationships in the Last House on the Hill database and their fictional interpretations. They serve as a scaffold for the exploration of one small corner of the BACH project—the burial of a woman under a platform in Building 3. Each micro-history builds from a single entity found in the LHotH database. From there, as with Spector's (1993) *What This Awl Means* or Gilead's Lysol bottle fragment in this volume, other fragments are related through relations that occur in the database. One micro-history builds from basket phytoliths found associated with a Neolithic burial of a mature woman known as Feature 634, or "Dido." Through its relationship between "basket" and then "Feature 634" in the LHotH database, this one small artifact is directly related to at least twenty other fragments (figure 2.3). Such fragments comprise text narratives attached to or embedded in media items in the form of captions and other metadata, or they might be textual descriptions (from diaries or archaeological contexts) that are enhanced in DWdTT by attached images or videos and alphanumeric data from the database converted into text or charts.

The entities or fragments of the "Basket in Feature 634" micro-history include images of this and several other baskets, including an attempt to preserve a basket, an image of another set of phytoliths interpreted as binding rope in the same burial, and two videos that record two events in "project time"—the discovery and the excavation of the remains of the basket. The people in the videos include Willeke Wendrich, a specialist in basket analysis,

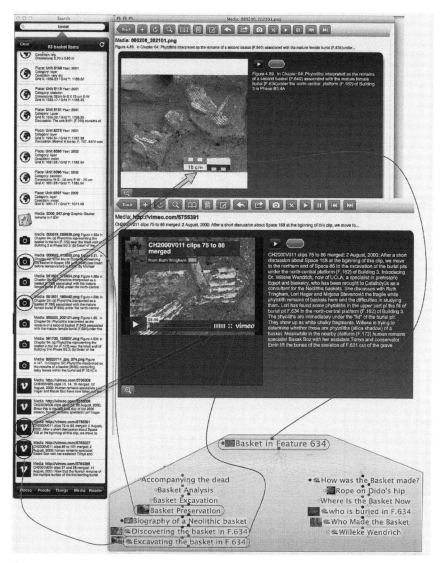

Figure 2.3. *Selection of source data from the LHotH database for the micro-history/ database narrative "Basket in Feature 634"*

and Lori Hager, the human remains specialist who excavated Feature 634. Exploration might encourage you to jump to another micro-history that focuses on Hager. Or you might follow links to other narratives in the "Basket in Feature 634" micro-history that go beyond the collection in LHotH. These narratives include an excerpt of a publication by Wendrich about excavating baskets at Çatalhöyük; in addition, there are fragments constructed as new narratives that I (the only user so far) have created as a result of exploring the web of media, texts, and other data and my imagination. These new narratives include giving the basket itself a voice so it can tell about its life (a literary trope used by a number of other writers) and scenarios of making the basket based on Wendrich's analysis.

One of the fragments in the "Basket in Feature 634" micro-history titled *Who Is Buried in F.634* is a video that remediates and remixes the primary data in the Last House on the Hill database describing how we came to designate the woman buried in F.634 as "Dido." This fragment, as with a number of others, also appears in three of the other micro-histories (figure 2.4), demonstrating not only the idea of entanglement but also the idea that the same fragment can be viewed multiple times and will have a different affect in each juxtapositional context. In the "Lori Hager" micro-history, the burial is seen from the point of view of the human remains specialist who excavated it; in the "Dido" micro-history, it provides the archaeological introduction to the life history of this mature woman; in the "Burials in Building 3" micro-history, this fragment is juxtaposed with other burials before and after F.634, providing Dido's context among the residents of Building 3 as a household.

Similarly, fragments from "Lori Hager," "Dido," and "Burials in Building 3," such as "Life History of Building 3," are also fragments in the "BACH Project" micro-history, again each with a different context and a different affect. Thus when landing on "Life History of Building 3" in the "BACH Project," a "traveler" could follow the path of archaeologists as they constructed the history with fragments drawn mostly from the LHotH database; by following a link such as "Life History of a Household," however, the context changes. The reader would follow a parallel path but one constructed from the archaeologist's imagined life of a single household or person in Building 3. From there the reader would travel onto a different set of narratives.

Such a tour of a recombinant history can be quite challenging. Steve Anderson, in the introduction to his online recombinant history of film *Technologies of History*, advises the user:

> Although certain aspects of the design may initially appear to resist easy navigation, our aim is neither to frustrate the user nor indulge in aestheticized design experiments . . . The experience of moving through the project is . . . intended to be partly experiential and partly curatorial; users may select from categories of content that are based on genre, format or (primarily) threads of historiographi-

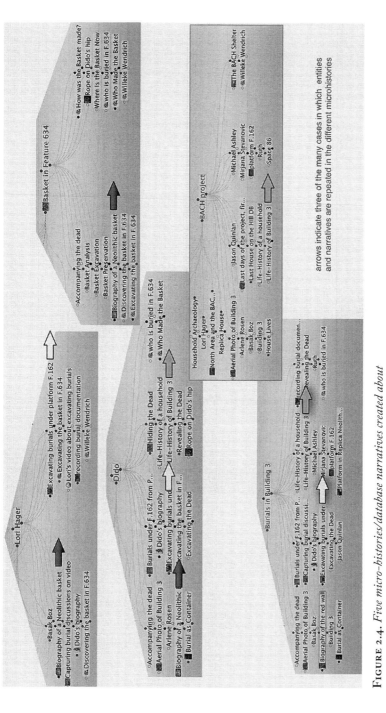

FIGURE 2.4. *Five micro-histories/database narratives created about Neolithic Çatalhöyük, Turkey, for Dead Women Do Tell Tales*

cal concern. The multiplicity of opportunities for revelation or chaos function as both a metaphor for history's own lack of resolution and as a rhetorical strategy for resisting narrative closure.[10]

With very similar aims in my project, the eventual cloud-based or mobile-device user interface of Dead Women Do Tell Tales may resemble Technologies of History or may more closely resemble a two- or three-dimensional computer game. Two requirements for the future user interface of Dead Women Do Tell Tales that are inspired by Technologies of History are, first, that it be connected to the LHotH database so entities can be searched for and harvested on the fly. The second requirement is that it should enable users to log their path of exploration to create (and contribute) new narratives and to create "new critical contexts in which viewers simultaneously interrogate the past and rethink the entangled relations of history, memory and media."[11] Just as users of a database are invited to save their search tables while exploring a "regular" online database, users of Dead Women Do Tell Tales would be invited to create their own recombinations of fragments/entities from those built into DWdTT and those they find by digging deeper into the LHotH database. Both of these requirements would satisfy my ambition of engaging a broader audience in the creation of narratives that are based in but challenge the boundaries of archaeological research.

The interface you see in this demonstration serves more to enable visualization of the underlying structure of DWdTT and its relationship to the Last House on the Hill database. Currently, the user interface of Dead Women Do Tell Tales is built in a free mind-mapping software called The Brain.[12] Like all proprietary software (remember Storyspace and Macromedia Director?), it is unlikely to survive the test of time. Moreover, it is not connected directly to the LHotH database. For the moment, however, it is useful to show how the "thoughts"—my fragmentary narratives—function sometimes as parents, sometimes as children (depending on context), or as nonhierarchical "jumps," as a 3D web of enormous depth and complexity (figure 2.5). The structure of Dead Women Do Tell Tales—the fact that the source of each fragment is embedded in the narrative "entity" as metadata—guarantees that any interpretive narrative will be firmly anchored in the empirical data of the projects by its relationship to other fragments in the micro-history, which themselves have been drawn directly from the LHotH database (table 2.1). Thus at every step the author could argue and even further embed the rationale for his or her interpretation in terms of plausibility by direct reference to a source in the LHotH database.

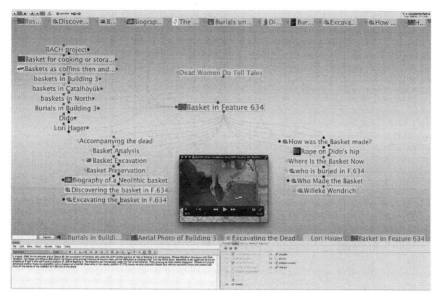

FIGURE 2.5. *Screenshot of the micro–history/database narrative "Basket in Feature 634" in the online The Brain interface*

The LHotH content, as the primary source of the archaeological project, has been created and prepared in a way that makes it sustainable, meaningful, and reusable for many generations. User interfaces—like Dead Women Do Tell Tales, the results of harvesting from a database—may be more or less sustainable depending on (1) whether they are built on open-source or proprietary software, (2) how easily the software and content can be updated, (3) how easily and how much they are accessed and used, and (4) how engaging they are. However, trends and fashions in interfaces change and are nevertheless relatively ephemeral.

For now, however, readers on their web browsers can explore this version of Dead Women Do Tell Tales with its five existing micro-histories and follow along as the recombinant history expands and begins to take shape in future months.[13]

In a chapter of *Last House on the Hill* titled "Sensing the Place of Çatalhöyük," I could do little more than suggest narratives such as these that might go beyond the strict empirical boundaries of the excavated data as tantalizing but disembodied fragments (Tringham 2012a). In the Dead Women Do Tell Tales recombinant history we will use the full power of digital technology to

TABLE 2.1 Details of the contents of three micro-histories/database narratives created for Dead Women Do Tell Tales about Neolithic Çatalhöyük, Turkey, showing their source as entities in the Last House on the Hill database or as texts of creative writing.

Micro-history/ Vignette	Narrative Title	Primary Medium	Narrative	Source
Basket in F.634	Introductory scaffold for the basket micro-history	audio	The basket of this micro-history was associated with burial in Feature 634, but was it as a container of the dead or as an accompaniment for the dead person? From the object itself, a wide net harvests many stories about the basket, many of them written as creative imagination	
Basket in F.634	Basket in F.634	text with photo	Description of phytolith remains of a basket designated Features 640 and 760	photo: CRP 080200_202443.jpg; text: LHotH feature description
Basket in F.634	Discovering the Basket in F.634	video	August 2, 2000: Willeke Wendrich discusses with Ruth Tringham, Lori Hager, and Mirjana Stevanovic the fragile white phytolith remains of baskets at Çatalhöyük and the difficulties in studying them	video: BACH CaTDV catalog; CH2000V011 clips, 75 to 86 merged; text: http://vimeo.com/575591
Basket in F.634	Excavating the Basket in F.634	video	August 2, 2000: human remains specialist Lori Hager is excavating the phytoliths at the top of the fill of burial F.634	video: BACH CatDV catalog; CH2000V011 clips, 85 to 101 merged; text: http://vimeo.com/5762027
Basket in F.634	Lori Hager	video	Lori Hager, one of two human remains specialists in the BACH area, is asked about her memory of Çatalhöyük through the senses	CatalViceoPlace CatDV catalog; LoriInterview_clip3.mov
Basket in F.634	Accompanying the Dead	text	Dido will have a basket as company. She remembers her child accompanied by much more	RET creative imagination

continued on next page

TABLE 2.1—continued

Micro-history/ Vignette	Narrative Title	Primary Medium	Narrative	Source
Basket in F.634	Basket Analysis	text	Analysis of some of the phytolith basketry from Çatalhöyük by basketry specialist Willeke Wendrich as to how the baskets are made	Willeke Wendrich. 2005. "Çatalhöyük Basketry." In *Changing Materialities at Çatalhöyük*, ed. I. Hodder, 333–38. Cambridge: McDonald Institute for Archaeological Research
Basket in F.634	Willeke Wendrich	video	Introducing Willeke Wendrich, who has been brought to Çatalhöyük as a consultant for the Neolithic baskets	Willeke_Intro_July2000-basket_or-H.264.mov
Basket in F.634	How Was the Basket Made?	text	Dido remembers how she was taught to make her first basket	RET: creative imagination
Basket in F.634	Biography of a Neolithic Basket	text with image	The basket in F.634 tells its life history	RET: creative imagination; photo: basket_02.jpg
Basket in F.634	Sedges	image	Some of the materials used to make baskets at Çatalhöyük	http://commons.wikimedia.org /wiki/File:Agropyron_cristatum_(382220852).jpg
Basket in F.634	Who Collects the Sedge?	text	Work song sung by sedge cutters of Çatalhöyük	RET: creative imagination
Basket in F.634	Where Is It Collected?	map		Google Earth
Basket in F.634	Who Made the Basket?	video	Animation movie created by Colleen Morgan with her avatar in the virtual world of Çatalhöyük on Okapi Island in Second Life	Colleen Morgan: machinima_1.mp4

continued on next page

TABLE 2.1—continued

Micro-history/ Vignette	Narrative Title	Primary Medium	Narrative	Source
Basket in F.634	Basket for Cooking or Storage in Building 3	photo with text	Phytoliths (plant remains) from a round basket found in the middle of the western room (Space 158) of Building 3, used for cooking	LHotH DB: 08700_12515
Basket in F.634	Baskets as Coffins, Then and Now	photo with text	Baskets used in burials to contain the dead; juxtaposition of two images, then and now	images: Then: John Swogger: Swogger_burial_6.jpg; Now: wicker-coffin.jpg
Basket in F.634	Basket Excavation at Çatalhöyük	text	Basket specialist Willeke Wendrich discusses the challenge of excavating baskets because of the fragmentary nature of their preservation	Willeke Wendrich. 2005. "Çatalhöyük Basketry." In *Changing Materialities at Çatalhöyük*, ed. I. Hodder, 333–38. Cambridge: McDonald Institute for Archaeological Research
Basket in F.634	Platform F.162	photo with text	The north-central platform (Feature 162) of Building 3 was a focus throughout the BACH excavation, with four different burial events cutting through it	LHotH DB 990728_r3450.jpg
Basket in F.634	Who Is Buried in Feature 634?	video	A movie remixed from LHotH media entities focuses on the excavation of a skeleton of a mature woman we have called Dido	Quinlan, Ashley, Tringham remix: http://vimeo. com/17146954

continued on next page

TABLE 2.1—*continued*

Micro-history/ Vignette	Narrative Title	Primary Medium	Narrative	Source
Lori Hager	Introductory scaffold to the Lori Hager micro-history	audio	Lori Hager, human remains specialist, with Basak Boz of the BACH project team. They excavated and documented all of the burials in Building 3. Lori is interested in thinking about the skeletons as people	
Lori Hager	Excavating the Basket in F.634	video		
Lori Hager	Lori Hager	video		
Lori Hager	Discovering the Basket in F.634	video		
Lori Hager	Lori's video interview of excavating burials	video	Interview, February 23, 2005, in Berkeley, California, in which Lori Hager describes her memory of the perception of touch while she excavates the burials and her experience of excavating this very intimate scale of archaeological practice—the investigation of human burial	LoriInterview_clip5-6.mov; http://vimeo.com/6182084
Lori Hager	Excavating Burials under Platform F.162	photo with text	Lori Hager and Basak Boz mapping, recording, and removing the uppermost layer of bones from the mass of human bones buried under Feature 162	LHotH DB: 06140I_115655
Lori Hager	Burials under F.162 from Phase B3.4A	photo with text	Feature 162 showing the multiple (four) burial pits beneath its floors in the later phases of the history of Building 3	LHotH DB: 06130I_145504

continued on next page

TABLE 2.1—*continued*

Micro–history/ Vignette	Narrative Title	Primary Medium	Narrative	Source
Lori Hager	Revealing the Dead, Then and Now	text with video	Then: Dido describes how they reveal the older burials as new burials are dug. Now: August 14, 2000: Ruth, Lori, and Basak figure out how to reveal the sequence of burials from the mass of bones.	text: RET creative imagination; video: CH2000V007C_clips03to04_08:400_cropped. mov, http://vimeo.com/5708213
Lori Hager	Capturing Burial Discussions on Video	photo with text	Project videographer Jason Quinlan records a discussion between BACH field directors Ruth and Mirjana and human remains specialists Basak and Lori about recording the mass of human bones under platform F.162	LHotH DB: 061401_074521: http://lasthouseonthehill.org /node/212
Lori Hager	Basak Boz	text	Introducing Basak Boz	
Lori Hager	Recording Burial Documentation	photo with text	Lori Hager fills in a Skeletal Unit sheet as colleague Basak Boz removes the bones from one of the burials under F.162	LHotH DB: 061701_154440: https://vimeo.com/album /112046/video/594126o
Lori Hager	Dido's Biography	text with illustration	Dido tells the story of her life, especially her memory of its dramatic events, including the births and deaths of her children	text: RET creative imagination; image: John Swogger: Swogger_g768_woman.jpg
Dido	Introductory scaffold to the Dido micro-history	audio	Dido is what we came to name the woman who was buried in Feature 634. In this micro-history I imagine much since no written trace exists, but we can build much information about her from the skeletal remains and the basket with which she was buried	
Dido	Dido's Biography	text		

continued on next page

TABLE 2.1—*continued*

Micro–history/ Vignette	Narrative Title	Primary Medium	Narrative	Source
Dido	Who Is Buried in F.634?	video		
Dido	Rope on Dido's Hip	photo	Phytoliths that mark the former presence of rope binding the hips of "Dido," a female excavated in 2001	LHotH DB: 06230_18172.jpg
Dido	Arlene Rosen	text		
Dido	Excavating the Dead	video		
Dido	Revealing the Dead	text		
Dido	Hiding the Dead	text with image	Dido tells of some of rules that regulate how the dead should be prepared for burial and how they should be hidden	text: RET creative imagination; image: LHotH DB: 072600_02205.jpg
Dido	Containing the Dead	text	Dido talks to the curious visitor about how she and her fellow villagers see burial as a container, like a womb or a cave	text: RET creative imagination; image: John Swogger, catal_swogger_burial.jpg
Dido	Burials under F.162 from Phase B3.4A	photo		
Dido	Excavating the Basket in F.634	video		
Dido	Lori Hager	video		

continued on next page

TABLE 2.1—*continued*

Micro-history/ Vignette	Narrative Title	Primary Medium	Narrative	Source
Dido	Who Made the Basket?	story		
Dido	Biography of a Neolithic Basket	text		
Dido	Aerial Photo of Building 3	photo with text	Aerial shot of the BACH area in 2000, looking west, showing a busy day in the life of the excavation of Building 3, where at least ten people are working comfortably. This might give an indication of how many people could have lived in Building 3 during its prehistoric life	LHotH DB: 081700_140917
Dido	Life History of a Household	story	The collective life history of the residents of Building 3 as told by Dido to a visitor	text: RET creative imagination
Dido	Life History of Building 3	image	Image of the changing floor plan of Building 3 through its ten phases defined archaeologically	LHotH DB: bach_ch4_Figure 03_ret.tiff
Burials in Building 3	Introductory scaffold to the Burials micro-history	audio	The burials in Building 3 are almost all under platforms (F.162 and F.173) at the north end of the main living room, as is usual at Çatalhöyük	

take these fragments—narratives—of created knowledge and audiovisual representation and combine and recombine them into an open-ended but always accumulating history of the BACH project, itself a (frequently forgotten) fragment of the larger Çatalhöyük Research Project. They are tangled with other stories from other forgotten archaeological projects in Serbia to create a new set of narratives that are themselves recombined to create a history that can never be grasped but that at the same time is not so far from "reality," because all of the narratives are embedded with some kind of empirical details.

ACKNOWLEDGMENTS

The "we" mentioned at many points in this chapter refers especially to the pleasure, inspiration, and guidance I have received in working with Michael Ashley, my "peer learner" from the beginning of our journey in building digital histories together to its most recent manifestation in the Center for Digital Archaeology (CoDA). We have created CoDA, a nonprofit organization, together with Meg Conkey, who has also been a tower of support and generosity on this journey, and Cinzia Perlingieri, without whom none of these projects would ever get finished.

NOTES

1. http://www.flashfictiononline.com/main/, accessed July 12, 2012.

2. http://www.eastgate.com/storyspace/, accessed January 1, 2012.

3. The Soft Cinema website includes samples of videos: http://www.softcinema.net/index.htm?reload, accessed March 16, 2011.

4. http://vectors.usc.edu/issues/6/techhistory/, accessed March 16, 2011.

5. One of the best known is "A Midwife's Tale," which was the subject of a PBS film with supporting materials: http://www.pbs.org/wgbh/amex/midwife/. But look also at this website in which the same original materials are put in the context of writing narratives: http://dohistory.org/, accessed September 16, 2011.

6. http://lasthouseonthehill.org, accessed July 12, 2012.

7. This term was first used by Shahina Farid at Çatalhöyük in 2005 (personal communication).

8. See Soft Cinema (Manovich): http://www.softcinema.net/index.htm?reload, and Technologies of History (Anderson): http://vectors.usc.edu/issues/6/techhistory/, accessed March 16, 2011.

9. http://www.ruthtringham.com/Ruth_Tringham/BACH_digital_publications.html, accessed November 15, 2013.

10. http://vectors.usc.edu/issues/6/techhistory/, accessed March 16, 2011.

11. Ibid.

12. http://www.thebrain.com/, accessed July 16, 2011.

13. http://webbrain.com/brainpage/brain/230E20DC-C9BC-7492-9B9C-297A3 84B4CCF#-67, accessed November 1, 2013.

REFERENCES

Anderson, Steve. 2011. *Technologies of History: Visual Media and the Eccentricity of the Past*. Boston: Dartmouth College Press.

Ashley, Michael. 2012. "An Archaeology of Vision: Seeing Past and Present at Çatalhöyük, Turkey." In *Last House on the Hill: BACH Area Reports from Çatalhöyük, Turkey* (Çatalhöyük, vol. 11), ed. Ruth Tringham and Mirjana Stevanovic, 481–502. Archaeologica Monumenta 27. Los Angeles: Cotsen Institute of Archaeology Publications, UCLA.

Ashley, Michael, Ruth Tringham, and Cinzia Perlingieri. 2011. "Last House on the Hill: Digitally Remediating Data and Media for Preservation and Access." *Journal on Computing and Cultural Heritage* 5 (4). http://dx.doi.org/10.1145/2050096 .2050098.

Beveridge, William. 1974. *The Art of Scientific Investigation*. London: Heinemann Educational Books.

Bolter, Jay David, and Richard Grusin. 1999. *Remediation: Understanding New Media*. Cambridge, MA: MIT Press.

Brown, Richard D. 2003. "Microhistory and the Post-Modern Challenge." *Journal of the Early Republic* 23 (1): 1–20. http://dx.doi.org/10.2307/3124983.

Crichton, Michael. 1977. *Eaters of the Dead*. New York: Bantam Books.

Davis, Natalie Zemon. 1984. *The Return of Martin Guerre*. Cambridge, MA: Harvard University Press.

Dewey, John. 1933. *How We Think*. Boston: D. C. Heath.

Ginzburg, Carlo. 1980. *The Cheese and the Worms: The Cosmos of a Sixteenth Century Miller*. Baltimore: Johns Hopkins University Press.

Ginzburg, Carlo. 2012. *Threads and Traces: True, False, Fictive*. Trans. John Tedeschi and Anne C. Tedeschi. Berkeley: University of California Press.

Joyce, Rosemary, Carolyn Guyer, and Michael Joyce. 2000. *Sister Stories*. New York: New York University Press.

Joyce, Rosemary, and Ruth Tringham. 2007. "Feminist Adventures in Hypertext." *Journal of Archaeological Method and Theory Special Issue: Practising Archaeology as a Feminist*, ed. Alison Wylie and Meg Conkey, 14 (3): 328–58.

Ladurie, Emmanuel Le Roy. 1997. *The Beggar and the Professor*. Trans. Arthur Goldhammer. Chicago: University of Chicago Press.

Lamoreaux, Naomi R. 2006. "Rethinking Microhistory." *Journal of the Early Republic* 26 (4): 555–61. http://dx.doi.org/10.1353/jer.2006.0069.

Landow, George. 1992. *Hypertext: The Convergence of Contemporary Critical Theory and Technology*. Baltimore: Johns Hopkins University Press.

Lopiparo, Jeanne, and Rosemary Joyce. 2003. "Crafting Cosmos, Telling Sister Stories, and Exploring Archaeological Knowledge Graphically in Hypertext Environments." In *Ancient Muses: Archaeology and the Arts*, ed. John H. Jameson Jr., Christine A. Finn, and John E. Ehrenhard, 193–205. Tuscaloosa: University of Alabama Press.

Lutz, John. 2007. "The Web Gives and It Takes Away." *Canadian Historical Association Bulletin* 33 (2): 38–39.

Manovich, Lev. 2001. *The Language of New Media*. Cambridge, MA: MIT Press.

Nesbit, Edith. 1899. *The Story of the Treasure Seekers*. London: Puffin Classics Books.

Piccini, Angela. 2007. "Faking It: Why the Truth Is So Important for TV Archaeology." In *Archaeology and the Media*, ed. Timothy Clack and Marcus Brittain, 221–36. Walnut Creek, CA: Left Coast.

Pratt, Mary. 2009. "How Technology Is Changing What We Read." *PC World*, May 5, http://www.pcworld.com/article/164355/e_books.html, accessed July 12, 2012.

Shanks, Michael. 2012. *The Archaeological Imagination*. Walnut Creek, CA: Left Coast.

Soar, Matt, and Monika Gagnon, eds. 2013. "Database, Narrative, Archive: Seven Interactive Essays on Digital Nonlinear Storytelling." http://dnaanthology.com /anvc/dna/index, accessed October 15, 2013.

Spector, Janet. 1993. *What This Awl Means*. Minneapolis: University of Minnesota Press.

Stewart, Kathleen. 2007. *Ordinary Affects*. Durham, NC: Duke University Press. http:// dx.doi.org/10.1215/9780822390404.

Szijártó, István. 2002. "Four Arguments for Microhistory." *Rethinking History* 6 (2): 209–15. http://dx.doi.org/10.1080/13642520210145644.

Tringham, Ruth. 1991. "Households with Faces: The Challenge of Gender in Prehistoric Architectural Remains." In *Engendering Archaeology: Women and Prehistory*, ed. Joan M. Gero and Margaret W. Conkey, 93–131. Oxford: Basil Blackwell.

Tringham, Ruth. 1994. "Engendered Places in Prehistory." *Gender, Place and Culture* 1 (2): 169–203. http://dx.doi.org/10.1080/09663699408721209.

Tringham, Ruth. 2000. "The Continuous House: A View from the Deep Past." In *Beyond Kinship: Social and Material Reproduction in House Societies*, ed. Susan D. Gillespie and Rosemary Joyce, 115–34. Philadelphia: University of Pennsylvania Press.

Tringham, Ruth. 2012a. "Sensing the Place of Çatalhöyük and Building 3: The Rhythms of Daily Life." In *Last House on the Hill: BACH Area Reports from Çatalhöyük, Turkey* (Çatalhöyük, vol. 11), ed. Ruth Tringham and Mirjana Stevanovic, 531–52. Archaeologica Monumenta 27. Los Angeles: Cotsen Institute of Archaeology Publications, UCLA.

Tringham, Ruth. 2012b. "The Public Face of Archaeology at Çatalhöyük." In *Last House on the Hill: BACH Area Reports from Çatalhöyük, Turkey* (Çatalhöyük, vol. 11), ed. Ruth Tringham and Mirjana Stevanovic, 503–29. Archaeologica Monumenta 27. Los Angeles: Cotsen Institute of Archaeology Publications, UCLA.

Tringham, Ruth, and Michael Ashley. 2012. "Afterword: Last House on the Hill: The Digital Mirror of House Lives." In *Last House on the Hill: BACH Area Reports from Çatalhöyük, Turkey* (Çatalhöyük, vol. 11), ed. Ruth Tringham and Mirjana Stevanovic, 553–54. Archaeologica Monumenta 27. Los Angeles: Cotsen Institute of Archaeology Publications, UCLA.

Tringham, Ruth, Bogdan Brukner, Timothy Kaiser, Ksenija Borojevic, Ljubomir Bukvic, Peter Steli, Nerissa Russell, Mirjana Stevanovic, and Barbara Voytek. 1992. " Excavations at Opovo, 1985–1987: Socioeconomic Change in the Balkan Neolithic." *Journal of Field Archaeology* 19 (3): 351–86.

Tringham, Ruth, and Mirjana Stevanovic, eds. 2012. *Last House on the Hill: BACH Area Reports from Çatalhöyük, Turkey* (Çatalhöyük, vol. 11). Archaeologica Monumenta 27. Los Angeles: Cotsen Institute of Archaeology Publications, UCLA.

Wardrip-Fruin, Noah, and Pat Harrigan, eds. 2004. *First Person: New Media as Story, Performance, and Game.* Cambridge, MA: MIT Press.

Wolle, Anja, and Ruth Tringham. 2000. "Multiple Çatalhöyüks on the World Wide Web." In *Towards Reflexive Method in Archaeology: The Example at Çatalhöyük by Members of the Çatalhöyük Teams,* ed. Ian Hodder, 207–18. Cambridge: McDonald Institute for Archaeological Research.

3

Authoritative and Ethical Voices

From Diktat *to the Demotic*

MARK PLUCIENNIK

In this democratic age, should archaeologists be considered primarily as conduits for putting certain kinds of data, information, and stories about the past into play for various groups to interpret as they wish? Or do the forms of their productions and interventions have more subtle and potentially political implications? If we accept that there are various ways and increasingly available different means of constructing archaeological stories, narratives, and texts, what might these alternatives mean in practice for archaeologists and consumers? I want to explore these issues initially through examining the notion of "authority" within archaeological representations, here referring to both their origin and status, and also the consequent ethical implications.

I use the term *diktat* to refer to the earlier position in which the printed texts produced by archaeologists (and specialists more generally) were relatively static, permanent, and unchallengeable on a day-to-day basis. By demotic I mean the ways changes in the costs of, access to, and nature of communication—increasingly beyond the power of states to regulate—have led to a proliferation of voices in which archaeologists are only one of many groups producing and consuming archaeologically relevant narratives and texts. This arises particularly today because many parts of the social, cultural, and scientific worlds have seen both a proliferation and an apparent democratization of texts. See, for example, the discussion on the explosion in

DOI: 10.5876/9781607323815.c003

numbers of archaeology journals over recent decades and the predicted rise in "open-access" academic publication (Rocks-Macqueen 2012), itself published on an open-access project—a blog and journal—run by postgraduate students (see also Hadley 2011; Rocks-Macqueen 2011).

This is largely driven by technology: the Internet and generally cheaper digital publication make texts and data more and more easily available, shared, manipulable, interactive, and potentially more inclusive—or offensive. Digital data capture in the field also assists this process. There are thus new ways of both producing and presenting archaeology and its interpretations (see, among others, Tringham, Bailey and Simpkin, Van Dyke, Tuwaletstiwa and Tuwaletstiwa, all in this volume, for many stimulating examples), including hypermedia, embedded videos, interactive databases, maps, and so forth. Form, style, and presentation (e.g., nonlinearity and mobile, global accessibility) may be more important, and differently evaluated and consumed in relation to content, when compared to past and primarily linear "hard-copy" texts and arguments. One result is that authority and hierarchy within academic disciplines and many other fields can much more easily be challenged or simply ignored, or the currencies of evaluation can be moved into other locations in relation to other forms of power—popularity, "hits," or finance, for example. Populism, crossover genres, and multimedia possibilities encourage differently constituted archaeologies, understandings of the past, and ideas about what "texts" and other versions of narratives should look like and contain. Under these circumstances it is worth asking if the duties of archaeologists, in their various roles as producers, interpreters, translators, authors, facilitators, teachers, and co-writers, have also fundamentally shifted, along with the ethical responsibilities we might demand of ourselves.

ARCHAEOLOGISTS AND THE PRODUCTION OF TEXTS

Where might one start thinking about the responsibilities of archaeologists as authors, as the people who put certain forms of representations, including traditional narratives about the past, into play? In a disciplinary sense, we excavate, collect, analyze, and review and then disseminate, debate, display, and otherwise produce material that relates to the past, whether objects, scientific analyses, images, data, public performances, or texts. Originally, it was unproblematic to consider the outcome of fieldwork or study to be the responsibility of an individual. Whatever the practical contributions of others, the final book, paper, or lecture would be recognized as a statement of an author, typically the "excavator" or, rather, site director.

However, changes in the nature and complexity of fieldwork, especially post-excavation, and other forms of study have since taken place. These include the organization of archaeological methods and practices, such as the spatial and intellectual dispersal of "fieldwork" (Jones 2001; Pluciennik and Drew 2000), as well as socio-political and socio-cultural expectations and an intellectual climate that require acknowledgment of collaborators. Technological conditions also enable multi-authored, dynamic, and dialogic "texts" to be put together in ways not previously practically possible and in multiple versions. Especially for some forms of digital, hyperlinked, and thus relatively unbounded texts, it may be difficult to ascribe or claim individual or even joint "authorship" of ideas and material or to constrain the form of narratives or certainly the reading of such narratives in any direct and simple way. The multiplication of publications, media, institutions, and recognized interest groups, along with increased specializations within the field, means it is also more difficult for individuals to claim public authority—to be able or to wish to speak for archaeologists or archaeology in some kind of representative, consensual way. These factors have led to a diminution or dispersal of individualized "authority," in the public sphere at least. With increasing numbers of sources of and channels for statements, the presence and presentation of archaeological stories and discussion have widened far beyond scholarly debate among small academic and other generally like-minded groups (such as enthusiasts in local societies) and dissemination through occasional popular books. Visible archaeological narratives (or counter-narratives) and potential dialogues now visibly encompass dissenters, creationists, and "the fringe," for example, as well as many other vocal and variously interested individuals and communities.

Thus, just as the notion of the "archaeological record" has long been criticized and the process of the construction of pasts (plural) been recognized as much more complex than once thought (Barrett 1988; Hamilakis 1999: 68–70; Patrik 1985), so, over a similar time period, has a series of related changes in the conception of archaeologists'—and other people's—relationships to those pasts occurred. These changes have not been confined to archaeology, of course, but are part of much wider postwar reactions—against positivism, for example—plus an interest in constructivism, relational philosophies and methodologies, and post-structuralist and postmodern doubts about the ontological and epistemological status of all narratives, *grands* and *petits*. It seems unlikely that, even if we wished, we could return to the idea of a single, in principle always archaeologically discoverable past, which could be captured by some kind of master narrative. This general outline of the recent parameters of western academic discourse is very well-known. But what about the specifics of archaeological authorship? Archaeology, like history, is a discipline with particularly close (if not always cooperative) relationships with many non-academic and nonprofessional groupings, from enthusiasts and amateurs to local communities of various kinds. This is the case because it is a subject of general as well as specific public interest, knowledge, and awareness. It is often part of the basis for identity politics of various kinds, for example. Archaeology as a discipline has very diverse and dynamic public, as well as professional and academic, concerns. Its members regularly interact with and are supported (and opposed), and their attitudes and disciplinary frameworks shaped and challenged, by commercial and government as well as educational institutions and organizations. Archaeology is consequently nowadays always producing a variety of texts for a wide range of audiences, arguably to a greater extent than many other disciplines.

In the light of all these changes, since the 1980s many have questioned the older model of what it is that archaeologists do and hence where our authority (and related responsibilities) might reside. One expression of this was the "ethical turn" familar across many disciplines, including philosophy, sociology, politics, literary theory, and geography (e.g., Bauman 1993, 1994; Davis and Womack 2001; Garber, Hanssen, and Walkowitz 2000; Proctor and Smith 1999). As Thomas (2005: 181) described for historians: "The debate over the presence of 'truth' and objectivity in historical scholarship has prompted many to arrive at a position where they recognize the impossibility of truthful representations of the past and have begun to question what, if not 'truth,' underlies the historical text. Likewise, if the historian . . . cannot present truth, what purpose does their work serve?" He repeats Jackson's (2001: 468) statement that "history is only present within language, and thereby shaped by material conditions, politics, ideology, and the very form of its saying and writing": the latter point has been much discussed in history, too, by those concerned with narrative structures, for example. However, for archaeology, "the form of its saying and writing" is typically more diverse and further complicated by the often collaborative (and sometimes confrontational) nature of the ways archaeological data and texts come into being. In archaeology, the ethical turn came at least as much from practical perplexities (Green 1984) and encounters with groups outside the discipline (e.g., World Archaeological Congress [WAC]: Ucko 1987) as from readings of French theorists.

Thus, wherever one stands on the relationship between representations and the past, there might be general agreement that archaeological authority—in some senses and some spheres at least—has become dispersed or fragmented and hierarchies challenged. New constituencies, participants, and interest groups have been recognized as having legitimate voices in what Hodder (1999) termed "the archaeological process," including the dissemination of interpretations (e.g., Colwell-Chanthaphonh and Ferguson 2008; Hodder 1999; McDavid 2002; Smith and Waterton 2009; Waterton and Watson 2010): site excavators, students, descendant communities, indigenous groups, local communities, amateur archaeologists, Druids and Mother Goddess groups . . . This has led some archaeologists to worry about the apparent loss of control—the inability to somehow enforce the boundaries and parameters of debate and authoritatively deny, correct, or challenge the circulation of "non-authenticated" versions in circulation. This position and these concerns are undoubtedly justified in the light of not just past but equally present experience of racist and extreme nationalist versions of history using archaeology (Kohl, Kozelsky, and Ben-Yehuda 2007). Of course, professional or academic archaeologists have never had a monopoly on publication or promulgation. It is rather that over recent decades alternative versions have become increasingly visible and the means of dissemination much more varied and accessible, from photocopying to desktop publishing and now especially the Internet and other forms of digital communication. At the same time, archaeologists have begun to explore "alternative narratives," including imagined pasts in which the fictional plays a part, as well as "normal" archaeological data presentation: see, for example, Tuwaletstiwa and Tuwaletstiwa (this volume); Van Dyke (this volume); and Pollock (this volume) for discussion of the epistemological and other issues involved in such hybrid texts.

Many have enthusiastically welcomed the possibilities of multiple authorship, both within projects and the discipline and beyond. Hodder (Çatalhöyük Research Project 2011), in considering his experiences with the Çatalhöyük Research Project, argued more than a decade ago that "as long as the interpretation by the excavators remains identifiable, wider debates do not threaten the integrity of the initial interpretations. Informed accounts can then be made by other groups and individuals . . . It is difficult to see why such a process should be seen as negative and undermining except in bastions of traditional academic authority where status rather than knowledge [is] the key concern" (Hodder 1999: 127).

In light of this, is it still useful to think of ourselves as *authors* at all, or does that overestimate the extent of our agency? Should we rather consider ourselves one among many *participants* in conversations, thought of as Bakhtinian dialogues—the "languages of archaeology" (Joyce 2002)—between and among contemporary, past, and future peoples? Is our role now rather as *facilitators* of such conversations (which will, however, still have asymmetric distributions of access to channels of communication and other people's ears and eyes)? Are we *privileged readers* of the past thanks to our specialized expertise, which enables us to pursue or extract meaning better than most? Or are we each now mere *individual readers,* without any special place or privilege, among a potentially infinite number? Do new media in particular mean there is little or no privileged communication left, only more and less popular communication, as the neo-liberal market increasingly measures the value of ideas monetarily too? Does the dispersal and expansion of authorship also mean the fragmentation of audiences, so that increasingly we archaeologists have to direct tailored texts to particular groups? If so, what might this mean for thinking about the form of our representations and their status? There are neither simple nor unambiguous answers to these questions. But we can perhaps sketch out some of the issues.

I want to start by setting out three contrasting and equally principled positions regarding the role of "authorship" and the ethical-political stance they claim or seem to entail. Because of brevity, they will inevitably seem caricatured, and in fact they overlap, but the contrast is sincerely meant.

Position 1 argues that archaeologists *are* authors in the traditional sense outlined earlier of diktat: they are the authoritative expositors and translators into language of material evidence of the past, in a more or less objective and neutral way. Archaeologists are the only ones with the necessary expertise to extract and decide meaning. This often characterized the view in 1960s and 1970s archaeology and, more generally, a modern mind-set in which a detached scientific final description and complete explanation were thought possible in principle. Here, objectivity and truth were the goals to be pursued; the philosophy and methodology implied a view *by* a universal subject *of* a universal objective past. One accepted in principle the ability to separate fact from value and the existence of a neutral universal language, generally understood to be that of science. One's duties as a scientist (actions, methodologies, means) were dictated by the ends (the ideals of objectivity and truth). Despite the wilder rhetoric of "anti-scientism" that surfaced in the 1980s, this was not and is not necessarily naive, apolitical, or amoral. A reasoned commitment toward ideals of objective neutrality and data, which is put into the public domain and open to question and testing, is at least as justifiable as one that claims transparent (i.e., "admitted") subjectivity and a recognition of one's situated-ness.

However, hard versions of such a scientific position have sometimes seemed to avoid nuanced discussion of ethical or political issues in the field of representation, precisely because it was seen as demanding rigorous, distanced neutrality toward outcomes or possible uses as a demonstration of the honest application of the scientific method. This could be interpreted in a laissez-faire manner, which seemed to support an abdication from responsibility for any possible consequences to other people or groups. In fact, much sociology of science shows us that choices (even if disguised as convention) about research directions are necessarily made all the time. In fact, nothing in the practice of good science needs preclude considering which line of inquiry would be the most acceptable in senses other than only the strict pursuit of knowledge, come what may. But under either scenario, the ethical duty and the epistemological remit is to be fair, open, and honest in laying the "facts" and methods before if not always the public per se, at least one's disciplinary and professional peers.

Implications: In this position, any authority resides within the discipline, with archaeologists claiming to be the only genuine arbiters and presenters of the archaeological facts of the past. The kinds of texts that are "honest" here are both descriptive and explanatory, though often in particular and perhaps arcane forms of language. Archaeologists may then also become translators of their own "proper" texts into "normal" or public language. Representation here is primarily of the archaeological record and to one's peers; some constituencies such as those of past people are either not seen as relevant or are only implied within the demand for methodological honesty. No concessions (apart from a general duty of clarity) are made to particular audiences. This is the status of much of the archaeological record in the "preservation by recording" sense and in fact is step 1 of the writing of most archaeological fieldwork—the so-called original data. While the archaeology doesn't change while it is in the ground, as soon as it is recognized as such and extracted, that happens under particular conditions "at the trowel's edge" (Hodder and Berggren 2003) and is recorded and written in particular ways. But most people would accept that here, if anywhere, is the locus of much archaeological authority (not unchallengeable but with some status): these archaeological data can by and large be accepted as an accurate representation of what was found *under the conditions of the time* and which probably bears some kind of proportional or consistent relation to what was "there" and hence the past.

Position 2 suggests that archaeologists act rather as readers or translators. In this view archaeology, in response to the linguistic turn and under the influence of post-structuralist semiotics, is rather seen as a contemporary cultural practice and at least as much about the present as the past; famously, for Shanks and Tilley (1987: 212) archaeology is "always a politics, a morality." They wanted "to find a place for the ethical, for values inherent in archaeological work . . . an embrace of the subjective and political dimensions of archaeological work: our living today, with its attendant biases, slants, value, politics, projects and aspirations is the condition of knowing the objective and material past" (Shanks and Tilley 1992: xviii).

These views have developed in many directions, but perhaps some weak version has become the mainstream position. That is, many practitioners would agree that even if there might be consensus about many aspects of the data, the particular ways in which such data are produced, the questions that are asked, and above all the meanings and values as such data are selectively used to build histories and other narratives are individually conditioned; everyone is "situated." If we embrace this wholly, then one cannot even claim to be a specialist *translator*; each archaeologist merely becomes one among many "*readers*." The "conditions at the time" of production are given much more weight than any "authority" resulting from privileged access to (supposedly) definite knowledge.

Although some may see this as more realistic (there are certainly multiple constituencies, interests, and interpretations, sincere and otherwise), others may view it as an abdication of professional and moral responsibility, this time from any commitment to a notion of truth or even reason, giving rise to fear of absolute relativism.

It is worth tracing the origins of this attitude. In part, this position was based on the Barthesian view of the "death of the author." Barthes (1977: 147–48) claimed that:

> To give an Author to a text is to impose upon that text a stop clause, to furnish it with a final signification, to close the writing . . . Once the Author is gone, the claim to "decipher" a text becomes quite useless . . . the true locus of writing is reading.
>
> The text is a tissue of citations, resulting from the thousand sources of culturea text consists of multiple writings, issuing from several cultures and entering into dialogue with each other, into parody, into contestation; but there is one place where this multiplicity is collected, united, and this place is not the author . . . but the reader . . .
>
> To restore to writing its future, we must reverse its myth: the birth of the reader must be ransomed by the death of the Author.

Barthes, of course, was writing as a literary critic and theorist—and hence himself a highly specialized and privileged (and authoritative) kind of reader/writer, albeit with an interest in examining many things—from images to contemporary fashion and entertainment, as well as books—as kinds of text. But to the forefront of his mind in this essay is still the model of books and poems (he commences with a quote from Balzac). Barthes presents what became a hugely influential model of a free-floating text wholly liberated from the intentions or meanings or values, of the author or instigator. That liberation was, theoretically speaking, extended to archaeologists as "interpreters" who may thus feel encouraged to give full rein to imaginative or even speculative versions of the past—as are many others. Post-processual archaeological theory at Cambridge in the United Kingdom in the 1980s and 1990s, deriving from or inspired by post-structuralist ideas, is often seen as the archaeological expression of this position (e.g., Bapty and Yates 1991; Shanks and Tilley 1987, 1992). One recent extension of this to what some might consider a cynical extreme—though one can see the logic—is found in the work of Cornelius Holtorf (2010). He recently argued that we should not be overly concerned about, for example, the publicity given to the Bosnian "pyramids." These are geological phenomena; the folding and subsequent erosion of the sedimentary strata has produced some surprisingly regular shapes on a massive scale. But a minority interpret these hills as ancient constructions and have run "archaeological excavations" and other ventures on this basis.[1]

For Holtorf, the "stories" are "at variance with academic convention." As I would express it, these particular stories are simply wrong, not only because I am speaking from within the discipline and disciplinary community (as is, of course, Holtorf) but because I am doing so in a conventional way regarding the archaeological status of these "sites." I accept that in this case the geological, stratigraphical, and archaeological rules are quite straightforward and enable a professional and academic judgment that is unambiguous—the pyramid was not built by human agency. Holtorf, though, is rather examining parts of the public context for these particular narratives. To Holtorf, "What matters is not so much the scientific accuracy, empirical richness or agreeable content of the story but the way in which we, as characters, are caught in the plot of the meta-story behind it" (ibid.: 388). Although Holtorf cautions that archaeologists "need to evaluate carefully the social consequences of their actions," he argues that "archaeology's social value lies first and foremost in well-told mystery stories that are appreciated by many . . . The quality of an archaeological story is in part determined by what its audience perceives the quality to be. Many of the historical details that make up the stories and meta-stories of archaeology are necessarily fictitious. In fact, neither the appreciation of archaeological stories nor the social impact of the meta-stories of archaeology depends on the degree to which their content corresponds to how it once 'really' was or might have been" (ibid.: 390–91).

While he might be right about what generates "impact," to imply that we should thus simply go along with the most salable version is highly dubious. Holtorf provocatively misuses the words *necessarily fictitious* here: this reads to me much better if we substitute *uncertain* or *speculative*. His warning to think about the possible consequences (of deliberately fictitious, crowd-pleasing productions?) seems a mere gesture. For otherwise he appears to be advocating outright capitulation to the logics of capitalism and populism—the triumph of the market. What archaeologists should be concerned with, in Holtorf's view, is primarily connecting to the public in their various guises (hence see also his argument *Archaeology Is a Brand*: Holtorf 2007). But we do not have to follow Holtorf to this extreme to accept that there are genuine concerns in pursuing the logic of this "readerly" position and the loss of authority for the right (as well as the wrong) reasons. One clear issue that arises is how one might consider the boundaries of archaeologically acceptable interpretations. While intepreting the Bosnian features as physically human-made pyramids seems demonstrably wrong in archaeological and geological terms, we have to accept that others may not subscribe even to these (to us wholly legitimate and justified) discourses (cf. LAW 1997). Many other instances may be far less obvious and much more ambiguous and contested even within accepted scientific or other fields. At that point at least, other factors such as prestige, authority, institutional status, and backing—all the trappings of social capital and socio-political power and influence—may well come into play to influence whose views and which narratives prevail and among which groups of people.

Of course, we *should* think about public impacts. If not, we may all too easily end up not with dialogues sensu Joyce (2002) but rather in preaching only to the converted or to our own subgroups—specialist academics speaking to specialist academics, fringe to fringe, professionals to each other and to developers: each has the tendency to produce and conform to what the audience might want to read or hear, in terms of style and format as well as content. The current proliferation of statements and narratives ironically means that much filtering necessarily goes on at an early stage about what communications we even scan or consider, let alone read or react to. The Internet has meant that rather than the ideal "of having everything connected to everything else, a structure of intense internal communication and sparse external links, a culture of networked unarticulatedness, has developed" (Reinhard Bernbeck, personal communication, 2011). Yet cross-fertilization and sometimes difficult dialogues with people using different "languages" are often the way to provoke new "readings."

However, and even bearing in mind Barthes's "Death of the Author," I would note also that it is a perfectly good and indeed desirable practice to ask of archaeological and any other texts (whether literary or material culture), What were the authors' (or agents') intentions in doing this? Why did they use this (word or image) rather than that? Why did they place this here rather than there? and so on—these are not usually fully or finally answerable questions. In other words, the agency of *how* a text (artifact, archaeological feature, narrative) was put together—as text, as material culture, as artifact, as a series of choices—is both legitimate and interesting and the very stuff of history. This is so regardless of whether we treat individuals, groups, or collective and hybrid entities as the authors and agents of the traces of the past in the present. But the implication of authorial death as usually construed and the consequent raising of the value of the archaeologist as "reader" is, in archaeological terms, a dismissal of the ethical demands of past or even present Others. This then enables the archaeologist to produce, typically from a somewhat privileged position (of access, resources, technical knowledge), stories often simply aimed at consumption within the discipline, or for personal or professional status, or for public popularity as proposed by Holtorf.

Position 3: Toward the demotic? Here we may consider archaeologists as participants in conversations. The most thought-out position here has been that presented by Rosemary Joyce (2002) in *Languages of Archaeology*, where she uses the Bakhtinian concept of dialogue. How should archaeologists relate to "heteroglossia"—the presence of many interrelated discourses (or "languages") and layers of meanings—and achieve genuine "polyphony" (multivocality), the equitable representation of those discourses and meaningful conversations? Joyce argues that archaeology necessarily incorporates a variety of authors, languages, audiences, understandings, meanings, timescales, and so forth. Her position is intellectually and politically attractive, but there are challenges. The implication is that as producers, writers, instigators of projects, co-collaborators, and facilitators of others' aspirations, narratives, histories, and community archaeologies, archaeologists should actively welcome the partial, accept situated selves and others, and be one among a plurality of voices.

However, as I have noted elsewhere (Pluciennik 2003: 644–45), "some voices are much louder than others! Multi-vocality is typically difficult to achieve—it has to be worked at. Being radical may consist of bringing different voices into play, but works best for those who are already engaged in a pre-existing dialogue. Is not the political implication of Bakhtin that we should *actively* work to give other people authoritative voices?"

We can also consider many archaeological narratives (especially those within contemporary media) much more as performance (going well beyond those presented and discussed by Praetzellis and Praetzellis and by Gibb in this volume) because, more generally, the archaeologists and other interested parties are often contemporary with, and sharing the same digital space and times as, other authors/readers. People in general are in principle both authors and readers at the same time; ideally, they are collaborative writers of dialogic pasts. As living authors, all can in principle explain, converse with, contradict, correct, intend, explicate meaning, and revisit their intentions, and so forth. The importance of *contingency* and open-endedness rather than narrative closure comes to the fore (cf., Critchley 2002); neither interpretations nor pasts nor meanings, politics, or actions are fixed. That is often going to be at odds with other groups for whom some kind of closure or at least certainty is a desirable outcome—those who want to "lay the past to rest" or who in their terms already "know" their past. Often, of course, this may be the view of the relatively powerful: nationalist groups that want a single, uncontested story of the awakening of national spirit, for example (see, e.g., Kohl 1998; Kohl and Fawcett 1995). Others, whether victims or not, may much prefer the past, ancient or recent, to remain open and never finalized (see, e.g., Crossland 2000; Gilead, this volume). For many groups, some degree of political power in the present will come from or lead to demands for sole or at least privileged authority over "their" past and the right to proscribe and prescribe the kinds of stories told.

The value of claiming (or waiving) "authority" will vary for different groups and constituencies in the present. Consider the extremes of positions 1 and 2 above. For example, is there a moral and political difference between the implications of authoring potential "fiction" (position 2) or actual "fact" (position 1), in the sense of attempted representation? One can imagine that the answers may be very different for (say) claimed descendant communities and for archaeologists. Holtorf implies that in the interests of our discipline and profession, we should pay the most attention to the quantity of present voices asking for our attention regarding the past. But that seems a highly problematic position, given the ways that globalization has increasingly enabled "predatory identities" and mobilized mass violence (Appadurai 2006). Linking ethno-nationalism and ethnic violence and other forms of terrorism in the 1990s, Appadurai (ibid.: 83) argues that in addition to physical migrations, "the global flow of mass-mediated, sometimes commoditized, images of self and other creates a growing archive of hybridities that unsettle the hard lines at the edge of large-scale identities." These circulating images and identities are, of course, also partly constituted by histories to which archaeology per se may contribute to a greater or lesser extent.

Position 3 suggests that we should act as mediators and facilitators of meaningful conversations—those in which we genuinely attempt to present, exchange, listen to, and amend views. Politically, that seems a good liberal position in relation to underrepresented or underprivileged groups in the present or the past. Is this a rather patronizing or paternalistic position? Actively attempting to enable dialogues and take account of differences—though the process may be difficult and will often highlight contested rather than consensual areas—seems to me both a more realistic and moral standpoint; a recognition of the changing landscapes of cultural, historical, and archaeological discourse and narratives. Often, of course, in relation to government or other bodies or interest groups and commercial organizations, archaeologists themselves will typically be in a subaltern position.

DISCUSSION

Whatever else authors or editors are doing, they are enabling some kinds of contemporary representation about the past, whatever they claim them to be—for example, representing reality, or a possible version of reality, or a plausible version of the past, or a possible past, or an idea about the past . . . What, then, might be the ethical duty or duties of archaeologists in relation to the kinds of "texts" they produce? It is probably uncontroversial to say that we might all generally accept broad and abstract notions that are similar to those expressed under position 1: for example, those of fairness and openness—the duty not to deliberately or intentionally mislead or conceal evidence, whatever we consider that to be. What other kinds of models might be helpful here? Tarlow (2001: 60) notes that one meaning of the word *representation* encompasses the idea of advocacy as "a moral obligation pertaining to those who normally enjoy advantages of power; acquaintance with the structures and establishments of power, fluency and articulacy in politically 'strong' languages and in the particular rhetoric of negotiation, and [who] possess greater material wealth and wider personal opportunities. All these are advantages that are in some measure acknowledged when they are exploited for the benefit of others."

In some socio-political and socio-economic contexts, archaeologists may enjoy advantages of power in getting their (and potentially others') voices heard; they will already be part of official or unofficial networks of communication, for example. In many other contexts (of development or the mass media or strong communities suffused with indigenous group politics, for example), archaeologists may find themselves toward the bottom of any hierarchy. However, in relation to the production of certain kinds of narratives about certain kinds of pasts, archaeologists are often in a relatively powerful position: technical, theoretical, and methodological competence allows us to make available particular kinds of knowledge/data. For present people and in addition to our own voices, we should presumably be endeavoring to empower (rather than disempower or silence) them and not unthinkingly claim or imply to be speaking in their place. Similarly, many communities have fought for and insisted on the right to their own voices and stories—whether alone, in opposition to, or with the support of archaeologists and many other interest groups, from mining corporations to regional authorities and national governments. Reaching that position has been a large part of the history of the last few decades in parts of the world previously subject to colonial settlement and archaeologies. More generally, then, we might accept that we should be attempting to make it possible to engage in conversations, for those who are interested. From our point of view, that might include ensuring that archaeologically derived data, for example, are reasonably intelligible and accessible.

What is less clear, though, is where the ethical relation to past people might reside—the narrativized subjects of some of these narratives and conversations. If archaeologists do have a particular constituency, it is surely here because these are people who can be made visible and whose "voice" is often made "audible" through our agency. Groups otherwise constituted, such as various actual or claimed descendant communities, may, of course, claim other forms of relevant rights, agency, and access—from spiritual truths to already-known traditions and cultural or other continuities. But in relation to past (and perhaps especially prehistoric) people, who themselves had little access to particular widespread and authoritative media of expression and perhaps no sense of or desire for dialogue with constituencies such as the future or "us," how should we be (re)presenting subjects? Should archaeologists sometimes or generally act as advocates of past people? What would that mean in practice? Answers to these questions will surely be highly variable, with markedly heterogeneous contexts of pasts, narratives about pasts, and relationships to such pasts.

One path will be to explore ways of collaborative working, including the roles of individuals with understandings of and responsibilities toward more than one community of interest, such as indigenous archaeologists in North America and elsewhere (e.g., Bruchac, Hart, and Wobst 2010; Colwell-Chanthaphonh and Ferguson 2008; Greer, Harrison, and McIntyre-Tamway 2002; Murray 2011; Nicholas 2010; Silliman 2008; Smith and Wobst 2005). Curiously, if anything, I think it brings us back to the notion of the (re)birth of the "author." We will and should have grounded authorial intentions—a denial of our agency in constructing these pasts would be a return to either position 1 ("I'm only the describer or translator of what's already there") or position 2 ("Make of this what you will, dear reader").

If we accept that narratives are constructed, often collaboratively, with awareness of various sensitivities and often for particular purposes (education, maintenance of community traditions, as part of a positive political process, and so forth), as well as more standard archaeological positions (public and academic information, preservation by recording), then this usefully highlights "agency" and the responsibilities of ourselves and others as authors of our own acts. Where no communities currently claim special relationships with particular past peoples and thus perhaps with particular interests and possible duties with regard to their representation in the present, archaeologists may feel (sensu Tarlow 2001) that—whatever their epistemological or theoretical position regarding relationships to the past—they do have forms of moral obligation to be fair, open, and transparent in their narrative representations and in demonstrating how such narratives are put together (cf. discussion of the ideas of construction and transparency in, for example, Bailey and Simpkin, Van Dyke, and Pollock, this volume). This seems a more realistic and achievable set of expectations than those discussed by more "readerly" understandings of what constitutes written history. Thus for Thomas (2005: 181), for example, the ethical difficulty with writing history arises from "the impossibility of truthful representations of the past." But his language is surely misguided here, just as much as Holtorf's "fictitious." If by "truthful" he means "unquestionably true," then it is indeed an impossibility; but for a historian or an archaeologist, the state of being truthful—meaning true to the facts as known and described—is possible and indeed demanded by an ethical commitment to fairness and balance rather than what people might want to hear. Of course, that does not imply that any single representation is or could be considered indubitably true. It is not even clear what that might mean, except possibly for the most trivial or banal of "facts," since the past is necessarily viewed from a different position than that from which someone in the past could have known or described it. But being at least partly verifiable and plausible, coherent and consistent are certainly possible and desirable qualities of archaeological representations of the past.

THE POWER OF NARRATIVES

But in the end, does it matter? If there are lots of competing voices, should we worry about potential effects that we cannot possibly compute or predict?

Is this fragmentation of authority and proliferation of discourses in fact highly democratic and to be welcomed? Should we then shrug our shoulders and go for what is likely to have the best result—whether in terms of immediate public response, or academic and peer group kudos, or future funding, or? Of course, we do all these things and have all these aims and more, singly and in combination. Any contemporary text is, even without considering "intertextuality," likely to have multiple authors/producers and contributions deriving from a variety of motivations and agencies and equally to have a range of audiences, readers, and consumers. But more generally, is the result of such deregulation, insofar as it leads to plurality, multivocality, and the plethora of (re)presentations and texts, a threat or an opportunity?

The availability of accessible outlets for archaeologically related views or comments, from blogs to peer-reviewed electronic journals or ebooks, as well as internal disciplinary specialization (Kristiansen 2004), suggests that it is increasingly difficult to influence or hold conversations even within the field as a whole in any obvious way. One can put ideas into play, but who reads and responds is highly uncertain. This dispersal of information and comment (of whatever source or validity) also means that people and organizations find new ways of assessing weight, status, and authority. We are all familiar with this: one component of the algorithms used by search engines on the Internet typically measures not only numbers of external links but also the "importance" or weight of the site from where those links derive, so that links from (say) a university or other ".edu" or ".ac" domain or a government website will count for more in assigning rank—and hence where a given website or digital article appears on a search results page. This is, then, one contemporary way of measuring the cumulative effect of authoritative, establishment views— "conventional wisdom"——along with popularity or "impact," the quantitative measure. Appadurai (2010) argues that cultural politics in our current "era of globalization" are primarily "characterized by high degrees of connectivity and circulation." He suggests that "we need to understand more about the ways in which the forms of circulation and the circulation of forms create the conditions for the production of locality." By "forms," Appadurai explains that he refers to "a family of phenomena, including styles, techniques, or genres, which can be inhabited by specific voices, contents, messages, and materials . . . The examples of nation and narration are a useful reminder that different forms circulate through different trajectories, generate diverse interpretations, and yield different and uneven geographies."

Appadurai is largely concerned with the production of difference through locality, but one could very clearly extend this to the production of difference through history rather than (or as well as) geography to make such considerations even more relevant to archaeological narratives. In his view, "We need to move decisively beyond existing models of creolization, hybridity, fusion, syncretism, and the like, which have largely been about mixture at the level of content. Instead, we need to probe the cohabitation of forms, such as the novel and the nation, because they actually produce new contexts through their peculiar inflection of each other."

CASE STUDY: CONTROVERSIES AND LOCAL LANDSCAPES

The effects of these new forms, technologies, and media on archaeology will require future studies. Meanwhile individually, because of their small readership, traditional academic publications in peer-reviewed journals or books seem unlikely to have much of an obvious or widespread impact, unless they can readily be assimilated to the agendas of the popular media or social networks by discovering "treasure," offering novelty or a celebrity (the discovery at Leicester of the bones of Richard III), or courting controversy (Bosnian "pyramids," Atlantis), for example. However, several have argued that perhaps especially for those working in the field of archaeology performed in areas of recent conflict (see, e.g., Horning 2010; Perring and van der Linde 2009), controversy in the sense of addressing painful issues and living memories can be a way of raising, confronting, and sometimes ameliorating past and present hurts. Thus Bernbeck and Pollock's (2007) suggested "archaeology of perpetrators" is carried out in landscapes identified as places of atrocities and squarely aimed at provoking and opening up public discussion; one should also see Gilead's chapter in this volume on the archaeology of Nazi extermination camps.

Colwell-Chanthaphonh (2007) has suggested that contested landscapes may actually be places where colonizers and the colonized eventually find common ground. Thus in many parts of the world that have been subject to colonial settlement and rule or more recent conflict, archaeology necessarily has to address difficult issues and deal with opposing or contrasting views within the various narratives produced (see also Tuwaletstiwa and Tuwaletstiwa, this volume, for another example of a landscape approach incorporating indigenous perspectives). In other areas, perhaps more distant from or with less controversy surrounding consensus interpretations of recent conflict zones, or in areas where classical civilizations have been the overriding focus of archaeological work, sites, surveys, and landscape histories may seem unlikely candidates for agents of either political conservatism or radical change.

Nevertheless, even in these less obvious places, one should not underestimate the potential importance of archaeologies and other published studies at regional, national, and international levels over the longer term and in a collective sense. Individual pieces may primarily reside in academic journals and university libraries and be of limited access and minority interest. But as they become exemplars of established narratives, they are likely to form the basis for more widespread education, especially as consensuses emerge and cumulatively form the basis of public as well as professional opinion and of state or other official policies. Certain approaches are likely to become the accepted version. Thus they help form frameworks or the starting points for policy decisions by political elites, as well as being instrumental in setting broader societal and cultural attitudes. Archaeology can typically form one of the pillars in these kinds of overarching frameworks, which reinforce cultural and political mores. The most obvious of these recent meta-narratives is that of progressive social evolution. The idea that history demonstrates that progress (material, cultural, spiritual, moral, intellectual) has not been equally shared across the globe has been used to ascribe different values to different peoples. This concept and ideology proved particularly powerful among nations with colonial ambitions and was used to denigrate native peoples, remove them from their homelands, and force them to settle and become a laboring underclass—or face slavery or genocide. This was not solely the fault or invention of archaeology, anthropology, or history, though all were complicit, but in the nineteenth and twentieth centuries archaeology played an important role in demonstrating the "facts of progress" and thus encouraging and supporting racist models and histories (Pluciennik 2005).

This can be illustrated through a brief consideration of past and present practice and textual effects in one area with which I have some experience: landscape histories, with particular reference to the Mediterranean. For example, Diana Davis (2007: xii) shows how after 1830 (when the French invaded Algeria), a new narrative was constructed that told of "environmental decline since what was presumed to have been the fertile and forested Roman period." The blame for desertification and the perceived currently poor state of environmental affairs was placed on pastoralists and their Arab predecessors. Similarly, in Sicily, as part of the so-called Southern Question, the fascist government blamed the "backward" peasants and conservative landowners for the lack of agricultural productivity, thus demonstrating their general decline from Classical times, and subjected them to political, rural landscape, and settlement reforms (Pluciennik 2008; Samuels 2010). Traditional academic reports and narratives—individually and collectively, specialized and popular, and drawn from fields including ancient history, agronomy, archaeology, ethnography, and history—informed such state policies and affected many people.

What of contemporary texts, their role, and the place of the demotic? In general, texts—from monographs to exhibition catalogs, brochures, and public lectures in ephemeral events or more permanent digital media and that deal with regional or subregional histories and archaeologies—interest various groups for various reasons. For those working professionally within the discipline or in related areas such as heritage or tourism, these texts may have a primarily intellectual or instrumental concern and help to put one's own knowledge, work, and research in context. If one is native to or a current occupant of the area, there may be a general or specific interest—one may know the landscapes and sites discussed in other ways and be interested to learn what archaeologists say about them, about how one's actual or putative ancestors lived, for example. Descriptions of the results of a particular project will often be given also in generally accessible publications and exhibitions (and conversations in a variety of media) and fulfill other roles and actions. These may include encouraging visitors to an area or to specific sites (for good or ill: publicity may also encourage metal detectorists or looters, for example) and contribute in a small and localized way to general education and leisure, tourism, and the economy. In Sicily, large archaeological parks benefit from regional and European Union funding.

But the demotic is also represented by many locally initiated and supported projects, often started by volunteers. These are typically small-town museums, focusing on rural practices and past peasant life (*civiltà contadina*) and predominantly displaying collections of old agricultural implements. A particular and arguably heavily romanticized notion of peasant life is increasingly displayed in practice and in digital and social media in Italy generally. Anecdotally, drawing on my own experience in central Sicily, there has been a marked change in attitudes toward recent past rural life since the early 1990s. While initially people were generally reluctant to discuss those times and conditions in relation to their own families, they can now be confronted and claimed as recognized hardship (exploitation in sulfur mines, peasant poverty and starvation) or even, especially in northern Italy, be linked to traditional practices, foods, and biodiversity and organic agriculture in a positive way.

Similar tensions and contrasting narratives continue to exist across the Mediterranean and elsewhere. The frameworks for deciding what it is possible to do politically and practically derive in part from interpretations of historical antecedents, involving archaeologists and many other specialists.

Narratives—both their content and their form—did and do matter. Appeals to and contributions from different sets of scientists, archaeologists, environmentalists, the media, and the public now occur within new forms of global capitalism, communication, kinds of corporate exploitation, and colonialism and through the medium of political and institutional bodies at regional, national, and international levels, as well as more easily voiced demands from groups that can be swiftly mobilized and claim political attention. Thus authority considered as the power to dictate or influence outcomes is still present and may draw upon texts and sources with particular kinds of weight and derivation. One cannot predict the consequences of deliberate misinformation or fictitious interpolations nor, of course, how any archaeological information may be used or abused. But notions of fairness (of consistent representation of the collected data, as discussed earlier) and some attempt at transparency of agenda, situation, and motivation, as well as a duty not to invent, exclude, or capriciously omit, would seem a good general ethical basis on which to proceed, whichever position one is persuaded by.

CONCLUSION

In this chapter I have tried to contrast previous styles and concepts of authorship of archaeological narratives understood as a single authoritative view of the past with the multiple languages and forms and styles of communication that can be seen as the eruption of the demotic—the people—into the visible spectrum of archaeological communication. The problem with the old-style diktat represented by single authorship from privileged sources is that such texts are typically difficult to challenge and dislodge by those outside or "below" easy means of access to the medium of publication. Because of the social structures and institutions from which the authors derived, they seemed often to speak the kind of "truth" to power that power preferred to hear—they were often perceived as, aligned with, or indeed members of the Establishment. Thus anthropology still struggles to distance itself from allegations of past colonialist complicity, just as archaeology is associated with nationalist excesses. Indeed, one might easily argue that both of these currents are still active, with political agendas for state building, and anthropologists and archaeologists are recruited as kinds of cultural liaison officers, among other roles, in Afghanistan and Iraq (see, e.g., Hamilakis 2009; Williams 2008). Thus the kind of supposedly democratized "free-for-all" that parts of the deregulated digital revolution and changes in intellectual climate seem to offer does not in itself change embedded power structures or the sites of authority or necessarily lead to better outcomes simply because there are more voices and even broader conversations with a wider range of participants.

Nevertheless, many kinds of apparently disinterested research and their often esoteric associated narratives, such as those of Mediterranean landscape survey, can feed into modern debates and policies, as discussed earlier. But in the cacophony, the deluge, of voices, texts, and information, it is arguably fashion, narrative style, medium, and forms of presentation (especially involving oversimplification) that are likely to play a larger part in what are commonly accepted as reasonable or plausible "truths" about the past than many of us would like, even if there is nothing objectionable in principle about, say, tweeting a new discovery or point of view. Holtorf argues that we should accept that pressure and recognize those limitations and by and large tell the kinds of stories people want to hear, as a way of at least attaining some kind of public audience. Others will want to remain more critically cautious, believing that different kinds of knowledge, skills, or experience do and perhaps should sometimes confer a "louder" institutionally, democratically, or politically recognized voice. But that conferral also demands certain ethical responsibilities and a mandate to involve others.

The kinds of narratives we produce do or potentially might matter, however esoteric or removed from the "real" world they might sometimes appear. In other cases, there is an obvious and direct potential impact of archaeological and historical intepretations that can be used to bolster political action in the present, including violence. We are aware of this from nationalist and terrorist events, such as ethnic cleansing and other means of activating and using cultural politics. In the kinds of circumstances recently discussed by Appadurai (2006, 2010), both the forms and contents of narratives, as well as modes of communication and circulation, can play out in unexpected and sometimes unwelcome ways. Other people may take our words and work and point to them as authority for their actions. How they do so will be beyond our control, just as we cannot and should not wish to police others' archaeological languages and dialogues. Nevertheless, an overly "readerly" position can lead to a denial of any responsibility for consequences that seem morally untenable or at least undesirable. Engaging with, being aware of, and sometimes assisting in the promotion of other voices is one side of this double duty.

But we should also retain our own sense of the "responsibilities of representation" discussed earlier and certain very general moral duties in terms of narrative presentation, such as transparency (cf. the arguments of Pollock, Van Dyke, this volume). This kind of critically aware attitude, which is open to continuous debate, would also seem to complement the form of much other archaeological practice. In many parts of the discipline, "authority" for statements is as much collaboratively conferred (among a team, a community), proposed, discussed, and justified rather than simply claimed or assumed. We should willingly accept the role of the demotic within our own specialist and professional field but neither bow to populism nor retreat to a readerly position that is ultimately a refusal to engage. Such a position constrains neither form nor content. Indeed, we should continue to explore the implications of different forms, modes, media, and technologies as demonstrated in this volume; see, for example, Bailey and Simpkin, Tringham, Nelson, and Tuwaletstiwa and Tuwaletstiwa for a range of thoughtful and stimulating examples. However, it does also demand that we continue to think carefully about what it is that we are doing and the implications, whenever, wherever, and however we put archaeological narratives into circulation.

ACKNOWLEDGMENTS

I am profoundly grateful to Reinhard Bernbeck and Ruth Van Dyke, not only for organizing a very stimulating session in the first place and for inviting me to participate but also for their extremely perceptive and critical comments on the first draft of this chapter. Their suggestions have very much helped to clarify and improve it. I am also delighted to have engaged with the other session participants from whom I learned much, including discussion with my friend and former colleague Cornelius Holtorf, with whom debate is always provocative and stimulating.

NOTE

1. For the geology, see Irna (2011), http://irna.lautre.net/-Bosnian-pyramids-.html., accessed March 14, 2012. For Semir Osmanagic's (the "discoverer" of the "pyramid") and his supporters' views, see "Archaeological Park: Bosnian Pyramid of the Sun Foundation," at http://piramidasunca.ba/eng., accessed March 14, 2012. For official reaction to Osmanagic's claims, see, e.g., Harding (2006), http://www.e-a-a.org/TEA25.pdf, accessed March 14, 2012, and the European Association of Archaeologists (EAA 2011), which thought the deception important enough to say this on the organization's home page (this quotation remained until 2011): "Following a visit to Sarajevo by the President, Secretary and Administrator, the EAA affirms its support for the small community of professional archaeologists in Bosnia-Herzegovina and urges the authorities, both cantonal, federal and state, to uphold the standing of the profession by providing adequate resources for museums, rescue archaeology and heritage protection, and to

withdraw all support for the absurd 'pyramid' project which is attracting world-wide media attention, misleading the public, and diverting political support and resources from the real issues of protecting and restoring Bosnia-Herzegovina's authentic and endangered national heritage." In a further statement the organization called the pyramid "explorations" "a cruel hoax on an unsuspecting public" that is "diverting attention from the pressing problems that are affecting professional archaeologists in Bosnia-Herzogovina on a daily basis"; http://www.e-a-a.org/statement.pdf, accessed July 15, 2012. For an excellent series of articles, blogs, exposés, and links, see Irna (2011), http://irna.lautre.net/-Bosnian-pyramids-.html, accessed March 14, 2012.

REFERENCES

Appadurai, Arjun. 2006. *Fear of Small Numbers: An Essay on the Geography of Anger.* Durham, NC: Duke University Press. http://dx.doi.org/10.1215/9780822387541.

Appadurai, Arjun. 2010. "How Histories Make Geographies: Circulation and Context in a Global Perspective." *Transcultural Studies* 1. http://archiv.ub.uni-heidelberg.de/ojs/index.php/transcultural/article/view/6129/1760, accessed September 11, 2011.

Bapty, Ian, and Tim Yates, eds. 1991. *Archaeology after Structuralism.* London: Routledge.

Barrett, John. 1988. "Fields of Discourse: Reconstituting a Social Archaeology." *Critique of Anthropology* 7 (3): 5–16. http://dx.doi.org/10.1177/0308275X8800700301.

Barthes, Roland. 1977 [1967]. "The Death of the Author." In *Image, Music, Text,* ed. and trans. Stephen Heath, 142–48. London: Fontana.

Bauman, Zygmunt. 1993. *Postmodern Ethics.* Oxford: Blackwell.

Bauman, Zygmunt. 1994. *Alone Again—Ethics after Certainty.* London: Demos.

Bernbeck, Reinhard, and Susan Pollock. 2007. "'Grabe, Wo Du Stehst!' An Archaeology of Perpetrators." In *Archaeology and Capitalism: From Ethics to Politics,* ed. Yannis Hamilakis and Philip Duke, 217–33. Walnut Creek, CA: Left Coast.

Bruchac, Margaret, Siobhan Hart, and H. Martin Wobst, eds. 2010. *Indigenous Archaeologies: A Reader in Decolonization.* Walnut Creek, CA: Left Coast.

Çatalhöyük Research Project. 2011. "Çatalhöyük: Excavations of a Neolithic Anatolian Höyük." www.catalhoyuk.com, accessed September 22, 2011.

Colwell-Chanthaphonh, Chip. 2007. "History, Justice and Reconciliation." In *Archaeology as a Tool of Civic Engagement,* ed. Barbara Little and Paul Shackel, 23–46. Lanham, MD: AltaMira.

Colwell-Chanthaphonh, Chip, and T. J. Ferguson, eds. 2008. *Collaboration in Archaeological Practice: Engaging Descendant Communities.* Lanham, MD: AltaMira.

Critchley, Simon. 2002. "Ethics, Politics and Radical Democracy—the History of a Disagreement." *Culture Machine* 4: 1–8.

Crossland, Zoe. 2000. "Buried Lives: Forensic Archaeology and the Disappeared in Argentina." *Archaeological Dialogues* 7 (2): 146–59. http://dx.doi.org/10.1017/S1380203800001707.

Davis, Diana. 2007. "Imperial Stories and Empirical Evidence." In *Resurrecting the Granary of Rome: Environmental History and French Colonial Expansion in North Africa*, by Diana Davis, 1–15. Athens: Ohio University Press.

Davis, Todd, and Kenneth Womack, eds. 2001. *Mapping the Ethical Turn: A Reader in Ethics, Culture and Literary Theory*. Charlottesville: University of Virginia Press.

EAA. 2011. "EAA Supports Professional Archaeologists in Bosnia-Herzegovina." www.e-a-a.org/.

Garber, Marjorie B., Beatrice Hanssen, and Rebecca L. Walkowitz, eds. 2000. *The Turn to Ethics (Culture Work)*. London: Routledge.

Green, Ernestene, ed. 1984. *Ethics and Values in Archaeology*. New York: Free Press.

Greer, Shelley, Rodney Harrison, and Susan McIntyre-Tamway. 2002. "Community-Based Archaeology in Australia." *World Archaeology* 34 (2): 265–87. http://dx.doi.org/10.1080/0043824022000007099.

Hadley, Patrick. 2011. "Opportunities and Obstacles to Community Knowledge-Sharing in the Digital Universe: Experiments with *Mesolithic Miscellany*." *Assemblage* (Features: State of the Arch, December 2011). http://www.assemblage.group.shef.ac.uk/features/state-of-the-arch/134-opportunities-and-obstacles-to-community-knowledge-sharing-in-the-digital-universe-experiments-with-mesolithic-miscellany, accessed March 17, 2012.

Hamilakis, Yannis. 1999. "La trahison des archéologues? Archaeological Practice as Intellectual Activity in Postmodernity." *Journal of Mediterranean Archaeology* 12 (1): 60–79. http://dx.doi.org/10.1558/jmea.v12i1.60.

Hamilakis, Yannis. 2009. "The 'War on Terror' and the Military Archaeology Complex: Iraq, Ethics, and Neo-Colonialism." *Archaeologies* 5 (1): 39–65. http://dx.doi.org/10.1007/s11759-009-9095-y.

Harding, Anthony. 2006. "That Bosnian Pyramid!" *European Archaeologist* 25: 2–4. http://www.e-a-a.org/TEA25.pdf, accessed March 14, 2012.

Hodder, Ian. 1999. *The Archaeological Process*. London: Routledge.

Hodder, Ian, and Asa Berggren. 2003. *At the Trowel's Edge: An Introduction to Reflexive Field Practice in Archaeology*. Boulder: Westview.

Holtorf, Cornelius. 2007. *Archaeology Is a Brand! The Meaning of Archaeology in Contemporary Popular Culture*. Oxford: Archaeopress.

Holtorf, Cornelius. 2010. "Meta-Stories of Archaeology." *World Archaeology* 42 (3): 381–93. http://dx.doi.org/10.1080/00438243.2010.497382.

Horning, Audrey. 2010. "Small Trenches: Archaeology and the Postcolonial Gaze." *Archaeological Diualogues* 17 (1): 27–30.

Irna. 2011. "Enquête sur les pseudo-pyramides de Bosnie." http://irna.lautre.net/-Bosnian-pyramids-.html, accessed March 16, 2012.

Jackson, Mark. 2001. "The Ethical Space of Historiography." *Journal of Historical Sociology* 14 (4): 467–80. http://dx.doi.org/10.1111/1467-6443.00156.

Jones, Andrew. 2001. *Archaeological Theory and Scientific Practice*. Cambridge: Cambridge University Press. http://dx.doi.org/10.1017/CBO9780511606069.

Joyce, Rosemary. 2002. *The Languages of Archaeology*. Oxford: Blackwell. http://dx.doi.org/10.1002/9780470693520.

Kohl, Philip. 1998. "Nationalism and Archaeology: On the Constructions of Nations and the Reconstructions of the Remote Past." *Annual Review of Anthropology* 27 (1): 223–46. http://dx.doi.org/10.1146/annurev.anthro.27.1.223.

Kohl, Philip, and Clare Fawcett, eds. 1995. *Nationalism, Politics, and the Practice of Archaeology*. Cambridge: Cambridge University Press.

Kohl, Philip, Mara Kozelsky, and Nachman Ben-Yehuda, eds. 2007. *Selective Remembrances: Archaeology in the Construction, Commemoration, and Consecration of National Pasts*. Chicago: University of Chicago Press.

Kristiansen, Kristian. 2004. "Genes versus Agents: A Discussion of the Widening Theoretical Gap in Archaeology." *Archaeological Dialogues* 11 (2): 77–99. http://dx.doi.org/10.1017/S1380203805211509.

LAW (Lampeter Archaeology Workshop). 1997. "Relativism, Objectivity and the Politics of the Past." *Archaeological Dialogues* 4 (2): 164–84.

McDavid, Carol. 2002. "Archaeologies That Hurt; Descendants That Matter: A Pragmatic Approach to Collaboration in the Public Interpretation of African-American Archaeology." *World Archaeology* 34 (2): 303–14. http://dx.doi.org/10.1080/0043824022000007116.

Murray, Tim. 2011. "Archaeologists and Indigenous People: A Maturing Relationship?" *Annual Review of Anthropology* 40 (1): 363–78. http://dx.doi.org/10.1146/annurev-anthro-081309-145729.

Nicholas, George, ed. 2010. *Being and Becoming Indigenous Archaeologists*. Walnut Creek, CA: Left Coast.

Patrik, Linda. 1985. "Is There an Archaeological Record?" *Advances in Archaeological Method and Theory* 8: 27–62.

Perring, Dominic, and Sjoerd van der Linde. 2009. "The Politics and Practice of Archaeology in Conflict." *Conservation and Management of Archaeological Sites* 11 (3-4): 197–213. http://dx.doi.org/10.1179/175355210X12747818485321.

Pluciennik, Mark. 2003. "Review of Rosemary Joyce et al., *The Languages of Archaeology*." *Antiquity* 77: 643–45.

Pluciennik, Mark. 2005. *Social Evolution*. London: Duckworth.

Pluciennik, Mark. 2008. "The Imaginary, the Ideal, and the Real: Recent Landscapes in Central Sicily." In *Monuments in the Landscape*, ed. Paul Rainbird, 199–211. Stroud: Tempus.

Pluciennik, Mark, and Quentin Drew. 2000. "'Only Connect': Global and Local Networks, Contexts and Fieldwork." *Ecumene* 7 (1): 67–104. http://dx.doi.org /10.1191/096746000701556563.

Proctor, David, and James Smith. 1999. *Geography and Ethics*. London: Routledge.

Rocks-Macqueen, Doug. 2011. "Archaeology Journals—Do You Get What You Pay For?" *Assemblage* (Features: State of the Arch, December 2011). http://www .assemblage.group.shef.ac.uk/features/state-of-the-arch/136-archaeology-journals -do-you-get-what-you-pay-for, accessed March 18, 2012.

Rocks-Macqueen, Doug. 2012. "The Last Days of Rome: The Rise of Open Access and the Fall of For-Profit Publishers." *Anthropologies: A Collaborative Online Project*. http://www.anthropologiesproject.org/2012/03/last-days-of-rome-rise-of -open-access.html, accessed March 18, 2012.

Samuels, Joshua. 2010. "Of Other Scapes: Archaeology, Landscape, and Heterotopia in Fascist Sicily." *Archaeologies* 6 (1): 62–81. http://dx.doi.org/10.1007/s11759-010 -9129-5.

Shanks, Michael, and Christopher Tilley. 1987. *Social Theory and Archaeology*. Cambridge: Polity.

Shanks, Michael, and Christopher Tilley. 1992. *Re-Constructing Archaeology: Theory and Practice*. 2nd ed. London: Routledge.

Silliman, Stephen, ed. 2008. *Collaborating at the Trowel's Edge: Teaching and Learning in Indigenous Archaeology*. Tucson: University of Arizona Press.

Smith, Claire, and H. Martin Wobst, eds. 2005. *Indigenous Archaeologies: Decolonizing Theory and Practice*. London: Routledge.

Smith, Laurajane, and Emma Waterton. 2009. *Heritage, Communities and Archaeology*. London: Gerald Duckworth.

Tarlow, Sarah. 2001. "The Responsibility of Representation." In *The Responsibilities of Archaeologists: Archaeology and Ethics*, ed. Mark Pluciennik, 57–64. Lampeter Workshop in Archaeology 4, BAR International Series 981. Oxford: Oxbow.

Thomas, Courtney. 2005. "History as Moral Commentary: Ideology and the Ethical Responsibilities of Remembrance." *Nebula* 1 (3): 179–96.

Ucko, Peter. 1987. *Academic Freedom and Apartheid: The Story of the World Archaeological Congress*. London: Duckworth.

Waterton, Emma, and Steve Watson, eds. 2010. *Heritage and Community Engagement: Collaboration or Contestation?* London: Routledge.

Williams, Jack. 2008. "The Ethics of Archaeologists Embedded in Military Structures during Armed Conflicts." Paper delivered at World Archaeological Congress 6, Dublin, June 29–July 4.

4

The Chacoan Past

Creative Representations and Sensory Engagements

RUTH M. VAN DYKE

We have much to gain through scholarly, sensuous engagements with the past. In this chapter I argue this point using two short, creative projects—an "imagined narrative" with accompanying PowerPoint file, and an audiovisual clip. Imagined narratives are creative nonfiction in which the author employs archaeological information to portray imagined fragments of past lives. Through the audiovisual clip, I attempt to convey a bundled, or entangled, set of relationships (Hodder 2012; Pauketat 2013) using nontextual aural engagement. In both, I am attempting to transcend the shortcomings of descriptive exegesis by following the writer's maxim "show, don't tell" (Kress 2006). I argue that creative projects can be analytical tools to provide us with alternative ways of thinking about, not just representing, the past. These efforts bring into focus the limitations of current empirical knowledge, and they raise new questions that can help guide future research.

But archaeologists pushing against the shared understandings of scholarly representation in our field (sensu Bourdieu) are subject to criticism from at least two quarters. The first problem is one of epistemological legitimacy. If the accepted formulae for conveying scholarly authority are missing, how does the reader decide whether to accept what she or he is reading as "knowledge"? How does the author give the reader explicit connections to empirical data, or "facts"? The second problem is ethical. If archaeologists imagine past voices, are we empowering and engaging with the

DOI: 10.5876/9781607323815.c004

FIGURE 4.1. *Pueblo Bonito, monumental great house at the heart of Chaco Canyon in northwest New Mexico (http://www.upcolorado.com/component/k2/item/2712-subjects -and-narratives-in-archaeology-media; photo by author)*

peoples of the past, or are we unethically appropriating and subjugating their voices? Below, I present the archaeological context for my examples, followed by the two creative projects. I close by addressing the potential epistemological and ethical problems with creative representations of the past.

RITUAL GATHERINGS IN CHACO CANYON

My archaeological work is centered around Chaco Canyon in northwest New Mexico. A millennium ago, Chaco Canyon was the center of an ancient Pueblo polity held together by ritual. Pilgrims traveled tens of kilometers to the canyon from their homes in outlier communities to participate in ceremonial events that probably coincided with equinoxes or solstices. These events were presided over by an elite group of Chacoan residents (e.g., Judge 1989; Kantner 1996; authors in Lekson 2006; Lekson 1999, 2008; Renfrew 2001; Sebastian 1992; Van Dyke 2007; Yoffee 2001). Although most Chaco scholars (but cf. Vivian 1990; Wilcox 1993; Wills 2000) see periodic ritual gatherings in the canyon as central to social and political organization, it is difficult to reconstruct the specific nature of Chacoan ceremonialism.

FIGURE 4.2. *Fajada Butte, the iconic landform in the center of Chaco Canyon, figured prominently in the spatial and ritual experiences of ancient inhabitants (http://www .upcolorado.com/component/k2/item/2712-subjects-and-narratives-in-archaeology-media; photo by author)*

The material evidence for ritual at Chaco consists of public architecture, rock art, unusual depositional events, and portable objects (figure 4.1). Clues to Chacoan cosmology are contained in the orientations, positions, and other aspects of great houses, great kivas, road segments, earthworks, and shrines (Fritz 1978; Lekson 1999; Stein and Lekson 1992; Van Dyke 2007) and in archaeoastronomical alignments and rock art (Malville 2004; Sofaer 2007). Chacoan landscape and monumental buildings encouraged particular kinds of bodily experiences, emphasizing dualism, balance, and Chaco Canyon as the center of the ancient Pueblo world (Van Dyke 2007) (figure 4.2). Archaeological signatures of feasting include unusual quantities of food remains, cooking vessels, cooking facilities, and special trash middens (Toll 1985, 2001; Windes 1987). Ritual paraphernalia include carved and painted wooden altar furniture (Vivian, Dodgen, and Hartman 1978), cylinder jars that held cacao (Crown and Hurst 2009), decorated baskets, cornhusk containers, and rush bundles (Webster 2011). Animistic artifacts bear the forms of animals associated with water, particularly birds and toads or frogs (Brody 1984; Pepper 1920: 91, 186; Vivian, Dodgen, and Hartman 1978). Chacoans interred turquoise, shell, and lignite objects and jewelry with burials, in sealed niches, and under roof support columns (Judd 1954: 338–39; Pepper 1909, 1920; Vivian and Reiter 1960). The caching of these inalienable objects (Mills 2004, 2008), the repeated obliteration and redecoration of cylinder vessels (Crown and Wills 2003), and the repeated remodeling of great houses and great kivas (Van Dyke 2004, 2007) suggest a concern with inscribed and embodied social memory (Connerton 1989).

VIDEO 4.1. Walking to Chaco *(2011), by Ruth M. Van Dyke (photo by Justin Rochell;
video available at http://www.upcolorado.com/component/k2/item/2712-subjects-and
-narratives-in-archaeology-media)*

The foregoing linear, textual description of archaeological evidence for ritual gatherings at Chaco is well-punctuated by references to scholarly works wherein the interested reader may consult the data. But the text fails to convey any hint of the real people involved in these events—there are no bodily experiences, no emotional or sensory engagements with Chacoan places or the objects. Sensory explorations (video 4.1) require us to expand our ranges of representational styles and media.

AN IMAGINED NARRATIVE: WALKING TO CHACO

It's early summer in AD 1050. The corn is just beginning to stretch green shoots upward from the dry fields planted along Coyote Wash, amid the beige-brown cliffs and the sandstone hoodoos. At Chaco Canyon, soon it will be time for the summer solstice ceremonies. I imagine that I am a ten-year-old girl living in the Whirlwind outlier community, about 35 km southwest of Chaco. This is the first summer I am old enough to join my grandmother and older sister on the journey to Chaco for the solstice ceremonies. We travel together across the rugged terrain, the desert gravels crunching in time with our footsteps. My early morning excitement dissipates gradually into fatigue because it's a long walk, and it's very hot during the day, and I have short legs. My sister runs ahead of me, gossiping with the other girls her age. We walk along the paths that connect the outliers, from our home at Whirlwind, north to the community at Escalon (figure 4.3), then east along the Chaco Wash to Lake Valley, and then further east to Casa del Rio. The paths are broad, straight, and well-trampled—many people have passed this way. Along the way, prominent, odd-looking landforms such as Bennett Peak and White Rock shift into and out of view. My grandmother tells me stories about things that happened to the ancestors

FIGURE 4.3. *Navajo archaeologist Davina Two Bears at the Chacoan outlier of Escalon (http://www.upcolorado.com/component/k2/item/2712-subjects-and-narratives-in -archaeology-media; photo by author)*

at those peaks long ago. And she tells me stories about other journeys she has made to Chaco, as a young mother and as a girl like me. One time a man was bitten by a rattler, and another time the special offering jars were left behind, and another time they met strange traders on the road who carried bracelets carved of white shell.

It takes us four days to make the journey. We stop each night at a different community, visiting the homes of relatives and cousins. My sister and grandmother catch up on the news and gossip; I play with my cousins and the other children. Some people are joining us on the journey; others are not. We share shelled corn and savory deer jerky we have brought, and people feed us and give us things to take to Chaco for them—offerings such as red dog shale pendants or Narbona Pass chert or pieces of special pottery. There are so many new experiences that each day seems to last a week. Each morning I wonder, who will we meet today? What will we eat? Where will we sleep tonight? We sing traveling songs as we walk. More and more people join us each day as we go—some come from distant communities to the north or south. Some speak with strange accents, and some we cannot understand at all.

On the fourth day of our journey we walk east up the Chaco Wash from the great house of Casa del Rio toward West Mesa. In the distance, I see a row of

FIGURE 4.4. *A collared lizard stands watch over the Chacoan great house of Peñasco Blanco (http://www.upcolorado.com/component/k2/item/2712-subjects-and-narratives-in -archaeology-media; photo by author)*

watchers standing atop the mesa edge, silhouetted against the sky . . . but as we move nearer I can see that these are not people but shrines. My heart pounds with excitement. Chaco at last! We round the edge of the mesa and enter the canyon, and suddenly we are assaulted by a cacophony of drumming and singing, dogs barking, voices in conversation. We climb the short staircase up the cliff to the great house of Peñasco Blanco (figure 4.4), where we will stay with our relatives for the week of the ceremonies. The building resembles our great house at home at Whirlwind, but it is much bigger. As we approach, we smell venison roasting, and we see people running to and fro along the third-story rooftops. Someone calls and waves to my grandmother, and we have arrived.

DISCUSSION

I originally wrote this imagined narrative because I was frustrated by the limitations of the empirical analytic methods I had been using to think about relationships among people who lived at outliers and ritual events at Chaco Canyon. We know such relationships exist because of architectural and arti-factual connections between communities such as Whirlwind and Peñasco Blanco. We know the stark, high desert landscape held complex meanings for Chacoans, as it does for Pueblo and Navajo peoples today. I used line-of-sight analysis in ArcGIS to demonstrate that outliers such as Whirlwind were connected to Chaco Canyon through shrines and high places (Robinson, Van Dyke, and Windes 2007). But I sought a way to think about the lived, embodied ways outlier residents would have understood this landscape and their relationship to Chaco Canyon. I wrote this imagined narrative from the perspective of a ten-year-old girl from the Whirlwind outlier because, like my archaeological self, this imaginary girl would have been a relative outsider at Chaco, old enough to undertake the pilgrimage but young enough to have only a naive and partial understanding of the events she witnessed. I juxtaposed the narrative with field photographs from archaeological survey and mapping projects along the route she would have traveled. This technique provides a visual dimension to the narrative, allowing a reader/viewer to "see" what the landscape looks like. It also emphasizes the constructed nature of archaeological knowledge, as archaeologists are depicted engaged in the research that resulted in the analyses that lie behind the narrative. Of course, the narrative and images are partial, constructed, and subjective—they represent only one fragment of one possible story. But there is a multidimensionality to the representation that moves us beyond an expository description of Chacoan pilgrimage. Imagined narratives are good to think with.

ENGAGING OTHER SENSES

It is not possible—and indeed, it is not necessarily desirable—to get away from visuality in constructing and representing knowledge. But humans experience a plethora of other kinds of sensory entanglements. Phenomenological archaeology provides one way for us to think about sensory, bodily experiences in the past. Much phenomenological archaeology is focused on the visual, revolving around inter-visibilities among monuments or shifting visual perceptions along routes of movement (e.g., Cummings, Jones, and Watson 2002; Cummings and Whittle 2003; Scarre 2002; Tilley 1994; Van Dyke 2007, 2011). However, there is an increasing interest in evoking the sounds, smells, tastes, and textures of the past (e.g., authors in Day 2013; Hamilakis 2002; Hamilton et al. 2006; Ryzewski 2009; Tilley 2009).

The emotional (and political) power of ritual is grounded in engagement with the senses (Geertz 1980; Smith 2000). Music, liturgy, costuming, feasting, drink, and dance all contribute to remembered, repetitive, body-centered, sensory experiences. Ritual can bring people together on many levels at once, creating and affirming a sense of identity on a scale that can range from households

Figure 4.5. *Colorado College students cross Chaco Wash after a thunderstorm (http://www .upcolorado.com/component/k2/item/2712-subjects-and-narratives-in-archaeology-media; photo by author)*

to regions. The cyclical repetition found in ritual can seem to conflate or suspend time, collapsing the past into the present. Ritual is a constitutive element of Pueblo life today (Ortiz 1969, 1972; Parsons 1939), and it is ritual that held Chaco together a millennium ago (authors in Lekson 2006; Lekson 1999, 2008; Renfrew 2001; Van Dyke 2007; Yoffee 2001). Elsewhere, I have explored the visual and spatial components of ritual at Chaco, but what about other sensory dimensions? What did ritual sound like at Chaco, for example? Pueblo ritual today involves songs, chanting, liturgies, rattles, drums, and other instruments. Although we have many odd objects from Chacoan contexts, we have no clear indications of musical instruments and no material evidence for songs or liturgies. But phenomenological engagement with the sensorium can provide some clues, if we are willing to work in the realm of intuition rather than limiting ourselves to deduction.

In the summer, northwest New Mexico is bright, sunny, and hot, with daytime temperatures in the 90s F. From mid-July to early August, however, the high desert receives over half of its annual precipitation in the form of heavy summer thunderstorms. Mornings are clear and bright, but in the afternoons, cumulus clouds gather around high peaks. The air thickens as swarms of

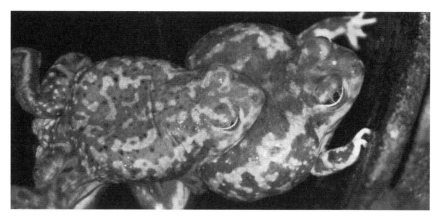

Video 4.2. Chaco Toads *(2014), by Ruth M. Van Dyke (photo by Michael Skinner; video available at http://www.upcolorado.com/component/k2/item/2712-subjects-and-narratives -in-archaeology-media)*

darkening clouds sweep across the heavens. Heavy, lightning-filled thunderstorms can pour several inches of water on one place in a few hours (figure 4.5).

These rains were and are critical for ancient and modern agriculturalists, and they figure prominently in Pueblo ceremonialism. The Hopi, for example, have a summer ritual cycle that revolves around bringing the clouds (who are also ancestors and spiritual beings called katsinas) from their nearby mountain home to lend life-giving rains to Hopi cornfields (Tuwaletstiwa and Tuwaletstiwa, this volume). The rains bring the sounds of thunder and running water. In their aftermath, they also bring another loud, unusual sound—the mating call of the spadefoot toad. These amphibians burrow into the desert soil where they hibernate for most of the year, emerging only for a brief period after summer rains to breed and feed before reburying themselves in the earth. So deafening and distinctive is their braying call that the spadefoot toad is the state animal of New Mexico.

The rain-toad association is well-known to Pueblo people—toads and frogs are associated with water, rain, fertility, and corn. The rain comes, the toads come, the corn grows and is harvested. Women grind corn on stone manos and metates into meal for stews and breads. Corn grinding—women's work—is of ritual importance for women going through puberty ceremonies and marriage ceremonies. At the final dance of the summer ritual cycle (Niman), there are *katsin'mana*, or katsina maidens, danced by men impersonating women. The katsin'mana perform the grinding of corn, using rasps to imitate the sound of the manos and metates. These rasps are sometimes decorated with frogs/toads.

When I heard the katsin'mana and then heard the toads following rains at Chaco, I made an aural connection: rain – toads – corn – women – food. Hopi people make this connection as well (Phillip Tuwaletstiwa, personal communication, April 2011). Given the unusual, short-lived, but deafening nature of spadefoot calls at Chaco and given the importance of toads/frogs, rain, and corn at Chaco, it seems very likely that these sounds and the associated bundles of ideas figured prominently in Chacoan ritual as well. But this textual description cannot convey my insight, nor can it convey the power of the aural relationships. To fully appreciate this, you have to hear it (video 4.2).

AUTHORITY AND ETHICS

Whenever one pushes against accepted disciplinary boundaries, the keepers of those boundaries push back. Alternative forms of archaeological representation raise epistemological as well as ethical concerns. When archaeologists build knowledge within a hypothetico-deductive framework, modern scholarship unquestionably accepts this knowledge as legitimate. Once we step beyond what we can "know" through science, however, we raise the specter of relativism and decenter our authority as archaeologists. How can we evaluate archaeological knowledge constructed and represented through interpretive, much less creative, methods?

McGuire (2008: 82–91) argues that archaeological knowledge should be evaluated according to four criteria: coherence, correspondence, context, and consequences. *Coherence* means interpretations of the past should be logical and rational, and they should fit with existing social theory. *Correspondence* means interpretations should be supported by empirical observations. *Context* requires archaeologists to be cognizant of our audiences, constituents, and stakeholders, including descendant communities, the public at large, and our disciplinary colleagues. *Consequences* ask us to consider the political impact of our work in the world—whose interests are served by a particular interpretation or analysis?

Coherence and *correspondence* are easily recognizable qualities in the two creative projects presented here. Clearly, when archaeologists write imagined narratives, we must ground them in empirical data (McCarthy 2003). Interpretations should resonate with multiple strands of archaeological evidence—encompassing rather than ignoring the interstices in the material, linking data into a coherent and plausible whole. My imagined narrative for the young girl's journey with her grandmother is not the only possible or indeed the only likely Chacoan pilgrimage experience, but it fits well with existing archaeological knowledge about outlier inhabitants and their relationships with Chaco Canyon.

How do we make correspondence more explicit? How do we point the reader toward the connections between material data and creative representations? Some contributors to the volume have dealt with this issue by incorporating multimedia links to data (e.g., Tringham, this volume). My solution here has been to introduce and follow my work with expository passages punctuated with copious scholarly references. With the continued development of electronic publishing, we have the technology to make all citations active hyperlinks to other online articles and data. Until academic publishing catches up with web technology, the interested reader must follow up these connections on his or her own.

Context and *consequences* present knottier problems. Do alternative narratives really help past voices to speak, or are they merely another way for archaeologists to appropriate and subjugate past peoples? If we imagine voices for subjects in other times and places, are we actually silencing them by placing our own words in their mouths (Bakhtin 1990: 27–36)? Historical archaeologists can sidestep this problem by juxtaposing their own words with the words of their subjects, taken from journals, letters, or other literary sources (e.g., Beaudry 1998; Gibb, this volume; Praetzellis and Praetzellis, this volume; Yamin 1998). Janet Spector (1991, 1993) was able to ameliorate the problem because she based *What This Awl Means* on interviews and close collaboration with direct descendants of her site's Wahpeton inhabitants. But without ethnographic informants or historical documents, are we merely giving voice to our own contemporary and perhaps overly romanticized notions about the past?

I counter this critique by arguing that we are already speaking for past peoples when we engage in any form of archaeological representation. We can avoid objectifying subjects if our work foregrounds the roles of the writer and the reader in constructing archaeological knowledge. Archaeological texts entail dialogue among writer(s), readers, and other archaeologists (Pluciennik, this volume). The active part the reader plays in constructing archaeological interpretations is brought sharply into focus by the websites created by Michael Shanks, Rosemary Joyce, Ruth Tringham, and others. Hypertexts enable/force viewers/readers to chart their own nonlinear pathways through interrelated bodies of content (Joyce, Guyer, and Joyce 2000; Joyce and Tringham 2007; Lopiparo and Joyce 2003; Metamedia 2010; Shanks 2012; Webmoor 2005). Although imagined first-person narratives are not hypertext, they are overtly constructed. Clearly, the imagined narrative above was not written by a ten-year-old Chacoan girl—rather, it was written by an archaeologist imagining one possible experience of a ten-year-old Chacoan girl. So, I argue that imagined narratives as I have described them here actually represent a more transparent authorial hand than does an oblique, ostensibly subject-less narrative.

Alternative representations have a great deal that is positive to offer audiences and stakeholders in the present, within and beyond the discipline. Narratives, video, acoustic representations, and hypermedia files grab the public imagination far more easily than scholarly prose. In an era when funding is scarce and the utility of archaeological research is difficult to defend in the face of other pressing concerns (such as energy development in the United States), the benefits of public outreach for our discipline are clear. A creative work that gets the public excited about archaeology is a project worth pursuing. And far better for archaeologists to direct this work than to leave the field to filmmakers, novelists, or other avocationalists whose enthusiasm may be great but whose engagement with the empirical data is necessarily shallow (see Thomas, this volume).

There are also benefits within the discipline. It is all too easy to follow the well-worn grooves of existing scholarship, widening and deepening the traces, perhaps, but seldom cutting new pathways across unknown terrain. Alternative, creative explorations and representations are good to think with. They help us ask new questions and see relationships that might not otherwise be apparent, infusing our scholarship with fresh energy. I advocate for legitimate, scholarly spaces for creative, sensuous engagements with constructed pasts, and I argue that archaeologists should be in the forefront of these undertakings.

ACKNOWLEDGMENTS

As I developed this chapter, I benefited from constructive criticisms, encouragement, and suggestions offered by many people. I especially want to thank Reinhard Bernbeck and Randy McGuire. Their input has made the chapter stronger, but I take full responsibility for the final product. In the *Walking to Chaco* video, photos from the Casa del Rio project are by Richard Moeller, and the rattlesnake photo is by Michael Skinner; the Kutz Canyon overlook photo is by Justin Rochell; all other photos are mine. In the *Chaco Toads* video, the jet frog photo appears courtesy of the Division of Anthropology, American Museum of Natural History, Washington, DC, catalog #H/10426. Two spadefoot toad photos are by Connie A. Darby, and the mating spadefoot toad photo is by Michael Skinner. The photo of restored mealing bins in Room 55, Pueblo del Arroyo, was taken by O. C. Havens in 1925 and appears courtesy of the National Park Service, Chaco Culture National Historic Park Museum Collection, slide #6839. The photo of Hopi women grinding corn was taken by Edward S. Curtis ca. 1906 and appears courtesy of the Library of Congress, Washington, DC. The drawing of katsin'manas grinding corn is from Fewkes (1903: 92, plate XXXII). The paintings of hemis mana katsinas with rasps are by Raymond Naha and appear courtesy of Adobe Gallery in Santa Fe. I thank Russ Bodnar for providing the sound recording of spadefoot toads in Chaco Canyon, and I thank Doug Gann and Jenny Adams for the recording of corn ground on metates. I am responsible for all media not otherwise attributed.

REFERENCES

Bakhtin, Mikhail M. 1990. *Art and Answerability: Early Philosophical Essays by M. M. Bakhtin*. Ed. Michael Holquist and Vadim Liapunov. Trans. Vadim Liapunov and Kenneth Brostrom. Austin: University of Texas Press.

Beaudry, Mary C. 1998. "Farm Journal: First Person, Four Voices." *Historical Archaeology* 32: 20–33.

Brody, J. J. 1984. "Chaco Art and the Chaco Phenomenon." In *New Light on Chaco Canyon*, ed. David Grant Noble, 13–18. Santa Fe: School of American Research Press.

Connerton, Paul. 1989. *How Societies Remember*. Cambridge: Cambridge University Press. http://dx.doi.org/10.1017/CBO9780511628061.

Crown, Patricia, and Jeffrey Hurst. 2009. "Evidence of Cacao Use in the Prehispanic American Southwest." *Proceedings of the National Academy of Sciences of the United States of America* 106 (7): 2110–13. http://dx.doi.org/10.1073/pnas.0812817106.

Crown, Patricia, and Wirt H. Wills. 2003. "Modifying Pottery and Kivas at Chaco: Pentimento, Restoration, or Renewal?" *American Antiquity* 68 (3): 511–32. http://dx.doi.org/10.2307/3557106.

Cummings, Vicki, Andrew Jones, and Aaron Watson. 2002. "Divided Places: Phenomenology and Asymmetry in the Monuments of the Black Mountains, Southeast Wales." *Cambridge Archaeological Journal* 12 (1): 57–70. http://dx.doi.org/10.1017/S0959774302000033.

Cummings, Vicki, and Alisdair Whittle. 2003. *Places of Special Virtue: Megaliths in the Neolithic Landscape of Wales*. Oxford: Oxbow Books.

Day, Jo, ed. 2013. *Making Senses of the Past: Toward a Sensory Archaeology*. Carbondale: Center for Archaeological Investigations, University of Illinois.

Fewkes, Jesse Walter. 1903. "Hopi Katcinas Drawn by Native Artists." In *The 21st Annual Report of the Bureau of American Ethnology*, 3–26. Washington, DC: Smithsonian Institution.

Fritz, John M. 1978. "Paleopsychology Today: Ideational Systems and Human Adaptation in Prehistory." In *Social Archaeology: Beyond Subsistence and Dating*, ed. Charles L. Redman, Mary Jane Berman, Edward V. Curtin, William T. Langhorne Jr., Nina M. Versaggi, and Jeffery C. Wanswer, 37–59. New York: Academic Press.

Geertz, Clifford A. 1980. *Negara: The Theatre State in Nineteenth Century Bali*. Princeton: Princeton University Press.

Hamilakis, Yannis. 2002. "The Past as Oral History: Towards an Archaeology of the Senses." In *Thinking through the Body: Archaeologies of Corporeality*, ed. Yannis Hamilakis, Mark Pluciennik, and Sarah Tarlow, 121–36. New York: Kluwer Academic/Plenum. http://dx.doi.org/10.1007/978-1-4615-0693-5_7.

Hamilton, Sue, and Ruth Whitehouse, with Keri Brown, Pamela Combes, Edward Herring, and Mike Seager Thomas. 2006. "Phenomenology in Practice: Towards a Methodology for a 'Subjective' Approach." *European Journal of Archaeology* 9 (1): 31–71. http://dx.doi.org/10.1177/1461957107077704.

Hodder, Ian. 2012. *Entangled*. Chichester, UK: Wiley-Blackwell. http://dx.doi.org/10.1002/9781118241912.

Joyce, Rosemary A., Carolyn Guyer, and Michael Joyce. 2000. *Sister Stories*. New York: New York University Press. http://www.nyupress.org/sisterstories (site discontinued), accessed March 14, 2010.

Joyce, Rosemary A., and Ruth Tringham. 2007. "Feminist Adventures in Hypertext." *Journal of Archaeological Method and Theory* 14 (3): 328–58. http://dx.doi.org/10.1007/s10816-007-9036-2.

Judd, Neil M. 1954. *The Material Culture of Pueblo Bonito*. Smithsonian Miscellaneous Collections 124. Washington, DC: Smithsonian Institution.

Judge, W. James. 1989. "Chaco Canyon—San Juan Basin." In *Dynamics of Southwest Prehistory*, ed. Linda S. Cordell and George J. Gumerman, 209–61. Washington, DC: Smithsonian Institution.

Kantner, John. 1996. "Political Competition among the Chaco Anasazi of the American Southwest." *Journal of Anthropological Archaeology* 15 (1): 41–105. http://dx.doi.org/10.1006/jaar.1996.0003.

Kress, Nancy. 2006. "Better Left Unsaid: Know What to Leave out of Your Tale to Keep Your Stories Lean and, Ultimately, More Satisfying." *Writer's Digest* 86 (3): 20.

Lekson, Stephen H. 1999. *The Chaco Meridian: Centers of Political Power in the Ancient Southwest*. Walnut Creek, CA: AltaMira.

Lekson, Stephen H. 2008. *A History of the Ancient Southwest*. Santa Fe: School for Advanced Research Press.

Lekson, Stephen H., ed. 2006. *The Archaeology of Chaco Canyon: An Eleventh-Century Pueblo Regional Center*. Santa Fe: School of American Research Press.

Lopiparo, Jeanne, and Rosemary A. Joyce. 2003. "Crafting Cosmos, Telling Sister Stories, and Exploring Archaeological Knowledge Graphically in Hypertext Environments." In *Ancient Muses: Archaeology and the Arts*, ed. John H. Jameson Jr., John E. Ehrenhard, and Christine A. Finn, 193–203. Tuscaloosa: University of Alabama Press.

Malville, J. McKim, ed. 2004. *Chimney Rock: The Ultimate Outlier*. Lanham, MD: Lexington Books.

McCarthy, John P. 2003. "More Than Just 'Telling the Story': Interpretive Narrative Archaeology." In *Ancient Muses: Archaeology and the Arts*, ed. John H. Jameson Jr., John E. Ehrenhard, and Christine A. Finn, 15–24. Tuscaloosa: University of Alabama Press.

McGuire, Randall H. 2008. *Archaeology as Political Action*. Berkeley: University of Calfornia Press.

Metamedia: A Collaboratory at Stanford University. 2010. http://metamedia.stanford.edu, accessed March 15, 2010.

Mills, Barbara J. 2004. "The Establishment and Defeat of Hierarchy: Inalienable Possessions and the History of Collective Prestige Structures in the Puebloan Southwest." *American Anthropologist* 106 (2): 238–51. http://dx.doi.org/10.1525/aa.2004.106.2.238.

Mills, Barbara J. 2008. "Remembering While Forgetting: Depositional Practices and Social Memory at Chaco." In *Memory Work: Archaeologies of Material Practices*, ed. Barbara J. Mills and William H. Walker, 81–108. Santa Fe: School of Advanced Research Press.

Ortiz, Alfonso. 1969. *The Tewa World: Space, Time, Being, and Becoming in a Pueblo Society*. Chicago: University of Chicago Press.

Ortiz, Alfonso. 1972. "Ritual Drama and the Pueblo Worldview." In *New Perspectives on the Pueblos*, ed. Alfonso Ortiz, 135–61. Albuquerque: University of New Mexico Press.

Parsons, Elsie Clewes. 1939. *Pueblo Indian Religion*. Chicago: University of Chicago Press.

Pauketat, Timothy R. 2013. "Bundles of/in/as Time." In *Big Histories, Human Lives: Tackling Problems of Scale in Archaeology*, ed. John Robb and Timothy Pauketat. Santa Fe: School of Advanced Research Press.

Pepper, George H. 1909. "The Exploration of a Burial Room in Pueblo Bonito, New Mexico." In *Anthropological Essays Presented to Frederick Ward Putnam in Honor of His Seventieth Birthday*, 196–252. New York: G. E. Stechert.

Pepper, George H. 1920. *Pueblo Bonito*. Anthropological Papers 27. New York: American Museum of Natural History.

Renfrew, Colin. 2001. "Production and Consumption in a Sacred Economy: The Material Correlates of High Devotional Expression at Chaco Canyon." *American Antiquity* 66 (1): 14–25. http://dx.doi.org/10.2307/2694314.

Robinson, Tucker, Ruth Van Dyke, and Tom Windes. 2007. "Chacoan Shrines in High Places: Intervisibility across the San Juan Basin." *Glyphs* 57 (10): 6–7.

Ryzewski, Krysta, ed. 2009. "Experience, Modes of Engagement, Archaeology." Theme issue of *Archaeologies: Journal of the World Archaeological Congress* 5 (3).

Scarre, Chris. 2002. "Coast and Cosmos: The Neolithic Monuments of Northern Brittany." In *Monuments and Landscape in Atlantic Europe: Perception and Society during the Neolithic and Early Bronze Age*, ed. Chris Scarre, 84–102. London: Routledge.

Sebastian, Lynne. 1992. *The Chaco Anasazi: Sociopolitical Evolution in the Prehistoric Southwest*. Cambridge: Cambridge University Press.

Shanks, Michael. 2012. *The Archaeological Imagination*. Walnut Creek, CA: Left Coast.

Smith, Adam T. 2000. "Rendering the Political Aesthetic: Political Legitimacy in Urartian Representations of the Built Environment." *Journal of Anthropological Archaeology* 19 (2): 131–63. http://dx.doi.org/10.1006/jaar.1999.0348.

Sofaer, Anna. 2007. *Chaco Astronomy: An Ancient American Cosmology*. Santa Fe: Ocean Tree Books.

Spector, Janet. 1991. "What This Awl Means: Toward a Feminist Archaeology." In *Engendering Archaeology*, ed. Joan M. Gero and Margaret Conkey, 388–406. Oxford: Blackwell.

Spector, Janet. 1993. *What This Awl Means: Feminist Archaeology at Wahpeton Dakota Village*. St. Paul: Minnesota Historical Society Press.

Stein, John R., and Stephen H. Lekson. 1992. "Anasazi Ritual Landscapes." In *Anasazi Regional Organization and the Chaco System*, ed. David Doyel, 87–100. Maxwell Museum of Anthropology Anthropological Papers 5. Albuquerque: University of New Mexico.

Tilley, Christopher. 1994. *A Phenomenology of Landscape*. Oxford: Berg.

Tilley, Christopher. 2009. *Interpreting Landscapes: Geologies, Topographies, Identities: Explorations in Landscape Archaeology 3*. Walnut Creek, CA: Left Coast.

Toll, H. Wolcott. 1985. "Pottery, Production, and the Chacoan Anasazi System." PhD diss., Department of Anthropology, University of Colorado, Boulder.

Toll, H. Wolcott. 2001. "Making and Breaking Pots in the Chaco World." *American Antiquity* 66 (1): 56–78. http://dx.doi.org/10.2307/2694318.

Van Dyke, Ruth M. 2004. "Memory, Meaning, and Masonry: The Late Bonito Chacoan Landscape." *American Antiquity* 69 (3): 413–31. http://dx.doi.org/10.2307 /4128400.

Van Dyke, Ruth M. 2007. *The Chaco Experience: Landscape and Ideology at the Center Place*. Santa Fe: School for Advanced Research Press.

Van Dyke, Ruth M. 2011. "Anchoring Identities: Iconic Landforms across San Juan Time and Space." In *Changing Histories, Landscapes, and Perspectives: The Twentieth Anniversary Southwest Symposium*, ed. Margaret C. Nelson and Colleen A. Strawhacker, 403–22. Boulder: University Press of Colorado.

Vivian, Gordon R., and Paul Reiter. 1960. *The Great Kivas of Chaco Canyon and Their Relationships*. Santa Fe: Monographs of the School of American Research and the Museum of New Mexico 22.

Vivian, R. Gwinn. 1990. *The Chacoan Prehistory of the San Juan Basin*. New York: Academic Press.

Vivian, R. Gwinn, Dulce N. Dodgen, and Gayle H. Hartman. 1978. *Wooden Ritual Artifacts from Chaco Canyon, New Mexico*. Anthropological Papers 32. Tucson: University of Arizona Press.

Webmoor, Timothy. 2005. "Mediational Techniques and Conceptual Frameworks in Archaeology: A Model in 'Mapwork' at Teotihuacan, Mexico." *Journal of Social Archaeology* 5 (1): 52–84. http://dx.doi.org/10.1177/1469605305050143.

Webster, Laurie. 2011. "Perishable Ritual Artifacts at the West Ruin of Aztec, New Mexico: Evidence for a Chacoan Migration." *Kiva* 77 (2): 139–72.

Wilcox, David R. 1993. "The Evolution of the Chacoan Polity." In *The Chimney Rock Archaeological Symposium*, ed. J. McKim Malville and Gary Matlock, 76–90. Washington, DC: USDA Forest Service, General Technical Report RM–227.

Wills, Wirt H. 2000. "Political Leadership and the Construction of Chacoan Great Houses, A.D. 1020–1140." In *Alternative Leadership Strategies in the Prehispanic Southwest*, ed. Barbara J. Mills, 19–44. Tucson: University of Arizona Press.

Windes, Thomas C. 1987. *Investigations at the Pueblo Alto Complex, Chaco Canyon, New Mexico, 1975–1979*, Volume 1, Volume 2, Parts 1 and 2. Chaco Canyon Studies, Publications in Archeology 18F. Santa Fe: National Park Service.

Yamin, Rebecca. 1998. "Lurid Tales and Homely Stories of New York's Notorious Five Points." *Historical Archaeology* 32 (1): 74–85.

Yoffee, Norman. 2001. "The Chaco 'Rituality' Revisited." In *Chaco Society and Polity: Papers from the 1999 Conference*, ed. Linda S. Cordell, W. James Judge, and June-el Piper, 63-78. Albuquerque: New Mexico Archaeological Council, Special Publication 4.

5

Landscape

The Reservoir of the Unconscious

PHILLIP TUWALETSTIWA AND
JUDY TUWALETSTIWA

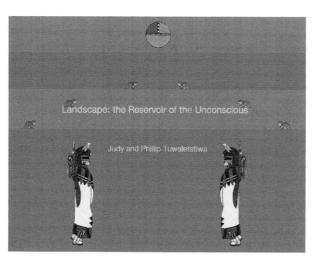

FIGURE 5.1. *(http://www.upcolorado.com/component/k2
/item/2712-subjects-and-narratives-in-archaeology-media)*

Our participation in this project respects the premise
of this book: to increase archaeological knowledge by
incorporating text, art, fiction, song, poetry, video, audio,
and Internet links. Within this array of approaches, our
chapter is a radical departure from a traditional archaeological presentation: we use fiction as an informing
device. This might not sit well with people accustomed
to a traditional archaeological approach. Consequently,
our chapter is similar to Swift's *Modest Proposal*: it
encourages exploratory avenues of thought outside an
established tradition.

DOI: 10.5876/9781607323815.c005

In this chapter, our references are to Pueblo people, specifically the Hopi of northern Arizona. Overarching characteristics of southwestern Pueblo people include farming, residing in one place for millennia, living in villages of multistory stone houses, and observing religious practices designed to bring moisture to their fields and villages. Corn, Water, and the Sun are the focus of everyday Pueblo life; reverence for these elements permeates all social and religious practices.

Our chapter is a combination of prose, song, and visual art that describes Pueblo life as it may have been in the past and as it exists today. We chose these excerpts from our novel in progress, *The Laughing Spiders*©, to suggest a variety of styles, narrative, and tone to illustrate different ways of "seeing" the past. We want to encourage various methodologies to examine the past in a way that immerses readers in the culture, pulling them away from their own cultural biases.

We offer no footnotes, attributions, or quotations. What we present stems from listening to Hopi Oral History, years of living on the Hopi Reservation, and reading from a wide variety of southwestern literature including fiction, history, ethnography, and anthropological and archaeological writings. Equally important are the personal experiences of watching Hopi religious ceremonies, participating in religious pilgrimages, socializing with Hopi friends and relatives, planting and harvesting corn, and understanding that life exists in Hopi Land because of the Hopi people's relationship to nature.

We have written a story. We attempt to bring the past into the present. Is it a true account? We do not know. But to the native eye and ear, it carries as much truth as fiction.

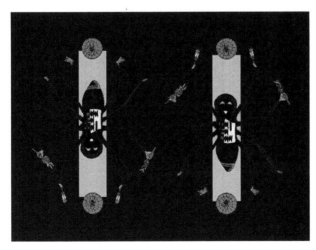

FIGURE 5.2.

THE NOVEL

We are collaborating on a novel, *The Laughing Spiders©*, that explores the thoughtful use of fiction to humanize ancient people. The first half of the novel takes place around 750 CE. The second half takes place in the late twentieth century. Both sections are set in the American Southwest.

In *The Laughing Spiders* we use a symbolic visual language and a written language. We do the same in this presentation. We are not illustrating the written word. We are trying to enhance the meaning of illustration and text by having them inform each other in a way that merges mythos and logos.

We write about landscape, an amorphous term that needs to be tethered. For example, Hopitutsqua translates as Hopi Land. Out of the people's relationship to their land, images and narratives emerged to form a history and a cosmology. That is what we mean when we say that landscape is the reservoir of the unconscious.

The images we use are ancient and contemporary. They express a cosmology that evolves from Hopitutsqua.

Before we read from our novel, let's explore the merging of mythos and logos in landscape through a dream Phillip had a few years ago.

FIGURE 5.3.

Above us stretches the firmament. Below us spreads the earth. The eagle glides and soars in the ethereal realm. The serpent crawls and burrows in the subterranean realm. Their spirits meet at the center place, the membrane between worlds. A transformation occurs and a new form, the feathered serpent, is born. This is the moment of creation, of human creation in relationship to the land and its inhabitants.

FIGURE 5.4.

FIGURE 5.5.

When the people first came to the American Southwest, the snake and the eagle were here, existing without us. Through the eyes of humans, the snake and the eagle became what never lived in nature, the plumed serpent. Through such creative acts, the people formed a spiritual life reflecting their relationship to their land and the land's relationship to them.

This is the preface to the ancient section of our novel.

FIGURE 5.6.

What is the voice of the earth?
Listen. You will know it.
The pale light before sunrise is a voice.
The sweet taste of roasted corn is a voice.
The succulent flesh of melon is a voice.
The dancing flame of fire is a voice.
The shadowy smell of smoke is a voice.
The soft skin of a baby is a voice.
The wrinkled face of an old woman is a voice.
The rumble of thunder is a voice.
Have you listened to a corn plant growing?

FIGURE 5.7.

Sit in the field. Sit very still. In the dark silence of night, you can hear the corn growing. In the bright light of day, you can hear the corn growing.

Do you hear wind humming?

Do you see bee filling her baskets?

Do you hear worm chewing?

Do you see *Yàapa* mockingbird watching worm?

The sound of corn growing is a farmer singing, the wind scattering his words across his field.

FIGURE 5.7*a*.

FIGURE 5.8.

"Throughout, along your fields here, the young corn plants are fluttering their pollen-laden wings. They will make themselves grow upward here.

They adorn themselves to go there, they adorn themselves to go there, the blue/green clouds adorn themselves." (Hopi Song)

FIGURE 5.9.

The sound of corn growing is a raven swooping and cawing.

The sound of corn growing is rain walking across the land from every direction.

We choose the seed carefully. The most beautiful ears of corn we choose. We choose them to be the Mother.

Figure 5.10.

We dig in the earth with our *sooya* (digging stick) holes like burrows, two hands deep. We drop our seeds into the moist earth. We give them a home so their roots will emerge to tunnel into the dark. We give them a home so their shoots will emerge to climb into the light.

They are coming up toward us. We cannot hurry them. We wonder, How can life come from something so small, so dry, so hard? We pray for rain. We sing for life to come again.

FIGURE 5.11.

The corn children stand up in the morning. We wait and we pray and we sing and we work, mounding the earth around them. We weave twigs to protect the young ones from the screaming wind. We pick off worms.

Raven is hungry. Porcupine is hungry. Cottontail is hungry. They are hungry for our corn. We sleep beside our corn children, sleep with one eye open.

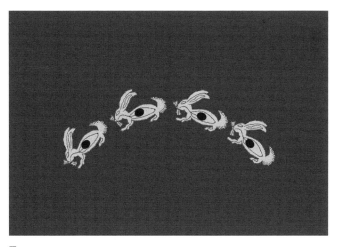

FIGURE 5.12.

In my field, early one morning, I found four newborn cottontails. All dead. Each smaller than a child's hand. Their eyes not yet open, they lay in a half circle on the ground, like someone set them there, just so. My dog grabbed one. She ate it. Ate it fast. I said, "Take no more."

Coyote carried away their Mother. Surprised her as she nursed them. No Mother to warm them. No Mother to feed them. In the cold of night, they died right away.

What is the voice of life?

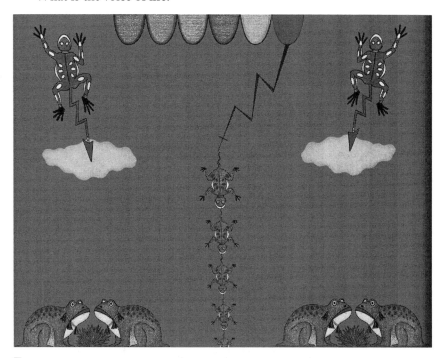

Figure 5.13.

The voice of life is the moaning of a woman giving birth.

The voice of life is the mewing of coyote pups hungry for their mother's milk.

The voice of life is the splashing of children playing in a puddle after a hard rain.

The voice of life is the laughter of a young man standing naked before thunder.

The voice of life is water sliding over rock, a snake like water moving.

The voice of life is the rattling of corn leaves as days grow short.

The voice of life is the silence of an old man dying, his time finished.

The voice of life is the silence of an old woman dying, her time finished.

The voice of life is a woman watching Taawa (Sun) rise where earth touches sky.

The voice of life is a woman watching Taawa set where sky touches earth.

The voice of life is a woman dreaming a world.

Our protagonist in the ancient section, Poovolli, Butterfly Woman, is the woman dreaming a world.

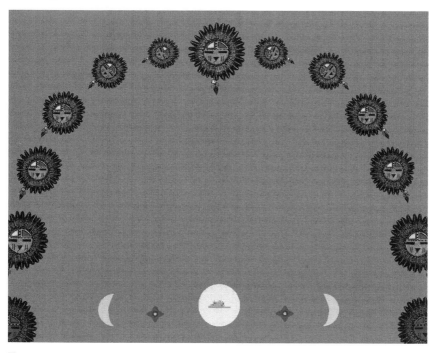

FIGURE 5.14.

Taawa led Poovolli's people. His arc measured their day.

Sprinkling meal they ground from corn Taawa helped them grow, the people prayed to him as he emerged.

He traveled as they worked. When he reached Taawanasami (the highest point of his journey), the people stopped to eat piiki and melon. They rested. Then they worked until Taawa stood a palm above the horizon.

When Taawa disappeared, moon, stars, and dreams illuminated the dark.

Taawa's travels measured the people's seasons.

Taawat aw (the Sun Watcher) tracked him when he emerged from where earth and sky lay together.

When Taawa stood halfway to his summer home, Taawat aw told the village crier, "We shall plant in two moons. Tell the people we must prepare."

For four mornings, the crier stood on a rock above the village, his voice splitting the stillness. "Listen, people. Listen. Planting is near.

"Lazy boys, get up. Clean the springs. Find the greasewood. Cut it for the *sooyat* (planting sticks).

"Men, make your prayer feathers. Take them to the fields. Sort your seed corn. Repair your hoes. The time of hard work approaches.

"Listen. Listen to my words. In two moons, we shall plant.

"Boys, stop looking at the girls. Get busy.

"Everyone, get up. Work! We must all work together.

"We must each have a good heart. An evil heart will spoil the seeds. An evil heart will make the wind blow. An evil heart will stop the rain.

"Men, in four suns, you will hunt rabbits.

"Women, stop your talk. Get busy. You will have rabbits to clean. Stew to cook. The boys and men will be hungry.

"Girls, stop your daydreaming. Quit looking at the boys. Help your mother carry water. You have corn to grind.

"Taawa will lead us."

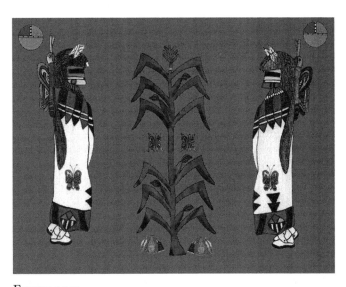

FIGURE 5.14A.

For five moons, the men and boys cultivated the fields. The women and girls cooked and tended the children. They dug clay and shaped vessels. They picked and stripped yucca leaves and wove baskets.

When Taawa reached his Summer House, the people asked the Creator to send clouds. They prayed for a gentle rain, a female rain, to nourish their crops.

After harvest, when Taawa stood halfway to His Winter House, they prepared for the cold. As the cold grew stronger, they entered the Dead Time, the time before the night of long dark. In their shelters, the people told stories about the migrations, about floods and fires. They told stories about the birds and animals, about the moon and the stars. They told stories about Coyote.

Figure 5.15.

They prayed that Taawa, after stopping to rest in his Winter House, would begin his journey back to the North, bringing warmth and rain again. Thus, they lived their lives in the rhythm of the land.

Following are two selections from the modern part of The Laughing Spiders. *In them, we suggest how the past remains present, as depicted in this seed pot transforming into an integrated circuit.*

FIGURE 5.16.

After a long day of branding and castrating bull calves, clipping yearling's ears, and doctoring the older cows, they grilled steaks and corn and now sat, bellies full, on Leroy's porch, facing southeast toward the Hopi Buttes. In the distance, near Giant's Chair, a line of dark rain clouds rumbled toward them, flashing lightning as they rolled across the land.

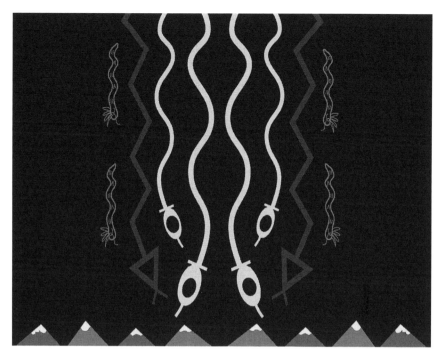

FIGURE 5.17.

Amanda pulled the striped Pendleton blanket tighter around her and Lenard.

Oliver Big Hat sniffed the air. "I hope it's a female rain," he said. "Can you Hopis do something to make sure it reaches my place?"

"Sorry, Hat," said Leroy, "We're going to hold it up at Second Mesa. By the time it hits Piñon, you'll be lucky to fill a thimble."

Seth chuckled and shook his head. "I hoped we could get by without another Navajo-Hopi dispute. You guys have been going at each other since we were in Vietnam."

Oliver laughed, "Our people were going at it way before then, Seth."

FIGURE 5.18.

Raindrops splashed in the dust, falling in a slow, steady cadence—the female rain Oliver had hoped for.

"Every drop is precious," said Leroy, looking at Amanda and Lenard. "Every drop."

"Gee, Dad," said Lenard, "Not every drop. There're so many of them. We wouldn't miss a few."

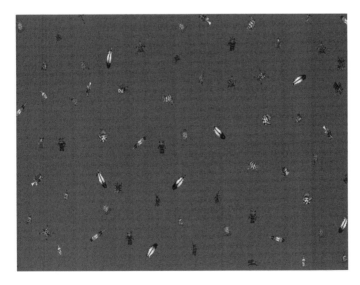

FIGURE 5.18A.

Watching the clouds, Leroy answered, "No, son, every drop."

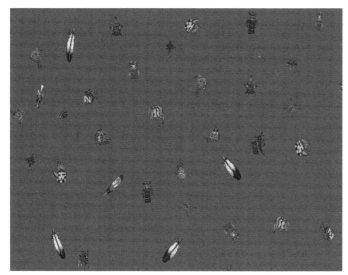

FIGURE 5.18B.

He looked at Lenard. "Suppose you were dying of thirst and you came to a place in the rocks, like the one I showed you on Ward Terrace, where you could drink only a drop at a time? As you drank, there would be a moment when you escaped Death's grip, a moment when one drop would decide whether you lived or died.

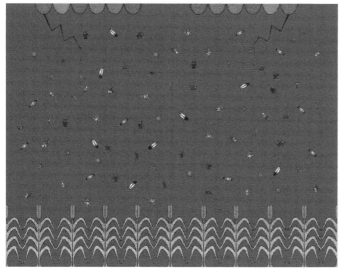

FIGURE 5.18C.

"So it is with the land. During a storm, there's a time when just enough rain falls for the corn, the cattle, the horses, the birds, the rabbits, and the grasses to continue living. Many drops together, but still one sacred drop touching the earth changes everything."

In a low voice, Seth murmured, "Amen."

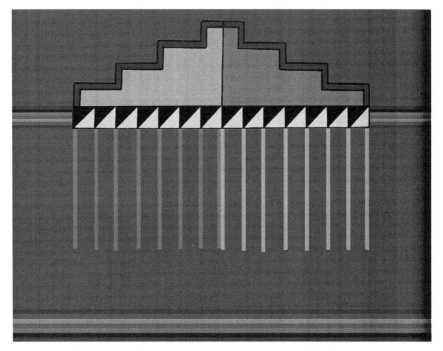

FIGURE 5.19.

Like a rainbow touching down, all was good that day on one mesa, in one village, at one house, on one porch, in the hearts of man and child.

One of our characters, Lenard, is a graduate student at the University of New Mexico. He tells his friend, Amanda, our protagonist, about a Hopi pilgrimage.

FIGURE 5.20.

Seven of us walked along the bottom of a small canyon, far west of Moenkopi, near the shrine Oongawuuti (Salt Woman), where the Salt Pilgrimage Trail forks west toward the Little Colorado River. The walls of the canyon offered little shade. The heat of the day fell on us like the breath of an oven. We stepped over cobble, atop small boulders, through sand, and around scrub brush, following the path engraved by the feet of generations of Hopi men.

We emerged into an open area, closed at one end by a narrow passage cut into the rocks. In a deep and wide hollow lay a pool of water. It was neither beautiful nor inviting. Hot to the touch, it had a green cast. Hopi tobacco grew around its edge. Hundreds of fat black tadpoles swam in the water. In wonder, I stared at this new life.

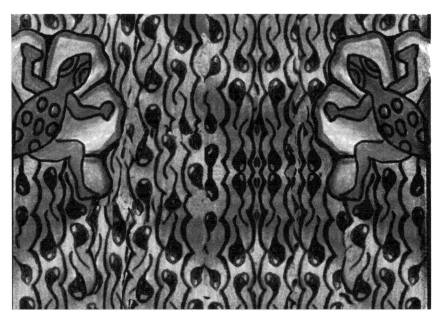

FIGURE 5.21.

Here, in one of the most isolated and harsh areas of northern Arizona, the pool of green water, heated sky, burning sand, and black tadpoles expressed the essence of our existence in our desert homeland. The sun gives food and warmth. Water gives life. The smoke of the Hopi tobacco growing beside the pool carries our prayers.

The water reflected the sky and the canyon walls and held the dark path to the lower world. I saw an unbroken line of ancestors who had walked this way, drank their fill, prayed, and given thanks for what the creator privileged us to know. I hoped they welcomed us.

The pool contained, in its simplicity, an intricate message. Staring through the water, past the tadpoles, I looked into the underworld, where I shall travel when I die. I saw the upper world of sky and clouds. In my reflection, surrounded by the canyon walls and tobacco plants, I saw the middle world. I stood at the center place where universes converge, where images real and not real merge.

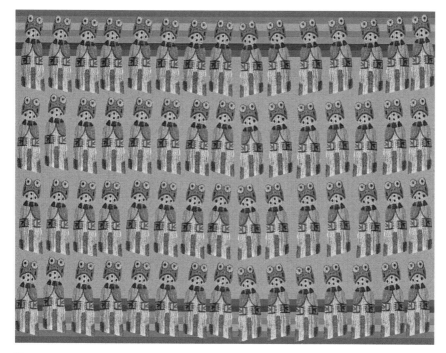

FIGURE 5.22.

6

Archaeologists as Storytellers

The Docudrama

WRITTEN BY MRS. MARY
PRAETZELLIS, WITH THE
ASSISTANCE OF DR. ADRIAN
PRAETZELLIS

Originally performed by Drs. Adrian Praetzellis
and Alexis Boutin

Adrian and I have always written stories. Perhaps we are frustrated artists, lacking the talent and discipline to create from scratch. But putting aside those personal failings, it is more likely that we write stories because our career paths through the emerging discipline of late-nineteenth-century, publicly funded historical archaeology provided the means and motivation to try something different, with few to advise or admonish us otherwise. Our archaeological work proceeded in the usual sequence: the development and implementation of a detailed social scientific research design, careful historical research and meticulous archaeological excavation, consistent artifact identification and analysis, a detailed technical report on all of the data addressing the research questions. We were blessed with rich deposits filled with nineteenth-century material culture generally complemented by a full documentary record, often replete with family papers and photos and sometimes firsthand memories. So, we went one step further. We prepared what might, but should not, be thought of as an extra-credit assignment—a monograph that presented our methods and findings in an accessible way to a wider audience (e.g., Praetzellis and Praetzellis 1984, 1985).

Later, on a lark and in an effort to liven up the tedium of professional meetings, we introduced "archaeologists as storytellers." We must not have been the only ones

DOI: 10.5876/9781607323815.c006

stupefied by the incomprehensible ramblings of our colleagues: storytellers proved an astounding success, transformational for many attendees. We did have rules: "Speakers will tell stories based upon information from a multitude of sources. These sources and their data will be referred to only parenthetically in slides and/or handouts. The stories may be about a person, place, or event . . . and will be readily understandable" (Praetzellis 2004: 84). We even debated the merits of our own forum: "How do stories created by archaeologists about the past deviate from a strictly processual explanation of culture? Is this a valid approach for historical archaeologists? Are we storytellers or scientists? How should we write the stories we tell? How much fiction is too much? What is meant by storytelling?" (Praetzellis and Praetzellis 2004). One of our personal criteria is that the stories we tell should have a modern message and, we hope, make the audience laugh in the process. We always knew we were having fun but, in retrospect, we were also playing (in the non-theatrical sense). Play is how humans and other primates learn and innovate. Just look at the young tech billionaires who as toddlers became comfortable with computers by getting the frog from one side of the street to the other without being smashed (Frogger) or at the influence of TV's *Colbert Report* on contemporary politics. Play and humor are wonderful tools.

The "docudrama" that follows explores the debate surrounding storytelling from our perspective and, it is hoped, in a humorous non-hurtful manner. Before presenting our drama, however, we outline the pedagogical and methodological underpinnings of our work. The drama covers the same ground, and the reader may skip our introduction if so inclined.

PEDAGOGY: PEOPLE AND PLACE

People like people. A past populated by characters of various genders and ethnicities, expectations and foibles, negotiating their paths through life will resonate more strongly with an audience than one illustrated by bell curves and solid objects. Most archaeologists retrieve things, not people, from their excavations. Archaeologists contextualize these things based on stratigraphic and temporal sequences and build increasingly complex explanatory models. The most stunning and historicitous (Adams 1977) of these objects fill museums worldwide. Visitors view and value these objects for their beauty and the familiar, yet foreign, connections to their own lives—an experience generally restricted to the aesthetic, often devoid of place and absent people. Linking people and place to objects (provenience) reduces this emotional separation: the difference between any old brass candlestick and the one that came from

Kalish in eastern Poland to London in the 1880s. The three-armed candlestick with the two lions, the Shabbat candlestick lighted every Friday night and passed down over the generations along with the stories of its owners. The old wax-encrusted candlestick had meaning to each generation. It could be a mirror or a vessel, reflecting or containing one's thoughts about the past, present, or future, depending upon vantage point.

We work on publicly funded archaeology, primarily historic-period sites about to be destroyed by construction, small windows of time and place in currently marginal, shifting environments. We work within a set of human issues—including contemporary ones—facing a particular place, with a particular set of remains and a particular set of memories. It is explicitly a relationship between past and present very much tied to place and people.

Place does not change; people change the landscape—leaving buildings, structures, and objects behind, buried belowground or surviving aboveground as remnants to be incorporated into later living surfaces. People move, bringing things with them, leaving things behind. Landscapes are layered with meaning, aboveground and belowground. A skilled excavator can uncover and untangle the living surfaces, structures, and hollow features, recovering threads of the lives of past peoples. These threads can be woven into many stories, each dependent on the skill, character, and perception of the weaver. But the story is still a construction. Archaeology only recovers fragments of the past; even when the full breadth of a documentary record is brought to play, our view is just through a keyhole to the past. Even with hundreds of keyholes into the same place in the past, there is no way to separate the interpreter's perception and role in editing the massive excess of material, in sorting marginal from important details. It could be said that the process of selection falsifies the past. But this assumes the existence of an omnipresent view of a solid past. If the past is seen as chasing the present and the views of all participants are acknowledged, then multiple meanings, multiple past realities, open to the interpreter.

Individual historical facts, archaeological layers, interfaces, features, and artifacts irrefutably exist. The archaeologist must assemble these pieces to create an image, an interpretation. The picture can only become clear by the imposition of an idea of meaning on the part of the archaeological observer. As mere compilation of un-interpreted archaeological and historical facts, the image is authentic but meaningless. When the archaeologist reassesses the image, converting facts into data in relation to an interpretive scheme, a new clarity appears. This new image might be either a keyhole view of a piece of historical reality or a fictional shadow, and even this attribution might depend on time, place, and observer.

How does one choose which stories to tell from those stockpiled in the layered time capsules that can be read in multiple ways and that change with the reader as either vessel or mirror? Three concepts guide our stories—clarity, power, and use. The clearer the connections between the archaeological and historical records, the greater authenticity a story will possess. The wealth of an archaeological deposit generally has nothing to do with its past or current value as commodities. Signature artifacts and constellations of artifacts leave footprints that are easier to follow and interpret. Some archaeological deposits are simply more evocative than others; the story almost writes itself. This is what archaeologists refer to as focus (Deetz 1996: 94).

We have argued that to meet legal criteria of importance and hence excavation and interpretation, an archaeological site must possess clarity (i.e., focus and integrity). Clarity refers to the quality of a site's data and its ability to clearly convey its importance as representative of a particular phenomenon. Is it possible to separate and interpret the behaviors represented by the site? Or is the site a hopeless jumble of activities, characteristics, and phenomena that cannot be disentangled each from the other? For some excavations we have written a story to go with every collection, but we have found that some stories are simply more evocative than others. When reenacted through a rich archaeological record, the intersection of large events or processes with households that lived in their shadow can make for powerful stories: the good, bad, ugly, and beautiful patterns that make life. The lives of African American porters, Chinese American miners, Japanese American florists, Jewish tailors, Irish American laborers, and American seamen and their families as translated through their archaeological stratigraphy, artifacts, and faunal remains can provide easily interpreted, often life-affirming stories that resonate through their former neighborhoods (see also the chapters by Nelson and Tringham, this volume). People as individuals and groups make the same mistakes over and over through the centuries. But individuals and groups can also learn from their mistakes, as well as their successes. Archaeology can be a tool for civic engagement (e.g., Little and Shackel 2007; Shackel and Gadsby 2011).

Archaeologists are privileged. We get to explore the past up close in a tactile process that destroys the record it discovers. Almost all archaeological investigations are publicly funded through government grants or legal requirements; days of the self-sponsored aristocratic archaeologist passed into extinction long ago. Our discipline has a responsibility to give something back: to provide publically available syntheses of our research and, where possible, to make them relevant to society's concerns. In the long view, this is not difficult. The same human problems continue with new backdrops. Where our work has intersected with questions of diet and health, the value of early childhood education, the importance of the individual in the face of the mob, and so forth, we have tried to write entertaining but useful stories to influence current behavior and events in a small way (see Pollock, this volume, for a discussion of the dangers of such stories).

Some things don't change. All archaeology is tied to place and to people who occupied that place in the past and in the present. We do our best to link the two through an interpretive format we call storytelling.

METHODS

Less than twenty years after the death of Queen Victoria, English critic and biographer Lytton Strachey declared, "The history of the Victorian Age will never be written: we know too much about it" (Strachey 1963: v). The quantity of information—written and material—left by Victorians and other cultures ancient and more recent is indeed staggering and quite possibly beyond synthesis. Strachey suggested a more subtle approach: attacks in unexpected places, searchlights into obscure recesses, that one "row out over that great ocean of material, and lower down into it, here and there, a little bucket, which will bring up to the light of day some characteristic specimen, from those far depths, to be examined with careful curiosity" (ibid.). Strachey's *Eminent Victorians* proved a brilliant and devastatingly ironic deconstruction of the Victorian era. There is a parallel between Strachey's characterizations of the Victorian era based on clinical biographies of four Victorians and our work in cities throughout Northern California. We have lowered our buckets and recovered archaeological collections associated with a few hundred households of widely diverse backgrounds. We have interrogated a few of these households, sometimes even individual iconic artifacts, to better understand their histories and the larger contexts within which they lived.

Our brand of storytelling is based on three methodological principles: ensuring authenticity, creating the unexpected, and devising a thought-provoking storyline. The process begins after the donkeywork of archaeological excavation and lab analysis, the archival research, and ordinary contextualization and interpretation. Conceived this way, storytelling is decidedly a *culmination* of research, not a way to skip the hardest part of archaeology—the interpretation.

As general practice we separate our data from our interpretation. For larger projects the team prepares Data Recovery or Site Technical Reports that describe in the usual detail methods and findings with voluminous tables, figures, and appendixes. Then the team prepares an Interpretive Report in which individual contributors are given the freedom to explore the data from their chosen theoretical perspective. Then, on occasion, we construct carefully woven narratives from the archaeological, archival, and interpretive data. For published public products, we generally supply a one-page graphic that connects sources and text (e.g., Praetzellis, Ziesing, and Praetzellis 1997: 2), along with a further reading list providing references to the technical reports. We endeavor to be clear on the separation between fact and fantasy. Our written introductions often discuss Objective Truth and the role of the author and label the effort as fact-based fiction. Our spoken presentations feature costumes and sufficient silliness to guide the viewer's reality compass. Of course, some confusion is probably inescapable. Some readers will always miss the distinctions, despite a hard copy full of quotes and references (see Pollock, this volume).

Methods are inextricably tied to goals. What is the *point* of storytelling? Our narratives are not merely efforts in "outreach." Although we have performed some for general audiences, the target is equally our professional colleagues, as well as ourselves. One purpose is to give scope to the imagination, which, often for good reason, is walled in by scholarly convention. It is hard to understand why historical archaeologists, whose discipline purports to give voice to the subaltern, display so little empathy with their subjects in their notoriously boring public presentations. When archaeological storytellers use humor, costumes, and theater, we are not backhandedly apologizing for our creativity by being outrageous (cf., Wilkie 2009: 342). We are, in fact, trying to shake things up by generating (we hope) feelings of surprise and jarring inappropriateness in our audience. Marshall McLuhan's (1994: 1) famous "the medium is the message" is apt here, for one principle is to inject the unexpected into the earnest atmosphere of the academic conference.

Effective theater creates atmosphere and tells a story. The playwright's imagination has few boundaries: she may invent the storyline from whole cloth and is limited only by the audience's ability to identify with the characters. Parallel to this, in an academic presentation authenticity is derived from the ritual order of the presentation that begins with an acknowledgment of the ancestors and continues through pronouncements grounded in well-sourced data. Storytelling is not so different. If the audience has no confidence in the sources and the honesty of the presenter, they doubt its authenticity and lose interest.

It all begins with the story. No, that's wrong—actually, it begins with the individual archaeologist who, immersed in the data and their context, becomes dissatisfied with the approved interpretive schemes of his or her profession (see also Gibb, this volume, for the use of storytelling as an interpretive method). Our fictional dialogue with Flavius Josephus impudently draws a parallel (which we hope the reader will forgive) between storytelling and the biblical hermeneutic method of midrash. Both assume the open-endedness of interpretation of the same text, and both use context to construct interpretations. In midrashic exegesis, the base text may be atomized on the assumption that every word has levels of significance, both individually and in its relation to others (Stern 1996: 20). In the same way, the germ of a story may begin with an archaeological "text" that may be a single artifact, an aspect of site structure, or a gap in the documentary history of an individual (see also Gilead, this volume, for alternative narrative structures based on the Torah).

DANGERS

While some colleagues boycott storytelling sessions and general rumblings persist about the dangers storytelling presents to one's career path, these critiques come down to different tastes and theoretical orientations. Leading figures in American archaeology, such as the late Lewis Binford, criticize all "post-processual archaeology," wherein storytelling decidedly fits, as "not archaeology" and "anti-science." In a post-processual framework, these critics claim, "the bottom line is that everybody's ideas are equally good, no matter how stupid they are" (Binford, cited in Thurman 1998: 52).

For those who do not believe archaeology is pure rational science but that it bridges humanities and the social sciences, there are many different analytical and interpretive schemes within which archaeologists should be free to pick and choose. While we have suggested that "every archaeologist should tell stories once in a while" (A. Praetzellis 1998: 1), we don't advocate that they should do it all the time or that it become the new orthodoxy.

The most significant criticism of storytelling is that of authenticity or lack thereof. "The storyteller's knowledge and expertise" must be "sufficient to lend credibility to the tale told," but if these tales are "published separately and distributed widely by an official source, they will be seen by their readers as the end products of research and therefore truthful accounts . . . Such hypothetical interpretive fiction can be misleading and create a biased picture of past peoples" (Lewis 2000: 7–8). Archaeologists have authority. People often believe what we say, so it is irresponsible—even unethical—to put words into the mouths of our research subjects. The practice chips away at the very boundary between fiction and scientifically derived conclusions. This is a legitimate criticism of storytelling and of all archaeological interpretation. As the critic continued, "The subjects of our studies deserve that the public hear stories about them that represent the cumulative results of our work" (ibid.: 8).

We agree entirely. Any archaeological interpretation should reflect careful excavation and analysis and should be confined to the available data that set limits to the archaeological imagination. The principal element storytelling has added is theatricality. It "mixes useful information with the pleasure of the telling" (Pearson and Shanks 2001: 66).

Since the premiere of the symposium Archaeologists as Storytellers in 1997, we have taken the show on the road touring the alphabet circuit—two more Societies for Historical Archaeology (SHAs), some American Anthropological Associations (AAAs) and Societies of American Archaeology (SAAs)—and numerous public and academic venues. The debate continues, as shown in our latest performance at the 2011 SAA meetings in Sacramento and recreated here. We based our docudrama on published sources. Quotation marks indicate an author's own words; uncited material represents our paraphrasing.

THE DOCUDRAMA

(http://www.upcolorado.com/component/k2/item/2712-subjects-and-narratives-in-archaeology-media)

CAST OF CHARACTERS (IN ORDER OF APPEARANCE)

JIM DEETZ: James Deetz liked a good story and told an even better one. His work inspired students and created a buzz seldom heard in archaeology. His influence as one of archaeology's brightest lights continues after his death in 2000, through the work of his students and children.

STANLEY SOUTH: Stanley South is one of the founders of historical archaeology as practiced in North America, providing many of the fundamental methods and tools that shape the discipline. A strict adherence to scientific principles and a distrust of the humanities ground his work.

BILL RATHJE: Bill Rathje died in May 2012, while this chapter was in revision. We miss him. A brilliant archaeologist and larger-than-life character, Bill's work in the archaeology of recent landfills and public education is a monument to his vision. He inspired others not just to change their behaviors but also to assist him in sorting through the gross debris of our modern lifestyles.

ROSEMARY JOYCE: Rosemary Joyce is an archaeologist at the University of California at Berkeley. She works primarily in Central America with the rich imagery and ruins of the Mayans; as such, her writings focus on complex topics of symbolism, gender, and power. Rosemary is active in promoting and improving archaeology as a discipline and in how we interpret and communicate our findings.

FLAVIUS JOSEPHUS: Born in 37 CE, Flavius Josephus was a Romanized Jewish historian whose work focused primarily on the first century, the Romano-Jewish War, and the destruction of Jerusalem. Covering such pivotal topics in western history, his work, life, and allegiances have remained controversial to this day.

THE SCENE: Set of the PBS talk show ARCHAEOLOGY TODAY *with Alexis Boutin.* In the background a KVIE logo and fundraising slogan: "We're PBS. Send Money." A perky anchorwoman in sexy newsroom attire sits behind her desk and shuffles papers.

ANCHOR. It has been nearly fifteen years since Archaeologists as Storytellers premiered to mixed reviews at the 1997 SHA meetings in Corpus Christi (M. Praetzellis 1998). And the controversy continues. Was the event a transformational experience for the discipline or the work of Satan (figure 6.1) packaged by hackneyed players seeking lucrative royalty payments (Gibb 2000)? With some difficulty we tracked down some participants—both actors and audience—along with their fans and critics, to uncover the truth. We'll begin with Dr. James Deetz, a beloved founder of historical archaeology and the discussant for that memorable session. Hello Jim, how are you?

JIM DEETZ. *[looking slightly distracted and otherworldly]*: Very happy and rather surprised to be here. It has been awhile since my last professional meeting, but I can't say I've missed them. Particularly, the "fixation on words, almost for their own sake . . . The liberal sprinkling of text with fashionable words and phrases, like jimmies on an ice cream cone [that] lead to what Henry Glassie aptly called a 'verbal gyre through which criticism

FIGURE 6.1. *Adrian as the Devil (http://www.upcolorado.com /component/k2/item/2712-subjects -and-narratives-in-archaeology -media)*

descends into cynicism, self complaint permutes into self fascination, political responsibilities evaporate into elitist abstractions, interest in the world is replaced by interest in the academical, and righteous action, numbed by paradox, stops'" (Deetz, quoted in Brown 2004: 117).

ANCHOR. *[Clears throat, embarrassed]:* Ah, . . . yes, . . . but what do you remember of that meeting, where you also received the SHA's coveted Lifetime Achievement Award?

JIM. Well, I had warned Mary Praetzellis of my skepticism. Wished I could have written my own story but settled on the sum-up. Some archaeologists

FIGURE 6.2. *Jim Deetz (http://www .upcolorado.com/component/k2/item/2712 -subjects-and-narratives-in-archaeology -media)*

boycotted it as dangerous, but "by the time the session ended, any reservations I may have held had completely vanished . . . I can honestly say that this was the first session that I have ever attended at *any* conference during which I did not look at my watch at least once or twice . . . It raised in my mind questions I think we might give some thought to as we go about our business. In short, what is it that we do and why do we do it? Simply put, archaeologists *are* storytellers. It is our responsibility to communicate to as wide an audience as possible the results and significance of our findings. Now any account of the past, whether based on excavated materials or documents[,] is construction . . . [and] qualification of our statements to avoid criticism of being 'subjective' does not make them any more objective, and indeed they are not, being the construction of the persons writing a report on their findings" (Deetz 1998: 94–95; figure 6.2).

ANCHOR. Well, of course, the storytellers were just taking a page out of your book *In Small Things Forgotten*, where you begin with seven first-person narratives (Deetz 1996: 1–4). They hark back to your 1967 classic *Invitation to Archaeology*, where you introduce the American public to

the topic in a wonderfully read-
able, complex, but clear book that
shows the "essential hows, wheres
and whys of archaeology" through
examples from your own work
(Deetz 1967: ix).

Not everyone would agree with
Dr. Deetz's approach. I'm thinking
of those processual archaeologists
who believe the archaeological
record is more or less objective
and that archaeologists should be
identifying patterns in the record
to help understand the structure
and dynamics of human behaviors. Lewis Binford suggested
that those who mine their sites
for answers to particular questions, such as gender roles, are "the
rapists of the archaeological record"

FIGURE 6.3. *Stanley South (http://*
www.upcolorado.com/component/k2
/item/2712-subjects-and-narratives-in
-archaeology-media)

(Binford, quoted in Thurman 1998: 47). Binford declined to be interviewed on this show, but we have it on good authority that he is not a
fan of the storytelling craze. Fortunately, Stanley South is here today: a
Binford colleague, historical archaeologist, and renowned storyteller of
a different bent. Stanley . . .

STANLEY SOUTH. "I see archaeology as the search for the truth" (figure
6.3). My basic philosophical belief is "Science: Seek life's truths to set
you free" (South, quoted in Joseph 2010: 135). "I take care that my stories
are not fiction . . . There are stories such as those being told by historical
archaeologists to embellish their findings to make them more palatable;
and there are lies that are euphemistically referred to as stories . . . I don't
normally combine science with a story of the time I shot the head off a
rattlesnake with a pistol a crewman just handed me, or when I beat down
a cottonmouth with a shovel, or when I was being chased by an alliga-
tor—those stories are real, not imagined . . . If I dig a ruin somewhere
else and find a pearl handled pistol, could I simply attach Clarence's
story about blowing the head off a chicken to that excavation report
as 'explanation' and call it historical archaeology? Think about it! I don't

call poetry or fiction, or story-telling—archaeology" (South 2005: 3, 350). "Archaeological explanation does not need fiction to enrich it; because it then becomes fiction" (South, quoted in Joseph 2010: 141).

ANCHOR. But some processualists have begun to see the value of story-telling and that it is simply the format through which archaeologists communicate their findings to others. Bill Rathje is perhaps the best-known and influential of contemporary archaeologists. His Garbage Project helped shape our understanding of the nature of landfills, influenced contemporary packaging and how people think about what they choose to purchase and discard. Bill is an incredibly popular speaker and media darling; he travels the world talking to people about garbage, meeting with government leaders and experts in the field, and making a difference in the long-term viability of our planet. He travels so much that a bumper sticker "Honk if you've seen Rathje" appeared on the University of Arizona campus where he taught for many years. Thus, we are very lucky to have Bill here with us today. So Bill, tell us about your closet storytelling career.

BILL RATHJE. "I am a bona fide, card-carrying 'processual' archaeologist. I am not Mike Schiffer, but I wrote an introductory textbook with him that is crammed full of discussions of test implications, forma-tion processes, and appropriate scientific procedures . . . with not one word about storytelling [Rathje and Schiffer 1982]. I thought telling stories was totally inappropriate for a 'processual' or any other type of archaeologist. In fact, when I read Mary Praetzellis's prologue to the first symposium where a group of archaeologists told stories at a professional meeting, I was instantly disgruntled. 'Yikes!' I thought, 'This is not science.'" Later, I "reviewed several slide presentations that I have given across the country concerning the Garbage Project's rig-orous scientific approach. Imagine, then, my horror when I discovered that these processual gemstones were embedded within a welter of stories—an average of one story every two to three slides. Golly jingo! I was a closet storyteller" (figure 6.4).

And this is why: "The length of time you can usually count on people watching and listening to you without the intervention of food or a beverage or a comment from someone else in the room or a phone call or a doorbell or a shout from someone outside of the room or a myriad of other interruptions is calculated by media gurus to be less than thirty seconds. Thirty seconds, that is, unless people are

FɪɢᴜRE 6.4. *Bill Rathje (*middle of photo*) embraces storytelling (http://www.upcolorado*
.com/component/k2/item/2712-subjects-and-narratives-in-archaeology-media)

riveted by what you're saying or doing. That's why when I give talks
or work with the media, I always tell stories. People get interested in
human stories and remember them better than they remember cold,
hard facts. There will always be people who miss your point, . . . but
if the points of your stories are what you want people to hear, stories
maximize communication. I tell stories to grab the audience's attention and make the points I wish them to take home." Simply put, "I
will keep digging and recording with processual rigor, but I'll also
keep telling stories" (Rathje 2004: 2–4, 14).

ANCHOR. I think all archaeologists would agree with Bill: the craft, or
art if you will, of archaeological excavation and analysis remains a
sacred trust. But many also believe, like Bill, that they don't have
the leisure to study that record for its own sake, without thought
to the pressing questions that face our planet. Cornelius Holtorf
(2010: 390) writes that "meta-stories of archaeology benefit society
by making people reflect upon what it means to be human and what
they share with others in the social groups to which they belong.
Archaeological story-telling," he feels, "is an opportunity for archaeology to fulfill itself in contemporary society by directly improving
the quality of people's lives, providing meaning, stimulation, and

guidance." Archaeology can make better people and a better future. And it doesn't matter that there are other, more straightforward ways to achieve this objective. In Holtorf's view, it's important to do what we can with what we have (see Pluciennik, this volume, for further discussion of Holtorf's work).

Moving right along, we are fortunate that the master of *The Languages of Archaeology*, Dr. Rosemary Joyce, is with us today. Rosemary . . .

ROSEMARY JOYCE. It is the multiple voices of archaeology that interest me most: the excavators, lab workers, researchers, and analysts who generate the findings. The archaeological forbears who passed down their insights. The descendant communities with their special knowledge and interests. The distributors of grants and regulators who supply the funds. The general public, to whom we are all accountable, seeking amusement, enlightenment, or a platform; not to mention those of us fortunate enough to write about archaeology. There are so many interests and so many potential stories. Of course, "the scientific report remains alive and well, the dominant form of writing in archaeology. And far from being opposed to narrative, scientific articles are nothing but narratives: narratives that obscure the speaking voice, that use 'professional jargons, generic languages, languages of generations and age groups, tendentious languages, languages of authorities of various circles and of passing fashion'" (Joyce 2002: 138, citing Bakhtin 1981: 262–63).

"Archaeological discourse strains to contain the determination of the past within specific disciplinary contexts: but the past always escapes us, as it should, since it is not our past (alone)" (Joyce, Guyer, and Joyce 2002: 127). One way to proceed is to "tell multiple stories in multiple voices" (ibid.:132). "This process of writing and rewriting, telling and retelling, which as a discipline has been our history, today has the potential to create a space to engage beyond disciplinary walls" (Joyce 2002: 143).

ANCHOR. Thank you, Rosemary (figure 6.5). Archaeologists have been writing narratives for decades—notably, the peopling of prehistory by feminist archaeologists in the 1990s in which Rosemary played a large role (Claassen and Joyce 1997). In one of my favorites, Janet Spector (1993) used a bone awl to artfully weave a narrative of her exploration into the life of a young Dakota woman. But, of course, history comes from story, and the link between the two goes back further than the written word. Welcome Flavius Josephus, author of *The Jewish War*, *Antiquitates Judaicae*, and other favorites. Or should I say Joseph ben Mattiyahu?

JOSEPHUS. Josephus, please. It sounds so much more . . . civilized.

ANCHOR. Naturally. Our guest was born in Jerusalem in about the year 37 of the Christian era. He had a thorough education in the important Jewish sources, as well as hermeneutics and other methods of biblical interpretation. Some call him an early archaeologist, but he is best known as a historian. Others have hinted that he is not always . . . as accurate as he could be. Millennia later, some still consider him a traitor for his acceptance of Roman ways.

FIGURE 6.5. *Rosemary Joyce (http://www .upcolorado.com/component/k2/item/2712 -subjects-and-narratives-in-archaeology -media)*

JOSEPHUS. There will always be people who criticize others to boost their own importance. But enough of trivialities. I don't know if I care for the title of archaeologist, but I *am* interested in the history of eretz Yisrael, of course. And in my twenty-volume *Antiquitates Judaicae* (Josephus 1824), I use traditional sources to calculate the dates of what you would call archaeological remains. As to my being imaginative in my writings, well, all I do is to fill in some of the unknowns. It's not so different from you archaeologists who have only the beginnings and the ends of things and must fill in the middle.

ANCHOR. Not sure I follow you, Mr. Josephus . . .

JOSEPHUS. Consider this scenario (the word derives from the Latin *scaena*, by the way): A Roman antiquarian lives in a house once owned by the great Marcus Tullius Cicero. The collector finds the shards of a pot in his garden. He examines them and concludes that the pot was made in Syria. At this point he knows two things: the pot was made *there* and is now *here*. But between the making and the breaking and the discarding, what does he know? Nothing. Did Cicero bring it back from his time in Syria? Did Cicero himself handle and break it? How? These are the things the man wants to know. But Cicero is dead and cannot tell us.

This was my problem writing *Antiquitates*. The documented history of the period is full of gaps. All those who had experienced it

FIGURE 6.6. *Titus Flavius Josephus (Josef ben Matityahu), as imagined by Adrian Praetzellis*

directly were gone. So on some occasions I may have been influenced by a hermeneutical approach the rabbis use to interpret the Torah— the first five books of the Hebrew scriptures—to fill in some of the gaps. The approach is called midrash (Stern 1996). You understand?

ANCHOR. Yes, but let me explain it to our audience. A midrash is a backstory that fills in a gap in a biblical narrative. It fills in the details the original story left out. Things like motivation and personal history. Midrash fleshes out characters. It explains the significance of a small event or the hidden significance of a particular word order. Is that right?

JOSEPHUS. Close enough. Let me give you an example. As you know, Abraham was the founder of our lineage, but the Torah tells us almost nothing about his early life: he was born in Ur and the next we're told he's seventy-five years old. This leaves us wondering why *he* was chosen to be the founder of our people. A midrash in *Bereshis Rabbah* helps us (Bialik and Ravnitzky 1992: 32; Neusner 1991: 34). It explains that Abraham's father was a maker of idols. One day, it is said, he left Abraham in the shop alone. When a customer asked to buy an idol, Abraham replied, "How old are you?" The man said he is sixty and

Abraham responds, "Woe to the man who is sixty and yet needs to worship an idol that is one day old!" Embarrassed, the man went on his way. This midrash shows the origin of our ancestor's insights that led to monotheism, and this explains much of his later career.

ANCHOR. So the method could also apply to archaeology for, like the Hebrew bible, archaeological sites are a type of canonical source. The objects and the places are fixed, in the same way in which the Torah text is unalterable. And both the text and our knowledge of these objects are incomplete. Archaeologists know what they say, but what do they mean?

JOSEPHUS. Of course. And it is through midrashim, stories if you will, that we can extract the range of possible meanings from both the text and the physical remains.

ANCHOR. Thank you, Josephus, for your . . . ah . . . unusual perspective. And now for our final interview—Adrian Praetzellis, one of the most shameless of storytellers. He has played everything from Jack London (Praetzellis and Praetzellis 1999) to a US surgeon general (A. Praetzellis and M. Praetzellis 2004) to a teenage female prostitute and a "john" (Costello 1998) to a character he created for his mystery textbooks (M. Praetzellis and A. Praetzellis 2004). Adrian, how did you get into storytelling?

ADRIAN. Well, it was all Mary's idea. I am an avowed ham. But Mary, who prefers to remain behind the scenes, is the producer/director of our shows. We believe that "every archaeologist should tell stories once in a while." We have found that sites "contain many potential stories, but every one is the product of the archaeological imagination that pulls together historical and archaeological facts into interpretation that is more than the sum of the parts of which it is made and more than its excavator can document in the usual way." There are no shortcuts to storytelling: it takes "years doing the donkeywork" and writing reports. Storytelling is "just an additional way of explaining" what our sites are about. We will never know if the motivations assigned our characters are authentic. And, of course, there is the danger that stories can misrepresent and manipulate the past for present gain. "Or archaeology may merge with fiction and psychological autobiography." The latter "is not necessarily a bad thing, but probably not an activity that merits public funding" (A. Praetzellis 1998: 1–2).

ANCHOR. We understand that recently you have moved away from storytelling into number crunching, rendering your "admiring colleagues . . . shocked" and "alarmed" (Beaudry and Symonds 2011: xvii). British archaeologist James Symonds went so far as to suggest you sold out, providing clients with "data per dime," and wished you would just continue to tell "informative and gloriously funny stories on the small scale" rather than deceive with statistics (Symonds 2011: 73–74). Is this true?

ADRIAN. Yes, quite right. And our friend Jim should be happy we aren't telling stories about him! All actors hate to be typecast, and as archaeologists we feel the same. There's room in our field for all. Some archaeology may be science; some may be art; some may even be psychotherapy. And most thinking people are pretty clear which is which. All archaeology must be respectful of the archaeological record—we only get to dig it once. And we have to do the most careful, scientifically controlled work possible. We have to provide technical reports that document our methods and findings. But at that point it is anyone's game for interpretation. You might not approve of my story, but the data are out there and you are free to write another.

After more years than I care to confess, we have developed enough data from consistently excavated, cataloged, and analyzed contexts to venture into statistics. We've changed our scale from small stories to larger ones, at the city scale. Our recent work in the San Francisco Bay area uses these data to look at large "patterns," including inequality and poverty (Praetzellis and Praetzellis 2009, 2011), in a way we hope even Lew Binford and Stan South might approve. But will we stop telling stories? Never!

ANCHOR. And in closing, is there anything you would like to tell our audience?

ADRIAN. We have a baseball autographed by Lew Binford in our bedroom that I bought at a silent auction for $150 and I've always wanted to . . .

ANCHOR [interrupts]: Sorry. Time for a message from our sponsor!

[On screen: Flashing ad for Rowman and Littlefield announcing the new 2011 edition of *Death by Theory: A Tale of Mystery and Archaeological Theory* by Adrian Praetzellis. Audience bursts into deafening applause. Cries of Encore! Genius! etc. Exeunt all.]

REFERENCES

Adams, William H. 1977. "History, Historicity, and Archaeology." *Northwest Anthropological Research Notes* 11 (2): 135–43.

Bakhtin, Mikhail M. 1981. *The Dialogic Imagination: Four Essays.* Ed. M. Holquist. Trans. C. Emerson and M. Holquist. Austin: University of Texas Press.

Beaudry, Mary C., and James Symonds, eds. 2011. "Introduction: Transatlantic Dialogues and Convergences." In *Interpreting the Early Modern World: Transatlantic Perspectives*, ed. Mary C. Beaudry and James Symonds, xi–xxii. New York: Springer.

Bialik, Hayim Nahman, and Yehoshua Hana Ravnitzky, eds. 1992. *Sefer HaAggadah.* Trans. William Braude. New York: Schocken.

Brown, R. Marley III. 2004. "Memorial: James Fanto Deetz, 1930–2000." *Historical Archaeology* 38 (2): 103–23.

Claassen, Cheryl, and Rosemary A. Joyce, eds. 1997. *Women in Prehistory: North America and Mesoamerica.* Philadelphia: University of Pennsylvania Press.

Costello, Julia G. 1998. "Redlight Voices." Paper presented at the Society for American Archaeology Annual Meeting, Seattle, March 25–29.

Deetz, James. 1967. *Invitation to Archaeology.* Garden City, NY: Natural History Press.

Deetz, James. 1996 [1977]. *In Small Things Forgotten: An Archaeology of Early American Life.* New York: Anchor Books, Doubleday.

Deetz, James. 1998. "Discussion: Archaeologists as Storytellers." *Historical Archaeology* 1 (32): 94–96.

Gibb, James G. 2000. "Forum: Imaginary, But by No Means Unimaginable: Storytelling, Science, and Historical Archaeology." *Historical Archaeology* 34 (2): 1–24.

Holtorf, Cornelius. 2010. "Meta-stories of Archaeology." *World Archaeology* 42 (3): 381–93. http://dx.doi.org/10.1080/00438243.2010.497382.

Joseph, J. W. 2010. "An Interview with Stanley A. South." *Historical Archaeology* 44 (2): 132–44.

Josephus, Flavius. 1824. *The Works of Flavius Josephus.* Trans. William Whiston. London: T. & J. Allman.

Joyce, Rosemary A. 2002. "The Return of the First Voice." In *The Languages of Archaeology*, ed. Rosemary A. Joyce, 133–44. Oxford: Blackwell. http://dx.doi.org/10.1002/9780470693520.ch6.

Joyce, Rosemary A., with Carolyn Guyer and Michael Joyce. 2002. "Voices Carry Outside the Discipline." In *The Languages of Archaeology*, ed. Rosemary A. Joyce, 100–133. Oxford: Blackwell.

Lewis, Kenneth E. 2000. "Imagination and Archaeological Interpretations: A Methodological Tale." *Historical Archaeology* 34 (2): 7–9.

Little, Barbara J., and Paul A. Shackel, eds. 2007. *Archaeology as a Tool of Civic Engagement*. Lanham, MD: AltaMira.

McLuhan, Marshall. 1994. *Understanding Media: The Extensions of Man*. New York: MIT Press.

Neusner, Jacob. 1991. *Confronting Creation: How Judaism Reads Genesis: An Anthology of Genesis Rabbah*. Columbia: University of South Carolina Press.

Pearson, Mike, and Michael Shanks. 2001. *Theatre/Archaeology*. London: Routledge.

Praetzellis, Adrian. 1998. "Introduction: Why Every Archaeologist Should Tell Stories Once in a While." *Historical Archaeology* 32 (1): 1–3.

Praetzellis, Adrian, and Mary Praetzellis. 1984. *Gone, but Not Forgotten: Historical Glimpses of the Lake Sonoma Area*. Sacramento District: US Army Corps of Engineers.

Praetzellis, Adrian, and Mary Praetzellis. 1999. "Telling a Story about the Past or When Jack London Met the Scientist." Paper presented at the American Anthropological Association Annual Meeting, Chicago, November 17–21.

Praetzellis, Adrian, and Mary Praetzellis. 2004. "Why Can't the Workers Teach Their Children How to Eat?" Paper presented at the Society for Historical Archaeology Annual Meeting, St. Louis, January 7–11.

Praetzellis, Adrian, and Mary Praetzellis. 2011. "'Progress and Poverty' Revisited: A Statistical Interpretation to the Archaeology of Wealth and Poverty in the San Francisco Bay Area." Paper presented at the Society for Historical Archaeology Annual Meeting, Austin, January 5–9.

Praetzellis, Adrian, Grace H. Ziesing, and Mary Praetzellis. 1997. *Tales of the Vasco*. Rohnert Park, CA: Anthropological Studies Center, Sonoma State University. http://www.ccwater.com/files/TaleOfTheVasco.pdf, accessed July 9, 2012.

Praetzellis, Mary. 1998. "Archaeologists as Storytellers." *Historical Archaeology* 32 (1) (entire volume).

Praetzellis, Mary. 2004. "Archaeologists as Storytellers 3: They're Back . . ." Symposium organized for the Conference on Historical and Underwater Archaeology Program and Abstracts, St. Louis, January 7–11.

Praetzellis, Mary, and Adrian Praetzellis. 1985. "Archaeology, History and a Hoag House Mystery." *Journal of the Sonoma County Historical Society* 1985 (2): 2–9.

Praetzellis, Mary, and Adrian Praetzellis. 2004. "Dr. Adrienne Pretzels (State of Ennui University) and Dr. Ian Tulliver (University of Invercargill) Debate the Merits of Storytelling." Paper presented at the Society for Historical Archaeology Annual Meeting, St. Louis, January 7–11.

Praetzellis, Mary, and Adrian Praetzellis, eds. 2009. *South of Market: Historical Archaeology of Three San Francisco Neighborhoods*. Ronhert Park, CA:

Anthropological Studies Center, Sonoma State University. http://www.sonoma
.edu/asc/west_approach/index.html, accessed July 9, 2012.

Rathje, William L. 2004. "Telling Stories." Paper presented at the Society for
Historical Archaeology Annual Meeting, St. Louis, January 7–11.

Rathje, William L., and Michael B. Schiffer. 1982. *Archaeology*. New York: Harcourt
Brace Jovanovich.

Shackel, Paul A., and David A. Gadsby, eds. 2011. "Archaeologies of Engagement,
Representation, and Identity." Theme issue of *Historical Archaeology* 45 (1).

South, Stanley A. 2005. *An Archaeological Evolution*. New York: Springer.

Spector, Janet D. 1993. *What This Awl Means: Feminist Archaeology at a Wahpeton
Dakota Village*. St. Paul: Minnesota Historical Society Press.

Stern, David. 1996. *Midrash and Theory: Ancient Jewish Exegesis and Contemporary
Literary Studies*. Evanston, IL: Northwestern University Press.

Strachey, Lytton. 1963 [1918]. *Eminent Victorians*. New York: Capricorn.

Symonds, James. 2011. "Stooping to Pick Up Stones: A Reflection." In *Interpreting
the Early Modern World: Transatlantic Perspectives*, ed. Mary C. Beaudry and James
Symonds, 63–84. New York: Springer. http://dx.doi.org/10.1007/978-0-387
-70759-4_4.

Thurman, Melburn D. 1998. "Interview with Lewis R. Binford." *Historical Archaeology*
32 (2): 28–55.

Wilkie, Laurie. 2009. "Interpretive Historical Archaeology." In *International
Handbook of Historical Archaeology*, ed. Teresita Majewski and David Gaimster,
333–45. New York: Springer. http://dx.doi.org/10.1007/978-0-387-72071-5_19.

7

*Constructive Imagination
and the Elusive Past*

Playwriting as Method

JAMES G. GIBB

In the 1970s and 1980s the hypothetico-deductive approach—its power and pitfalls—dominated much of archaeological discourse. Clear statement of postulates and questions, logical derivation of testable implications, and testing of null hypotheses—essentially trying to disprove one's hypothesis—offered objectivity, replicability, and verity. The approach prompted discussions of the relative primacy of deduction and induction in the development of postulates and in research in general, and it focused interest on epistemology. The approach bespoke science. Largely omitted from the debates were the nature and role of imagination in research. The ineffability of imagination seemingly places it beyond positivist science. It is a subject of research, not a research tool. But most scientists no doubt would agree that imagination has a place in research—perhaps, if it is possible to weigh such abstractions, the most important place.

As a first foray into the subject, imagine Dr. Phil D. Science serving on a panel at a professional conference. Dr. Science roundly criticizes "foofoo philosophizing" and storytelling that passes for rigorous research. "Our job," says Dr. Science, "is to provide a body of knowledge for its own sake and to inform decision-making at all levels of society. We don't do just-so stories; we leave those to the Modern Language Association and writers' workshops." Dr. Science's critique may be justified in responding to imaginative interpretations of data that have not been tested and that might not be

DOI: 10.5876/9781607323815.c007

testable, imaginings that pass for knowledge. If directed solely at constructive imagination as a means for identifying unrecognized data and relationships, the criticism may be invalid. The question *is not* whether one person's musings constitute knowledge: imaginings and beliefs cannot inform the practices and policies of a diverse society without leading to chaos and inaction. They can pass as one person's understanding of the world but not as knowledge. The question *is*, how can we use constructive imagination in a particular research endeavor? Can an idea of uncertain parentage find a productive place in mainstream research?

The nature of imagination is best left to philosophers and psychologists, but imagination serves archaeologists well. One needn't know how an aspirin works; that it does so is reason enough to take two when head or joints ache. Users, however, must understand the basics of when aspirin might help, how many to take and how often, and potential side effects that might warrant discontinuing use and visiting the doctor. Imagination, similarly well used, can contribute to historical studies and to all scientific endeavors, even if the processes of idea generation and analogizing remain uncertain and the sources of specific ideas indefinable. We are unready for comprehensive guidelines, but there is value in experimentation to better understand how researchers can harness constructive imagination in ways that do not undermine the fundamental strengths of science and, indeed, render explicit the paths by which a researcher arrives at novel ideas.

In these pages I examine imagination as a way of exploring a particular place—the Colonial period port town of Port Tobacco in southern Maryland, USA—at two points in the past and, particularly, as a way to gain insight into a problem for which there are no obvious sources of data. I use playwriting as a tool for structuring the inquiry, discussing aspects of the art, and then developing ideas about a specific environmental problem: sedimentation, more particularly, community responses to sedimentation. In keeping with conventional approaches, I begin with background on the particular research problem, present a methodology for addressing that problem, and then apply the method and review the results.

BACKGROUND TO THE RESEARCH PROBLEM

European powers carved up the New World in the sixteenth century, the various monarchs and oligarchs asserting and defending their territorial claims while discrediting those of indigenous peoples. The Chesapeake Bay region became one of the principal targets for English colonization early in the seventeenth century, first in coastal North Carolina (1585) and Tidewater Virginia (1607) and then in Maryland (1634). Although supported by Queen Elizabeth I and her Stuart successors, these were largely private undertakings. A joint stock company founded Virginia and retained control until after the disastrous Powhatan attacks in 1622, when King James I transformed it into a royal colony (1624). Cecil, Lord Baltimore founded Maryland as a private undertaking through which he attempted, unsuccessfully, to introduce the rapidly fading manorial system to British North America (Gibb 1996). Virginia and Maryland engaged in the fur trade and flirted with iron making and ship building, but agriculture dominated both economies. By the middle of the seventeenth century, the Chesapeake colonies were shipping large quantities of tobacco to England for domestic use and re-export, as well as increasing quantities of wheat, livestock, and leather to the "sugar" colonies in the British West Indies. By the mid-eighteenth century, Virginia and Maryland had become two of Great Britain's most treasured colonies, creating through agricultural commodity production the capital and markets for Britain's growing industrial base and turning Scotland into a commercial and cultural center within a few decades after unification with England in 1707 (Karras 1992).

The settlers were primarily English, but they included Irish and French, Dutch, Bohemians, and small numbers of other Europeans, as well as increasing numbers of Scots after the 1715 and 1745 uprisings. Enslaved Africans were relatively few until the late seventeenth and early eighteenth centuries, after which they dominated the labor force and constituted a large minority of the colonial population (Walsh 1977). Native American communities persisted in the face of increasing pressure throughout the late seventeenth century but had become socially, politically, and economically peripheral in the Tidewater region by the early eighteenth century (Rountree and Davidson 1997). (They remained powerful into the late eighteenth century, however, in the piedmont and mountainous regions to the west of our immediate place of interest, the Chesapeake Bay portion of the Atlantic coastal plain.)

European settlement of the Chesapeake Tidewater region was profoundly rural at the outset, with plantations spreading initially along the coastline to take advantage of floodplain soils and navigable water. Maryland colonists "took up" land, which is to say they exchanged credits earned by transporting themselves or others to Maryland for rights to land. They held the land in usufruct, subject to payment of modest semiannual rents and sworn oaths of fealty to Lord Baltimore by which they acknowledged his ultimate right to the land. Failure to fulfill either of these requirements could result in the escheatment of a settler's land and all that was on it—house, barns, livestock, crops in the field—to Lord Baltimore. (Fee-simple conveyances began under the sixth and last Lord Baltimore in the 1750s.) Tobacco dominated production in most parts of the colony, although wheat production rapidly increased in southern Maryland and on the Chesapeake Bay's Eastern Shore during the late seventeenth century.

Bulk commodities and extensive navigable waterways, coupled with liberal access to arable land, encouraged dispersed settlement. With little need for banking facilities (tobacco is labor-intensive rather than capital-intensive) and ready access to imported goods offered by factors (merchants' agents) eager to secure merchantable commodities, Marylanders and Virginians felt little need to create towns (Jones 1724: 35); indeed, the lack of towns inhibited the collection of import and export duties, an important source of Lord Baltimore's revenues and those of the king and a drain on planters' resources.

The Calverts, lords Baltimore (a small Irish barony), understood the value of urban centers for accumulating and investing capital, establishing effective government, and enhancing their own political and social stature. With their encouragement, the Maryland General Assembly enacted a series of "town acts" between 1668 and 1708 (Miller 1988; Pogue 1984; Reps 1972). Each law specified up to sixty town sites located on tracts possessed by individual landholders, with many of the same locations designated in subsequent acts. Some sites were platted, on paper if not necessarily on the ground, and the lots were offered for sale with the usual conditions applying to general tracts but also requiring construction of a 400-ft^2 dwelling on the lot within eighteen months of acquisition. Failure to meet those conditions resulted in the lots retroceding to the original possessor. Few of these town sites developed, and even fewer grew beyond a few buildings (Thomas 1994). Some, such as Calverton in Calvert County and Moore's Lodge in Charles County (figure 7.1), provided governmental and judicial services, as well as ordinaries for feeding and boarding court attendees and other travelers, but little else and only briefly (King, Strickland, and Norris 2008; Pogue 1984).

Despite forces against urbanization, some towns formed and persisted, particularly those the Maryland General Assembly designated ports of entry. In 1945, L. C. Gottschalk—a soil scientist specializing in problems arising from sedimentation—published a study of several of the larger drainages in Maryland, highlighting the towns of Joppa, Georgetown, Bladensburg, Elkridge, and Port Tobacco, as well as Virginia locations along the Potomac River. He noted that Maryland's legislature tended to select town sites near heads of navigation (Gottschalk 1945a: 222). While these locations provided merchants with maximum reach into the hinterland, they were also the most

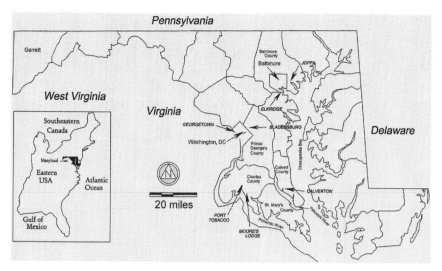

FIGURE 7.1. *Map of Maryland depicting the locations of places noted in the text*

vulnerable to sedimentation, with the heaviest loads of material precipitating in the shallowest, lowest-energy portions of the streams. Most of the port towns in Gottschalk's study became landlocked before the American Revolution. Recent investigations completed by the Port Tobacco Archaeological Project team confirm both the process and the timing of sedimentation that Gottschalk described (Gibb 2011; Hayward 2010). Joppa, the onetime seat of Baltimore County as yet unexamined by archaeologists, serves as an example.

The Maryland General Assembly established the town of Joppa in 1707, stipulating twenty acres to comprise forty lots, a two-acre public square, streets, and alleys. The act required lot holders to erect a 400-ft^2 dwelling with masonry chimney within eighteen months of the conveyance or lose their rights in the lot. Joppa developed with a number of dwellings, warehouses, wharves, a customs house, and other public buildings (Scharf 1879) indicative of institutional development. Sedimentation, caused by extensive clearing in the Gunpowder River watershed, led to significant degradation of the harbor facility by around 1750 (Gottschalk 1945a: 223). The county seat was moved to Baltimore, an aggressively expanding community on the Patapsco River sixteen miles to the southwest, in 1768. In 1945, Gottschalk (ibid.: 219, 225) found evidence of port facilities at Joppa Town two miles distant from navigable water. The process was understood at least as early as 1857 when engineer Alfred M. Rives commented on sedimentation in the Potomac River at Georgetown, discountenancing the claim that it was caused by a bridge. He recognized the connection among agriculture, erosion, and the loss of ports (Rives 1857, cited in Gottschalk 1945a: 227).

The process varied in its particulars but occurred throughout the region, destroying waterways and burying wharves at town sites and at individual plantations. The fact that it was generally recognized much earlier than Rives's 1857 description is evidenced in Patrick Henry's oft-quoted but unreferenced dictum: "Since the achievements of our independence, *he is the greatest patriot who stops the most gullies*" (e.g., Franklin 1942: 30; Gustafson 1961: 109).

ARCHAEOLOGICAL RESEARCH QUESTIONS

Gottschalk (1943, 1945b) conducted studies throughout the eastern United States, focusing largely on municipal reservoirs and calculating lost capacities caused by twentieth-century sedimentation, and he used his understanding of current processes to explain eighteenth-century events. Gottschalk identified a principal cause: sedimentation resulting from deforestation and poor farming practices, both of which concerned federal and state authorities during the first half of the twentieth century. (An Act of the General Assembly [Laws of 1753, Chapter 27] identified the "opening and digging into the banks of Patapsco river for iron stone" as another cause of sedimentation that was damaging access to Elkridge and Baltimore.) Gottschalk also determined the general time frame in which this sedimentation occurred, or at least when it most directly degraded urban harbors, by reference to a small number of documents: the second and third quarters of the eighteenth century.

There are several things Gottschalk did not document, and the best way to build on his work is to fill some of those gaps. Details about each of the towns are wanting, particularly in terms of specific dates and sources of sediment (colluvial, alluvial, or combinations), and this is an area in which conventional archaeological investigations, aided by soil studies, could provide sound data (e.g., Gibb 2011). The effects of sedimentation on individual plantation wharves lie outside the scope of Gottschalk's study, but data on loss, repair, and extension of private wharves will contribute to a larger understanding of the problem for this society accustomed to moving people, livestock, and goods by water (Shomette and Eshelman 1981). This is a point on which terrestrial and underwater archaeology can inform (Leone 1983). A critical issue on which Gottschalk shed little light—perhaps because there is little direct information on it—is the manner in which Marylanders responded to sedimentation. What did they know, when did they know it, and what did they do about it, if anything? Mark Leone (1983) hypothesized a positive relationship between the development of town life, particularly the formation of institutions, and a population's efforts to counter environmental degradation; but this is a difficult hypothesis to test. Disconfirming data would be negative if there were no material responses or if analysts do not suspect, hence recognize, those responses. In the absence of explicit responses to erosion and sedimentation, such as improved farming practices and dredging, a nonconventional approach may help.

METHOD

The anthropological approach to identifying individual and group attitudes and responses to events is to interview the subjects of the study. In historical research, where the subjects are usually dead and the perceptions of their descendants are not of primary interest, questioning takes the form of collecting and analyzing texts produced by the people in question. Letters, newspaper editorials, commissioned reports, legislation, court proceedings, maps, diaries, ships' logs, and travelers' accounts are among the more common sources, and Gottschalk used some of these for the Chesapeake Tidewater region. Few of these sources likely survive or have been identified, as implied by the small number Gottschalk and other writers (e.g., Reps 1972) cite. Their citations also represent the views of engineers responding to conditions long after the fact, merchants concerned about increased costs of shipping, and travelers observing a situation and perhaps inconvenienced by disruptions in transportation. Farmers and lumbermen, whose activities directly created conditions for erosion and sedimentation, are mute, as are the many people whose livelihoods depended indirectly on the ready flow of commerce through their communities. The challenge is to evoke those responses in a manner that informs research. The object is not necessarily to create those responses and test them—such a direct if/then approach is probably not feasible in most cases—but to use hypothetical responses to identify relationships and conditions not previously considered, recognizing the previously unrecognized. These newly discovered relationships may have their own archaeological residues that can be sought, sampled, and analyzed. The reader might draw a parallel here with exploratory data analysis, wherein a researcher uses statistical techniques to seek underlying patterns not otherwise apparent and then statistically analyzes those patterns.

Art, playwriting in particular, provides means for investigators, well steeped in archival and archaeological data, to explore past attitudes toward events and processes for which there is no apparent direct evidence. Playwriting seems best suited because it functions largely through dialogue, requires no technical skills, and can involve little more than snippets of dialogue without necessarily producing a complete work with well-developed plots. A brief scene with a few lines of dialogue may be all that is required to provide illumination; the production of a full-length literary work for the stage, although rewarding, is not the object. The method does not require a commitment to stage or screenwriting any more than running a series of cluster analyses means the researcher must become a statistician. I have discussed elsewhere (Gibb 2003) the method I use for playwriting and offer only a brief summary here. The steps are relevant whether one intends just a few lines of dialogue, a full scene or act, or an entire play.

I start with an abstract or argument that establishes the time and place of action and defines the subject, or central reflector. Any general comments about emotional intensity or ramifications of what will ensue are also appropriate. The abstract is the tool I use to envision the story, even if the plot and outcome of the narrative aren't clear. I then compile a list of characters—sometimes more than eventually appear in the scene—describing each with a biographical sketch that is referenced to archival and archaeological sources or to characters from period literature. I could appear among the characters, or I might create a composite representation of an archaeologist such as Kent Flannery's (1976) Real Mesoamerican Archaeologist, Great Synthesizer, or Skeptical Graduate Student. With these basic components in place, the task largely becomes one of writing and rewriting dialogue, letting the characters take the story where they may within the constraints of their internal logic and the setting. Period literature, newspapers, and other sources provide cultural context to minimize presentism, but make no mistake: as playwright, I pick the words and the mouths from which they emanate. I do so not to give life to dead persons and cultures but to experiment in the expectation that the fictional interactions within a partially reconceived cultural context will lead me to previously unrecognized relationships and attitudes and potential material residues of those patterns. Each step in this process should be written as if for publication, regardless of how the product will ultimately be used.

This is the method; as in any scientific undertaking, the method must be thoroughly documented so the writer and others can evaluate the results. A summary, or perhaps a select few lines of dialogue, might appear in the resulting report or publication, rendering what might have passed for brilliant insight into an obvious progression. An exegesis, unnecessary in a full-length fictional treatment, substitutes for plot and more narrowly identifies the insights and newly recognized research avenues that circumvent previously perceived research obstacles. Here is an example of what I think it should look like in abbreviated form.

SETTING THE SCENES

(http://www.upcolorado.com/component/k2/item/2712-subjects-and-narratives-in-archaeology-media)

MUD FIGHTS: A PLAY IN ONE ACT, TWO SCENES

ACT I, SCENE 1: Port Tobacco, present. A board and wire fence, house in the background, a road, and a steep rise beyond that. Upstage of the fence, the elderly resident of the house. He is unwell and not able to linger. Downstage of the fence a middle-aged man—an archaeologist, managing director of the Port Tobacco Archaeological Project—in work clothes, the blade of a small trowel stuck downward between his belt and jeans, just above the right hip pocket. Both are white men, middle class. Voices in the background obviously distract the archaeologist as his crew of professional and avocational archaeologists excavates complex deposits off stage right. The two talk in strained tones, longtime resident to outsider. The subject: the history of Port Tobacco.

ACT I, SCENE 2: Port Tobacco, 1760. The open door of a store in which stands a man of middle years, Scots merchant John Semple, engaged in conversation with an English planter and officeholder, John Hanson. The two talk in strained tones, outsider to resident. The subject: Port Tobacco.

CAST OF CHARACTERS

JOHN SEMPLE: A Scotsman in partnership with James Lawson in Glasgow, Semple maintained a store in Port Tobacco between 1757 and 1768 (figure 7.2). Profligate spending and self-advancement, coupled with ill-advised investments and trade disrupted by the French and Indian War (1755–63), would eventually drive the partnership into bankruptcy. Knowledge of Semple comes from business letters and court documents. Drawing on Martin (2008: 18–19) and Karras (1992: 93–98), we can learn something of his character: an ambitious, risk-taking entrepreneur who looked to the spectacular successes of his countryman John Glassford and other Scots whose early appearance on the Chesapeake and British West Indies frontiers enabled them to amass great wealth. Like his fellow Scottish merchants, he was increasingly vilified by his neighbors, most of whom were English planters,

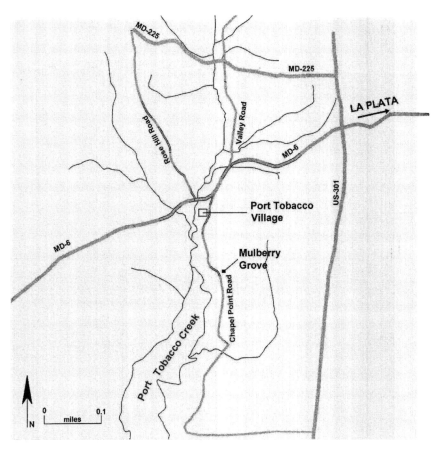

FIGURE 7.2. *Map of the Port Tobacco Valley, depicting current road system and houses of prominent planters and statesmen*

for sharp business practices. Unlike many of them, he flagrantly defrauded his partner (brother-in-law James "Jemma" Lawson). Karras (ibid.), drawing on court documents and business correspondence, does not offer a flattering portrait.

JOHN HANSON: Of Swedish ancestry, he was born on the family estate called Mulberry Grove, just south of Port Tobacco, six years before the town's official founding in 1727. Hanson served as a Charles County delegate in the general assembly, where he was a member of the Country Party in opposition to the Lord Proprietor's party, and he played a prominent role in financing Maryland's participation in the French and Indian War. He represented Maryland in the Stamp Act Congress in 1765 and moved to Frederick on Maryland's western frontier in 1769, where he became a leader in regional politics. The State of Maryland sent him to the US Congress in 1780. After he delivered Maryland's acceptance of the Articles of Confederation in 1781 (the last state to ratify), Congress elected him the first president of the new United States government. He served his one-year term and died a year later at the home of relatives in southern Maryland on the Potomac River. In this scene, it is 1760 and Hanson is a mature, politic man, a member of the landed aristocracy that controlled much of southern politics.

JAMES BEARD: James is the third generation of his family to have lived in the colonial port town, which in Scene 1 consists of just eight households and a massive brick courthouse built in 1970 as a replica of the 1819–92 courthouse. In middle age he steered the restoration society his father co-founded decades earlier, working unsuccessfully toward the creation of a sustainable restoration that is both living village and museum. He is retired from a large corporation in which he held a middle-management position.

ARCHAEOLOGIST: By training and experience, he is all of the characters in Kent Flannery's parable and none of them. The realities of working with a resident descendant community defy the adoption of any of these academic personae. Of working-class background and public-school education, he lacks some of the tact and grace that many of similar background have managed to develop, and he is often pedantic. The son of a Glaswegian, he is in the unfamiliar position of studying "his own people," the Scots who formed the mercantile core of Port Tobacco and whose network of compatriots, although frequently at odds with one another, exercised far more economic and political control in the region than warranted by their numbers.

ACT I, SCENE 1

JAMES BEARD. [*feigning surprise*]: You're back. What are you looking for now?

ARCHAEOLOGIST. Good morning. Yeah, back again. I think we're finally going to nail down the whole sedimentation problem. The soil layers around the Burch House will allow us to date and describe the process.

James Beard. Burch House? Oh, Catslide House. Don't know why you feel a need to change the name.

Archaeologist. Well . . .

James Beard. Anyway, why don't you talk to Wearmouth or just read his and Roberta's book. They'll tell you what you want to know.

Archaeologist. [*restrained, but visibly irked*]: Well sure, they talk about the creek silting in but not about precisely when or how or what residents did about it or the landslides that . . .

James Beard. Landslides! There weren't any landslides. What makes you say landslides?

Archaeologist. As I was saying, the layers of soil around the Burrr . . . Catslide House . . . tell us about massive flows of sand and gravel from the heights across the street, depositing up to two-and-a-half feet of sedi . . .

James Beard. There is nothing in the *Port Tobacco Times* about landslides . . . you would think the local newspaper would mention landslides.

Archaeologist. This is long before the *Times* existed and the sediment covered the eighteenth-century land surface with . . .

James Beard. When did these landslides supposedly happen?

Archaeologist. It looks like before the American Revolution but there is this much [*showing with his hands, one above the other, about two-and-a-half feet apart*] sediment . . .

James Beard. Oh, well, that is way back. But look at my father's map of the town as it was in the 1880s and you can see that the town was fine, nothing buried, and there were lawyers and shops and a blacksmith and livery and hotels . . .

Archaeologist. Well, sure; I'm not saying that the whole town got buried like Pompeii, but periodically large amounts of sand and gravel washed down those ravines across the street and in fact created those ravines [*perceiving a quizzical look*] . . . you can't see them without going into the woods, but the hillside was denuded in the eighteenth century . . . the ravines . . .

JAMES BEARD. Really [*the first hint of boredom appears on his face*]: Well, landslides or not, this was a vibrant town in the 1880s until we lost the county seat in 1895. If there were landslides I don't see that they had much of an effect. Town's still here. John and Roberta cover all of this in the book and you should read up. We've been researching town history all our lives.

ARCHAEOLOGIST. [*Frustration and indignation welling*]: Well, sure, I've read their book and we've been compiling a huge digital database . . .

JAMES BEARD. Betsy is waiting . . . I've got to go . . . [*sotto voce*] arrogant jerk.

ARCHAEOLOGIST. Yeah, I need to get back to the crew . . . see ya [*James is already walking away. Sotto voce as he walks toward the excavation*] Tiresome old bastard . . .

ACT I, SCENE 2

Note: Translations of Scots and Scoticisms appear between brackets after Semple's lines. The Scots idiom is that of the late eighteenth century and draws from works of the poet Robert Burns; some of the Scots phrases, therefore, are more florid and romantic than might have come from a Scots expatriate of the 1750s and 1760s.

JOHN SEMPLE. [*caught unawares as he is just leaving the store; speaking deferentially in a gentle Lowland brogue easily comprehended by English speakers*]: Ah, Mr. Hanson!

JOHN HANSON. Mr. Semple.

JOHN SEMPLE. You've come to see me?

JOHN HANSON. [*condescendingly and imperious*]: No. I'm here to see my tobacco.

JOHN SEMPLE. I assure you . . . all is well.

JOHN HANSON. I'll assure myself. The storm washed out the road and Mrs. Kinsman's ground [Washington Burch House] is buried in stones and mud. I hope not to find your warehouse in similar circumstances.

JOHN SEMPLE. [*anxious to allay fears and slipping deeper into brogue and Scotticisms*]: The Lord surprised us but dinna [didn't] catch us unprepared. A' [All] but a few sticks of lumber were well off the ground and untouched by mud and stanes [stones].

JOHN HANSON. [*reprovingly*]: Then it is to the Lord that we both owe thanks because the safety of my crop owes nothing to your efforts. You've not yet repaired that east door, have you? For all the money you take for handling my crops, you might make a fit place to store them.

JOHN SEMPLE. [*deferentially*]: There's few sae bonnie, an nane sae guid in a' King George' Dominion . . . if ya shud dout the truth a this . . . [There are few so well-built and none so good in all of King George's dominions . . . if you should doubt the truth of it . . .]

JOHN HANSON. [*irritably*]: I've no time for prattle and braggadocio . . . show me my crop.

JOHN SEMPLE. At once . . . [*sheepishly*] I'm raisin the handlin by a pence a hund'rweight fer the langer haul. The lighters refuse to cum above the point for the shallows. [I'm raising the handling fee by a penny per hundredweight for the longer haul. The boatmen refuse to sail above the point because of shallow water.]

JOHN HANSON. I've already paid to cart the damnable hogsheads up here, now you want me to pay to cart them back down to my own wharf! I'm paying you to store my crop, not to dance it about the countryside!

JOHN SEMPLE. [*defensively*]: Isna ma doin . . . the creek's full of mud and yestere'en's spate has worsen'd it. The boatmen dunna wan ta . . . [It's not my doing . . . the creek's full of mud and yesterday evening's storm worsened it. The boatmen don't want to . . .]

JOHN HANSON. Damn the boatmen and damn you!

JOHN SEMPLE. We've talk'd a diggin out the burn but itsa lang way and the mud keeps comin, freathin and tumblin brown, roarin frae bank ta brae. Jemma suggested we dump the yirth on yer auld wash'd fields alang the creek. [We talked of digging out the creek but it is a long way and the mud keeps coming, frothing and tumbling brown, roaring from bank to hillside. Jemma (Scots Jimmy, referring to his brother-in-law, James Lawson) suggested that we dump the dredge on your old washed fields along the creek.]

JOHN HANSON. [*contemplatively and more conciliatory*]: Do you think we can?

JOHN SEMPLE. Aye, but it'll cost . . . we spoke of borrowing yer people [slaves] and those of the Browns, Craiks, an' Chandlers . . .

JOHN HANSON. [*skeptically*]: Borrow?

JOHN SEMPLE. Ya know I'd help if I cud, but I ha na a boddle tha' isna Jemma's. [You know I would help, but I don't have a penny that isn't Jemma's. Reference is to a half groat, actually worth far less than a penny, of base metal and obsolete long before the time of the action.]

JOHN HANSON. You've got boddles enough, sir, for all you charge us in freight and interest. Well . . . we'll see . . . now, my crop!

JOHN SEMPLE. [*deferentially again*]: Here, sir.

DISCUSSION

Originally, I had envisioned a stage play in which the action alternated between the two scenes, 250 years apart, but was addressing the same subject. Lights would come up on one scene and dim on the other as the conversation moved back and forth, contributing dimensions to the discussion elusive in linear discourse. Dialogue in one scene could inform that of the other, even though the actors of each scene are incognizant of those in the other, the dialogues leading in tandem to the question of the cost of wealth: what burden does the public bear in the individual's accumulation of wealth, specifically, how the accumulation of wealth led to that of sediment, to the detriment of all. In more skilled hands that might have been the case, and the results likely would have been different but not necessarily more valid. The intent is not necessarily to write a great play or to stumble on some historical fact or enduring truth. It is to circumvent those limitations of data and conventional methods that stymie research; in this case, understanding the responses of the people of Port Tobacco to processes that eventually destroyed their economic well-being.

Superficially, these two brief scenes deal with a common issue, but in actuality they don't. Scene 1 isn't about sedimentation, although it was my intent to deal with it in a modern setting (storm-water runoff and failing septic systems continue to degrade Port Tobacco Creek and the Chesapeake Bay). A different choice in protagonists might have been necessary. The old codger, like virtually everyone else living in the town who cared at all about the town's history, isn't interested in sedimentation. He isn't particularly interested in the town's Revolutionary War history, much less the pre-war years. Mr. Beard is interested in the town of his grandfather; he is interested in the town's waning years. He is interested in the place it used to be before the county government moved to the growing railroad town of La Plata two miles to the east, a move that reduced Port Tobacco to a cluster of deteriorating tenements and the village green to a tobacco field within thirty years. He is interested in Brigadoon and the community's need to control social change, not the complex environmental issues that have vexed the area for three centuries.

I already knew that most of the town residents are either ambivalent toward the work of the Port Tobacco Archaeological Project or think it is a waste of time and resources (Gibb, Beisaw, and Walter 2010). The town's history has already been written and "the archaeology has already been done," as a local author and onetime amateur archaeologist testified before the county commissioners. If this scene tells me anything new, it is that what the project team has to share with town residents, especially those with deep roots in the community, doesn't interest most of them. I had attributed this indifference to the residents' preoccupation with the town of their ancestors (Reconstruction Era to the residents' formation of the Society for the Restoration of Port Tobacco in 1947). They simply weren't interested in the eighteenth or early nineteenth centuries. I was wrong.

There are differences of interest that may correlate with period but are not explained by period. The exercise of writing a few lines of dialogue, in the context created by the descriptions of setting and characters, illuminated in a controlled, structured way the seemingly inexplicable lack of support for our archaeological research. Port Tobacco lost its vitality and deteriorated into a clump of dilapidated buildings because the county seat was ripped from it, aided by the deliberate torching of the courthouse in 1892. Environmental degradation doesn't interest residents; politics, particularly conservative politics, do.

Our archaeological research is well suited to the exploration of the changing environment and the dynamic relationship between human activities (particularly commerce, agriculture, and government) and the larger environment, each changing in response to the responses of the others. There is a constituency for this kind of research; it just isn't in Port Tobacco. It is in the surrounding community, which is beset by developmental pressures that threaten quality of life. The politics of the struggle for the county seat—between the ancient town and the upstart railroad community of La Plata—are not as well-suited to (although not entirely beyond) the strengths of archaeology. If archaeological work at Port Tobacco is to serve the people of the town and the county, it will have to expand to address the material correlates of the struggle for the county seat as well as the degrading environment.

The second scene is less well grounded than the first. The first scene is a dramatization, from my perspective, of my encounters with a living member of the Port Tobacco community. The second scene is completely imaginary although informed by some facts, most unsourced because of the necessary brevity of the scene. The characters are based on known persons who lived and worked in and around the town. Whether the words forced from their fictional mouths are truly in keeping with their attitudes and sentiments is beside the point. The objectives here are to lay out for myself and my readers a possible scenario that might help us understand the issues, motivations for and limitations to action or inaction, and identify avenues of research that may be amenable to more conventional approaches.

Two variables that come to the fore are the closely related dimensions of class and ethnicity. John Hanson was a member of the native-born elite of Tidewater society, a landed aristocrat in fact if not in title. He operated in a climate of social deference, common throughout the colonies before the revolution and in the southern states for years after, indeed, through the Jim Crow era (approximately the 1880s through the 1960s, during which laws codified and supported racial discrimination). John Semple was a Scot from Glasgow or its environs. Fifteen years before the action in Scene 2 took place, the English army brutally suppressed a Scottish rebellion and the intensifying Highland Clearances, forcibly evicting families and selling them into American servitude. Although of Swedish ancestry, Hanson regarded himself as English or at least not Scottish and, as such, would have inspired a good deal of antipathy in many a Scot. At the same time, he may have regarded Scots like Semple as traitors, and Semple's work as a merchant no doubt lowered him in Hanson's estimation. Suspicion of price manipulation and engrossment (monopolization) further diminished the prestige of Scottish merchants in the Chesapeake Tidewater region.

For all that, these people had to work together—aristocrats and merchants, English and Scots, Anglicans and Presbyterians (even Francophile Scottish Catholics). The causes and sources of sediments in the waterways were obvious to all. The means of stopping sedimentation and reversing its effects may also have been obvious: witness Patrick Henry's aphorism, quoted earlier, which suggests application of method, not a call to invent solutions. But planters like Hanson relied on tobacco and wheat and timber, not cover crops, to pay their growing debts to Scottish and English merchant houses; and Scottish and English merchants wanted large quantities of tobacco and other commodities, speedily and efficiently gathered for shipment. Land, previously cheap and plentiful, rapidly became scarce and, along with slaves, the principal form of collateral for loans. Recognition of the value of domestic markets was years in the offing and longer in the development. Determining who would fund waterway restoration would also have been difficult. Public funding of infrastructure remained a matter of controversy many years after our fictional dialogue took place (and continues to the day of Beard's conversation with the archaeologist), and the networks of debt for planters and merchants alike would have disinclined both from investing in dredging, especially for as long as the cause of sedimentation went uncorrected. Semple couldn't or wouldn't reinvest in his own warehouse, which, of course, wasn't his. It belonged to the partnership, more particularly to the senior partner, James Lawson. In the end of the exchange, Hanson—a planter with considerably more wealth at risk than many of his neighbors—also failed to act, concerning himself instead with his current tobacco crop.

This brief scene between eighteenth-century planter and merchant illuminates another issue that is not peculiar to Port Tobacco and that has been raised by Leone (1983). If the paucity of Chesapeake towns deprived Marylanders and Virginians of centers of capital accumulation and places of common identity and pride, why did so many of the Tidewater towns discussed by Gottschalk (1945a) succumb so dramatically to sedimentation? Ethnic and class schisms, exacerbated by religious controversy, certainly did not foster the trust on which cooperation builds. But it is also possible that only the very largest towns (Annapolis, Baltimore, Williamsburg) truly accumulated capital. In the complex relationship of core to periphery (sensu Paynter 1982; Wallerstein 1974), capital in small towns was enmeshed in debt. One might have considerable assets on paper, but the rates and forms of debt collection encumbered capital and stinted efforts at large-scale investment. Bankruptcy was as much a matter of liquidity as an imbalance between debits and credits. Chesapeake town dwellers, like surrounding planters, were cash-poor. Semple did invest large sums in personal accommodations and in the purchase of an iron furnace in Virginia, but he did this largely at the expense of his brother-in-law in Scotland, with credit, or with bills of exchange. James Lawson spent ten years in the Chesapeake region, away from his wife and children in Glasgow, trying to recoup the debts owed to him by Semple and by their debtors, ultimately with little success.

Scene 2 allows us to think about societal divisions and the stifling effects of complex creditor-debtor relations in a merchant capitalist economy. It has not identified any potentially useful archival sources that might aid research into sedimentation: we are left with gleanings about individual efforts to combat the effects but not the causes of sedimentation from the private papers of George Washington—he set enslaved women to the task of filling field gullies in April 1788 (Jackson and Twohig 1979: 297)—Thomas Jefferson, and other noted agriculturalists of the period and the observations of occasional travelers like John Honeyman in 1775 (see also Weld 1807): "Port Tobacco is about as big as New Castle [Delaware] and is seated between hills at the top of Port Tobacco Creek which two miles below falls into the Potomac, and only carries small craft now" (Honeyman, quoted in Klapthor 1958: 55). The scene, however, suggests archaeological research questions: where is the Lawson-Semple warehouse, and is there evidence of repair or expansion or just of decay and abandonment? Can we identify in archaeological deposits the timing and nature of capital reinvestment, and can we use archaeological evidence of capital investment as a measure for individual and community responses to sedimentation?

Leone (1983) applied Fernand Braudel's (1981) concept of the town to explain archaeological survey data from the Patuxent River (Shomette and Eshelman 1981)—a large drainage east of Port Tobacco Creek—and failed attempts at town founding, tentative defensive efforts during the Revolutionary War and the War of 1812, and the failure to dredge the river on which so many relied for their livelihood: "The relationship among land use, river conditions, towns, and boat life is a function of capitalism, as a particular kind of economic system, and is not just a function of ecological change or industrial development" (Leone 1983: 174). London and later Baltimore impeded town formation by drawing off capital. Urban cores contributed to the processes that reduced the abilities of those who lived along the Patuxent River to create and protect the source of wealth. The fictional discussion between Hanson and Semple suggests further complexity that might enhance Leone's model. Their wealth was not liquid; even if it were, the enormity of the undertaking brought Hanson back from contemplation to more immediate concerns. No amount of privately raised capital and slave power could maintain one mile of river during the Colonial period in Charles County, Maryland. The cause had to be corrected; the manner in which staples for an international market were produced had to change. A consideration of how the people we study might react to these issues fosters understanding and directs us toward more sophisticated hypotheses.

Penning lines of dialogue, verse, or short stories as a means of scientific inquiry is unorthodox and threatens those centuries-old boundaries the western world has erected around science, the arts, and the humanities. It is an unconventional solution to those problems scientists largely ignore: how do we pursue important questions where there are no evident sources of data, and how can we explore phenomena we do not yet recognize? Few would disagree about the importance of imagination in overcoming these problems, but how can we use imagination in a structured way that documents both roads taken and those spurned? How can researchers not only guide others in paths taken but leave trails for themselves that allow them to retrace their steps to firmer ground when the way becomes soft and uncertain? And how can we hope to use non-western ways of knowing the past if we reject our own pre-Enlightenment traditions of understanding the world?

The method, like any approach to knowing, has pitfalls. The cultural contexts created for scenes will be incomplete at best, nonsense at worst. Persons real, fictitious, and composite become objects in whose mouths we place words they may never have uttered or have used in the situation in which we have placed them. They are dolls dressed as we would have them dress and acting in ways we understand from our own cultural perspective. But the scenes above are experiments, not statements about past events or persons. Even Scene 1, the model for which occurred only two or three years before I wrote those lines of dialogue, does not represent a past reality, only my perception as an outsider and one I use to further explore apparent paradoxes. After all, the aims of Port Tobacco residents and those of the Port Tobacco Archaeological Project were very similar. Why were the leaders of the two undertakings so at odds with one another? Analyzing the semi-fictional scene illuminated the different interests at work. Scene 2, although entirely fictional, suggests conflicts and the class, ethnic, and historical dimensions along which they may have been expressed, even identifying material manifestations of those conflicts (e.g., a commercial storehouse in which capital was or was not reinvested).

Playwriting served as a structured method for imaginatively organizing data from Port Tobacco. The resulting insights can be tested. The archaeological project could try tailoring its research more closely to the interests of the town's current residents, examining the material bases for those politics that created and sustained the fight for the county seat over the course of twenty years. For example, the county surveyed the village and drew a plat in 1888, just four years before the torching of the courthouse and seven years before removal of the county seat. Since the 1940s, residents have produced a number of images and descriptions of the town as it existed around 1890, all suggesting charm and antiquity. The 1888 survey appears to have served as their base map. Conventional archaeological data recovery and analysis techniques can determine the number, condition, and siting of dwellings and business establishments extant in the last quarter of the nineteenth century. Were they neatly organized in a quadrangle around a central green, much as contemporaries imagined the ancient New England villages in which American democracy was born? Were they all occupied and maintained at the time of the survey? Lacking direct evidence of responses to sedimentation prior to the Revolutionary War, perhaps the project team needs to identify and analyze indirect evidence suggested by the fictional discourse, examining how residents of all periods used their wealth and political power.

As a form of constructive imagination, playwriting is a promiscuous method, available to couple with any theory, because it is a tool for exploring what we know about a time and place without the strict limits imposed by conventional sources and forms of data. It is not a means for testing hypotheses, but it may lead to hypothesis formation. Imagination already pervades archaeological analysis and interpretation and has done so since the earliest days of the field. Playwriting is merely a method for making explicit that which has long been done implicitly.

REFERENCES

Braudel, Fernand. 1981. *The Structures of Everyday Life: Civilization and Capitalism, 15th–18th Century*, vol. 1. New York: Harper and Row.

Flannery, Kent V. 1976. "Research Strategy and Formative Mesoamerica." In *The Early Mesoamerican Village*, ed. Kent V. Flannery, 1–11. New York: Academic Press.

Franklin, Jay. 1942. *Remaking America*. Boston: Houghton Mifflin.

Gibb, James G. 1996. *The Archaeology of Wealth: Consumer Behavior in English North America*. New York: Plenum. http://dx.doi.org/10.1007/978-1-4613-0345-9.

Gibb, James G. 2003. "The Archaeologist as Playwright." In *Ancient Muses: Archaeology and the Arts*, ed. John H. Jameson Jr., John E. Ehrenhard, and Christine A. Finn, 25–39. Tuscaloosa: University of Alabama Press.

Gibb, James G. 2011. "Phase III Archaeological Data Recovery at the Burch House Site (18CH765), Port Tobacco, Maryland." Gibb Archaeological Consulting, Annapolis, MD. Port Tobacco, MD: Submitted to the Society for the Restoration of Port Tobacco.

Gibb, James G., April M. Beisaw, and Kelley Walter. 2010. "'No, It's over There!' Asking Questions a Community Has Already Answered." Paper presented at the

Annual Meeting of the Society for Historical Archaeology, Amelia Island, Florida, January.

Gottschalk, L. C. 1943. "Report on the Reconnaissance Sedimentation Surveys of Loch Raven and Prettyboy Reservoirs, Baltimore, Maryland." Washington, DC: US Soil Conservation Service Special Report 5.

Gottschalk, L. C. 1945a. "Effects of Soil Erosion on Navigation on Upper Chesapeake Bay." *Geographical Review* 35 (2): 219–38. http://dx.doi.org/10.2307/211476.

Gottschalk, L. C. 1945b. "Sedimentation in a Great Harbor." *Soil Conservation* 10: 3–5, 11–12.

Gustafson, Axel F. 1961. *Conservation in the United States.* Ithaca, NY: Cornell University Press.

Hayward, Anne T. 2010. "Sands of Time: The Sedimentation of Port Tobacco." Paper presented at the annual meeting of the Council for Northeastern Historic Archaeology, Lancaster, PA.

Jackson, Donald, and Dorothy Twohig, eds. 1979. *The Papers of George Washington*, vol. 5 of the series *The Diaries of George Washington.* Charlottesville: University Press of Virginia.

Jones, Hugh. 1724. *The Present State of Virginia: Giving a Particular and Short Account of the Indians, English, and Negroe Inhabitants of That Colony.* London: J. Clarke.

Karras, Alan L. 1992. *Sojourners in the Sun: Scottish Migrants in Jamaica and the Chesapeake, 1740–1800.* Ithaca, NY: Cornell University Press.

King, Julia A., Scott M. Strickland, and Kevin Norris. 2008. "The Search for the Court House at Moore's Lodge, Charles County's First County Seat." St. Mary's City, Maryland: Submitted to the Citizens of Charles County.

Klapthor, Margaret Brown. 1958. *The History of Charles County, Maryland: Written in Its Tercentenary Year of 1958.* Bowie, MD: Heritage Books.

Leone, Mark P. 1983. "Land and Water, Urban Life, and Boats: Underwater Reconnaissance in the Patuxent River on the Chesapeake Bay." In *Shipwreck Anthropology*, ed. Richard A. Gould, 173–88. Albuquerque: University of New Mexico Press.

Martin, Ann Smart. 2008. *Buying into the World of Goods: Early Consumers in Backcountry Virginia.* Baltimore: Johns Hopkins University Press.

Miller, Henry M. 1988. "Baroque Cities in the Wilderness: Archaeology and Urban Development in the Colonial Chesapeake." *Historical Archaeology* 22 (2): 57–73.

Paynter, Robert. 1982. *Models of Spatial Inequality: Settlement Patterns in Historical Archaeology.* New York: Academic Press.

Pogue, Dennis J. 1984. "Town Rearing on the Maryland Chesapeake Frontier: A Reinterpretation." Paper presented at the Annual Meeting of the Society for Historical Archaeology, Williamsburg, VA, January.

Reps, John W. 1972. *Tidewater Towns: City Planning in Colonial Virginia and Maryland.* Williamsburg, VA: Colonial Williamsburg Foundation.

Rountree, Helen C., and Thomas E. Davidson. 1997. *Eastern Shore Indians of Virginia and Maryland.* Charlottesville: University of Virginia Press.

Scharf, J. Thomas. 1967 [1879]. *A History of Maryland from the Earliest Period to the Present Day.* Hatboro, PA: Tradition.

Shomette, Donald G., and Ralph E. Eshelman. 1981. *The Patuxent River Submerged Cultural Resource Survey, Drum Point to Queen Anne's Bridge, Maryland: Reconnaissance, Phase I and Phase II, 2 vols.* Maryland Historical Trust Manuscript Series 13.

Thomas, Joseph B., Jr. 1994. "Settlement, Community, and Economy: The Development of Towns on Maryland's Eastern Shore, 1660–1775." PhD diss., Department of Geography, University of Maryland, College Park.

Wallerstein, Immanuel. 1974. *The Modern World-System: Capitalist Agriculture and the Origins of the European World-Economy in the Sixteenth Century.* New York: Academic Press.

Walsh, Lorena S. 1977. "Servitude and Opportunity in Charles County, Maryland." In *Law, Society, and Politics in Early Maryland,* ed. Aubrey C. Land, Lois Green Carr, and Edward C. Papenfuse, 111–33. Baltimore: Johns Hopkins University Press.

Weld, Isaac. 1807. *Travels through the States of North America and the Provinces of Upper and Lower Canada during the Years 1795, 1796, and 1797.* 2 vols. London: John Stockdale.

8

The Archaeologist as Writer

Jonathan T. Thomas

> If you want to understand what a science
> is, you should look in the first instance not
> at its theories or its findings, and certainly
> not at what its apologists say about it; you
> should look at what the practitioners of it do.
> —Clifford Geertz (1973: 5)

As anthropological archaeologists, we spend the majority of our time writing. Although we might envision our lives as ones spent working long hours in the field, the lab, or the classroom, in reality the longest hours are often spent in front of the keyboard, writing site reports, lectures, articles, books, reviews, and grant proposals—turning abstracts from last year into conference papers this year, only to turn those papers into articles or book chapters the next. The amount of daily correspondence we are expected to maintain with colleagues and students alone is staggering.

Yet despite all this time spent writing, there seems to be a broadly held yet opaque attitude that attention to the style or rhetoric is a secondary or perhaps even trivial matter. Even as scholars with feet in both the humanities and the sciences, an unapologetic focus on the rhetorical positioning of one's writing can be viewed as slightly suspect. To say "I'm really focusing on making it well-written and interesting" or "I'm working with different types of historical narratives" is easily misconstrued as "it's not systematic" or an even worse epithet, "it's non-scientific." It arouses skepticism.

DOI: 10.5876/9781607323815.c008

As Clifford Geertz (1988: 2) described this problem in his book about literary forms in anthropology, *Works and Lives*, "'Good' anthropological texts are plain texts, unpretending. They neither invite literary-critical close reading nor reward it . . . somehow, attention to such matters as imagery, metaphor, phraseology, or voice is supposed to lead to a corrosive relativism in which everything is but a more or less clever expression of opinion." Although I have read these words many times, they still give me pause to examine the different types of rhetoric embedded (often unconsciously) in the writing I produce.

Intellectually, however, the majority of archaeologists recognize that rhetoric and historical or scientific accuracy are not directly related. Engaging, compelling writing need not come at the expense of science or an abuse of the "facts"—it is not a zero-sum game. But if we are fully conscious that it is *not* a zero-sum game, why does the perception linger? To begin with, there is a widely held sense that most anthropological texts, similar to texts in other sciences, should adopt an anonymous, omniscient, and typically jargon-laden passive voice that is explicitly but duplicitously not self-referencing or self-aware, which is itself a sort of rhetorical device used to impress upon the audience the author's or authors' scientific impartiality. The passive voice is slippery, a potential way to mitigate blame should things go wrong: it is not "I say" or "we say" but rather the "results" doing the "saying." However, the passive voice doesn't ensure accuracy, and as epistemological critics such as Jürgen Habermas and Jonathan Marks have repeatedly pointed out, actual scientific impartiality is virtually never the case; scholars of all types are intrinsically vested in their arguments—rightly or wrongly—in ways not necessarily rational or even conscious (Habermas 1972; Marks 2009). If it were otherwise, they likely would not be passionately devoted to their work in the first place. Thus, the passive voice of the anonymous, omniscient narrator (the "scientific voiceover from above") has become a natural choice of voice for many anthropologists, particularly archaeologists and biological anthropologists, *precisely* because it is such an easy, accessible shortcut to creating credibility with an audience and it is a safe voice from which to project scientific professionalism. Compounding this, because we routinely produce the majority of archaeological texts for our own consumption or to be consumed by our students, there is a tendency to drift toward this voice generation after generation by how others write anthropology, by what has passed (see Joyce 2002; Pluciennik 1999).

SCIENCE VS. THE RHETORIC OF SCIENTISM

The real problem in terms of archaeological writing is less about creating historical narratives than it is the confusion between technical scientific writing and what others have dubbed "scientistic" writing. Scientific writing begins with a question, sets up hypotheses to test it, and presents the results for falsification. It is a very specific form of technical writing. *Scientistic* writing is more a way of writing that reaches for a scientific-sounding voice laden with impenetrable jargon, a calculated rhetorical device that uses the formality of technical scientific writing as a means of establishing scholarly credibility or establishing the general importance of the research question if it needs bolstering. For all of its embarrassing lack of critical self-awareness, scientism is an extremely popular and pervasive "voice" in archaeology in particular, and it has tended to drown out alternative styles of how archaeology could be written.

Whether alternative narratives[1] or creative historical narratives belong inside or outside the discipline is a matter for debate, but I would venture that your opinion on this issue probably has a lot to do with your standing or cultural capital in the discipline (graduate students, independent researchers, adjuncts, tenured and untenured professors, and all manner of contract archaeologists), the types of knowledge you think anthropologists should produce, what epistemologies are valid for the production of anthropological knowledge, and for whom this knowledge is produced. But if *ultimately* we are interested in the dissemination of knowledge at any level—publicly, academically, scientifically, popularly, or pedagogically speaking—it seems clear to me that anthropological archaeologists need to engage in a wide range of different types of writing. While academia, much like Hollywood, rewards conformity and hewing to formulas that were successful in the past, archaeologists should reward innovations and find better ways to connect our interests with the public interest so we might have empathy for people in the past as well. Moreover, we need to recognize that, for all intents and purposes, the taboos about how anthropological and archaeological texts should be constructed are really ours and ours alone.

This comes with caveats. For instance, archaeologists are the public arbiters of the ancient past, in a sense responsible for assembling the broader interpretive picture of prehistory that emerges from fragmented archaeological facts. However, unlike freelance writers, in our role as social scientists we also have an ethical obligation not to misuse or misrepresent our findings in ways that can be used to perpetuate structural violence or socio-political injustice upon people of the present. There is a perception that scientific writing somehow guarantees protection from this, although the history of the twentieth century contains numerous examples of the misuse of science that demonstrate this is not always the case. At the same time, in tandem with the development of technology, our discipline has undergone a continual analytical transformation over the past half century. While this transformation has dramatically improved our ability to recover fine-grained information from the archaeological record, for instance, it hasn't necessarily been accompanied by an analogous leap in our interpretive or rhetorical abilities.

TELLING STORIES ABOUT THE PAST

It is not as if creative nonfiction or alternative narratives or whatever you like to call it about the past don't exist—there are scores of them, too many to mention here. It's simply that most of these narratives—with notable exceptions, such as Janet Spector's (1993) *What This Awl Means*, Steven Mithen's (2004) *After the Ice*, or more recently Kelli Carmean's (2010) *Creekside: An Archaeological Novel*—are written by people outside the discipline. The popular success of "epic" prehistoric fiction series, such as Jean Auel's *Earth's Children®* series or Kathleen O'Neal Gear and W. Michael Gear's *People of the . . .* books, has made the prehistoric or ethnographic novel not only a daunting task but to many an intellectually questionable one, marked not as much by the perception of a lack of scientific accuracy as by a lack of scientific *specificity*—a problem endemic to fiction set in the distant past, which can been seen in such works as Craig Childs's *House of Rain*.

When we do engage with these narratives, it tends to be at a critical arm's length, as with archaeologist John Whittaker's (2010) excellent meta-analysis of a number of different novelistic portraits of life in the pre-Columbian city of Cahokia ("Novels of Cahokia") or socio-cultural anthropologist Virginia Dominguez's (2009) meta-analysis of how different anthropological texts, from dissertations to journal articles, use separate and distinctly codified rhetorical forms and norms and how deviation or "wiggle room" from these forms and norms is negotiated ("Wiggle Room and Writing"). What seems clear is that there a persistent readership for alternative narratives—one that would no doubt benefit from our relative expertise—but that anthropologists are more often than not averse to allow such texts to be written by people active within the discipline. It is frowned upon.[2] Thus, we are left to stand at the sidelines, nitpicking during our lectures and cocktail parties at the historical or scientific accuracy of alternative narratives written by non-archaeologists. I believe this is what in literary terms is called a double-bind.

We should face the fact that our prior unwillingness to participate in the production of interpretive reconstructions of the past has not in any way hindered these texts from being published; they will continue to be produced whether we write them or not. And I am not talking about the Erich von Dänikens of the world. There are plenty of credible scientists who are not anthropologists willing to misinform in the name of anthropology, as the debate surrounding the "truthiness" of Jared Diamond's 2008 *New Yorker* article on Papua New Guinea illustrates. Likewise, there are non-anthropologists doing a much *better* job of explaining the direct relevance of archaeology to the general public than we are, such as writer Jack Hitt's (2006) exploration of race and the Kennewick Man controversy for *Harper's Magazine* titled "Mighty White of You" or John Jeremiah Sullivan's (2011) essayistic meditation on the confluence of archaeological looters and the Southeastern Ceremonial Complex, "Unnamed Caves." I would argue that because of both our expertise and our ethical obligation, we are perhaps uniquely situated to ensure that writing about the past accurately represents archaeological facts but also to ensure that this writing is done in a way that is reflexive, less androcentric, and sensitive to the potential for the prehistory to be used for political propaganda (see, for example, Arnold 1990; Härke 1972, although there is a substantial corpus of literature on this subject).

I look forward to the time when debates about alternative narratives are less concerned with arguments about their epistemological validity, as this chapter is, and more concerned with how the deployment of characters embedded in these narratives is used to challenge or reify existing ideas or stereotypes about the past and to spark new questions, new hypotheses to test, new avenues of inquiry. Think about how the complexity of the human past could be represented through the use of multiple narrators discussing the same phenomenon but from different viewpoints. Does archaeology need such a Rashomon effect?[3] I don't know, but it is a conversation I want to be part of.

WRITING INDULGENCES

> I would like to see more people think about how anthropological
> texts are constructed. How they make their arguments, how
> rhetoric plays into it. The language in which they are cast.
> —CLIFFORD GEERTZ, 2004 INTERVIEW

My essay thus far has been standing in the shadow of Clifford Geertz, starting with the title—itself an allusion to the subtitle of Geertz's (1988) well-known book about anthropologists as writers, *Works and Lives: The Anthropologist as Author*. Unfortunately for me as an archaeologist, much of what Geertz has to say in this book is primarily concerned with how ethnographies are written. There are excellent technical books written to instruct archaeologists on how to shepherd archaeological texts to publication (specifically Brian

Fagan's [2006] *Writing Archaeology*) and books that critically apply literary theory to archaeological texts (e.g., Rosemary Joyce's [2002] *The Languages of Archaeology*), but the closest text to providing some sort of guidance as far as constructing alternative narratives is likely Janet Spector's (1993) *What This Awl Means*. Strangely, however, even though *Works and Lives* is largely about ethnography, I find that it may be a keystone for archaeologists attempting to construct alternative narratives. If we accept that the central thesis of Geertz's work is essentially true, that anthropology is not an experimental science in search of law but rather an interpretive science in search of meaning—and I fully believe this to be the case, perhaps even more so for archaeologists, who by necessity must interpret information resulting from events that are unobservable—then we must grapple with how to interpret information and create meaning from events in the past in ways that are historically accurate, ethical, and epistemologically sound. I'm sure there will be numerous disagreements about how archaeological data are deployed in alternative narrative texts, but the point is that we cannot even begin to have these debates until we allow ourselves to "indulge"—and it's telling that this word even seems appropriate in this instance—in this type of writing. For archaeologists, alternative narratives of the past are our *thick description*. Not thick description in the same sense as an ethnography attempting to sort out cultural structures of signification (winks upon winks upon winks [Geertz 1973: 9] do not preserve well in the archaeological record) but thick description in the vein of John Whittaker's (2010) "Novels of Cahokia," a recognition that the cultural meaning we derive from the evidence of the past is created though a critical dialogue between the scientifically derived "facts" of the past and texts that interpret this evidence using any number of rhetorical strategies or voices, but neither alone.

PREFACE TO THE ALTERNATIVE NARRATIVES

> The strange idea that reality has an idiom in which it prefers to be described, that its very nature demands we talk about it without fuss—a spade is a spade, a rose is a rose—on pain of illusion, trumpery, and self-bewitchment, leads to the even stranger idea that, if literalism is lost, so is fact.
>
> —CLIFFORD GEERTZ (1988: 140)

The final section of this chapter is experimental. It is an attempt to provide a few potential examples of the different types of alternative narratives proposed in this edited volume, narratives that not only use the archaeological record and anthropological theory to convey to the reader something of a thick description of human life and human culture in the distant past but which juxtapose several interpretations of an archaeological topic to bring to light hidden subjectivities within ostensibly objective scientific analyses. Like historical fiction, most alternative narratives follow a single character, such as the grandmother narrator in Kathleen King's (1983) *Cricket Sings*, or a number of characters set in distinct time periods, such as in Bryan Sykes's (2002) reconstructions of our matrilineal ancestors in *The Seven Daughters of Eve* or the intertwining plots in Kelli Carmean's (2010) *Creekside*. Some, like Steven Mithen's (2004) *After the Ice*, follow a single time-traveling character through many different time periods, so that a number of different archaeological pasts can be explored in a single narrative thread. In other alternative narratives, like Kent Flannery's (1982) "The Golden Marshalltown" or Timothy Pauketat's (2007) *Chiefdoms and Other Archaeological Delusions*, the authors use fictitious or fictionalized archaeologists to carefully explore various theoretical problems or controversies.

I started by picking a subject matter that has a lot of popular interest, which I was well acquainted with and eager to spend a good deal of time writing about, and that had a rich body of archaeological and theoretical literature: Paleolithic art. I then narrowed my focus to explore ideas and theories about the Gravettian era (ca. 27–22 kya) Eurasian Venus figurines, largely because people are fascinated with them and seemingly have been since their discovery over a century ago. I felt this quality would "guarantee" a compelling narrative (more on this later). The Upper Paleolithic Venus figurines also present a recurrent theoretical problem in anthropology, as their use and meaning have been continually contested by Paleolithic archaeologists, art historians, and anthropologists since the end of the nineteenth century. I began to envision a set of fictionalized vignettes that juxtaposed different historical interpretations of the Venus figurines within the texts themselves.

Although I was attempting to be entertaining (a quality essential to the suspension of disbelief in fictionalized exposition), my much loftier theoretical hope was that by standing diverging interpretations of the Venuses next to one another, I would be able to shed light not only on Paleolithic art but also on how changing anthropological interpretations reflect historically constituted cultural constructions as much as they do what the Venus figures "meant" to people 20,000 to 30,000 years ago. In my mind, these Venus figurine vignettes would in part be a recognition of the bleed-over between the facts and how these facts are interpreted and of the recursive process of knowledge construction and attribution of meaning (Geertz 1973: 27): interpretations of the Venuses have always been in many ways inseparable from what ur-anthropologist Johann Gottfried Herder first referred to as zeitgeist. I hoped to conclude this exercise by demonstrating the powerful contribution feminist archaeologists in particular have made to the interpretation of the Venuses (see Adovasio, Soffer, and Page 2007; Conkey 1997; Eller 2000; Nelson 1990, 2004).

Then a basic fact reared its ugly head: I had never written anything like this before! I experimented with constructing the vignettes from an etic scientific perspective, as well as from an imaginary emic perspective (one admittedly informed by a number of years of research on Upper Paleolithic art). I tried different narrative voices as well: the passive voice of academic writing and voices associated with various narrative forms—first person, third person, omniscient narrators, limited narrators, multiple narrators, and so on.

Echoing a modern academic or scientific tone was problematic for a number of reasons. Primarily, introducing a lot of specific dates, terms, locations, or other types of data into a narrative is immediately and alarmingly pedagogical and generally prevents the suspension of disbelief that is necessary for storytelling. Second, from a narrative perspective, the scientific voice is often antiseptic and overly jargon-laden—you have to go to a great deal of effort to read academic writing because it is not overly concerned with seducing the reader, as are fiction and creative nonfiction. Finally, academic and scientific writing typically uses the passive voice. While the passive voice is often used in narratives for expository purposes, bereft of an assertive first-person subject, it does not really lend itself to character development. It is hard for the reader to emotionally "get behind" the passive voice, which is not a problem when you are writing a scientific article but certainly is if you are trying to construct a narrative arc.

Alternately, using an imaginary first- or third-person omniscient narrator, the most common narrative voices in fiction and creative nonfiction, was no easier. Would the omniscient narrator be omniscient of the past but not of the present? How much "bleed-over" of my knowledge about the present could I allow to seep into this character in the past? This seemed highly problematic to me. How would the character speak? Was coming up with an imagined prehistoric way of speaking *really* any better than using modern cultural and scientific vocabulary, or would it just sound hokey?[4] Stripped of all modern knowledge, I was left with a prehistoric protagonist that was vague and uninteresting. I then tried the first-person limited voice—that is, a narrator who possesses only the knowledge of a single person—which suffered from the same lack of specificity but to an even greater degree. It turns out that you can't really convey *enough* archaeological information about the past this way;

the voice itself is too interior. It also seemed slightly insensitive to attempt some sort of emic Paleolithic voice coming from the back of the cave. How could I pretend to speak for these people so far removed from myself, both temporally and culturally? Does this appropriate their agency in some way? As writers, we have the problem of entertaining the audience through narrative arcs and dialogue. But as anthropologists and social scientists, we have certain ethical obligations to all people, past and present. But how can you be empathetic to a fictional character from a distant past that you did not experience? In other words, it's complicated.

Choosing any one of these narrative voices seemed limiting and limited. I was struggling with denying my characters vocabulary from the present in an attempt to present some sort of "*etic-ly cleansed*" version of the past that, rather dishonestly, pretends *not* to be informed by the present. I was not only stuck for failing to locate a believable narrative voice but for epistemological reasons as well. As the archaeologist Sarah Milledge Nelson (1990: 12) has noted, the collective interpretations of the Venus figurines represent a modern mythology of sorts, a folklore particular to anthropologists and art historians. At worst, their meaning is irresolvable, and we will likely never understand them very well (Eller 2000: 136; Soffer, Adovasio, and Hyland 2000). Although we are confident that the figurines are predominantly female, their original (Gravettian) structures of signification are gone. In this way, the Venus figurines are less a part of Gravettian culture than they are part of our own culture: they have become deeply embedded in our own structures of significance—they are firmly trapped in twenty-first-century webs of meaning. More people now know about, talk about, see, admire, and argue over these 200-odd figurines than ever did in the Upper Paleolithic.

I decided that the only way to accommodate these particular technical, rhetorical, and epistemological problems was to embrace the methods of postmodern meta-fiction (e.g., comments about or critiques of the text within the text, a rejection or deconstruction of traditional literary conceits, fragmentary, fractured, and often digressive narratives, and in a sense an ongoing self-conscious "wink upon wink upon wink" at the reader by the author. The work of the late David Foster Wallace and his heir apparent, David Mitchell, epitomizes this genre of fiction, although it has its roots in writers such as Thomas Pynchon, Don DeLillo, and Donald Barthelme).

So, I began. I wrote fictitious letters of correspondence from real nineteenth-century archaeologists about actual historical events related to the acquisition of specific Paleolithic figurines (see Delporte 1987, 1993; Piette 1894a, 1894b, 1894c, 1894d, 1894e; White 2006). I wrote first-person accounts of prehistoric adolescent boys, explaining why they made seemingly "erotic" (i.e., unclothed) female figures in an attempt at critiquing the "Paleoporn" explanation of Paleolithic art (see Absolon 1949; Adovasio, Soffer, and Page 2007; Berenguer 1973; Eller 2000; Guthrie 1984, 2006; Kurtén 1986; Nelson 2004;). I wrote third-person accounts of Paleolithic priestesses throwing wet clay figurines into the campfire, terrifying the surrounding crowd with their violent explosions, as an act of both performance and religious ritual (see Soffer 1993) and of Paleolithic women teaching others how to weave (see Adovasio, Soffer, and Page 2007; Soffer, Adovasio, and Hyland 2000). I wrote out a dream of Abbe Breuil's (the "Pope of Prehistory") that examined his application of sympathetic magic to Paleolithic art (Breuil 1928, 1952; Breuil and Peyrony 1930; Frazer 1992; White 2003). I wrote a transcription of a fictitious lecture by André Leroi-Gourhan that laid out the structuralist interpretation of Paleolithic art (see Leroi-Gourhan 1966, 1967, 1968; Nelson 2004). I wrote excerpts from a fictitious 1970s textbook on the Mother Goddess movement, describing its interpretation of the Venus figurines as peaceful, regenerative deities (see Eller 2000; Gimbutas 1974, 1989, 1994; Meskell 1995; Nelson 2004). I wrote the interior thoughts of a fictitious graduate student, comparing her pregnant body to that of the Venus of Willendorf (the "Autogenous Hypothesis"; see McCoid and McDermott 1996; McDermott 1996). I wrote out the notes of a fictitious undergraduate listening to the lecture of a well-known Paleoanthropologist explaining the Adiposity paradox (i.e., the paradox of how Upper Paleolithic people would have been familiar with obesity considering their generally fit hunter-gatherer lifestyle) of the Gravettian figurines (see Trinkaus 2005). I wrote and I wrote and I wrote some more, all of it extensively footnoted and cited.

As it turns out, the methods of postmodern meta-fiction are not particularly well suited to writing stories about the ancient past. As I found out from different readers (and as the editors of this volume can attest to), the vignettes were *too* experimental and confusing (or perhaps just poorly written). Readers were unable to understand where the facts stopped and the fiction began. It turns out I could not be the servant of contemporary literature, the archaeological record, and critical theory all at once.

BACK TO THE DRAWING BOARD

I decided that I needed to simplify the narratives, jettison the techniques of postmodern meta-fiction, and return to my idea of constructing the alternative narratives using a Rashomon-like effect—that is, a scene witnessed by different viewers who interpret what they are seeing in decidedly subjective ways. The ways my characters would "see" the scene reflect diverging anthropological theories dealing with the same subject of the use and meaning of Paleolithic art. I have arbitrarily used Finnish (a non-Indo-European language) place names for people's names in the narrative. Coming up with fictitious Upper Paleolithic names that were not distracting or hokey was much more difficult than I anticipated.

(1) Sympathetic Magic and Structuralism

This narrative explores the work of rock art pioneer Abbe Breuil (1928, 1952; Breuil and Peyrony 1930) who, looking for an alternative to the dominant "art for art's sake" (*L'art pour l'art*) explanation for prehistoric art, turned to Frazer's (1992) concept of the "law of similarities" in which Paleolithic people created art as a form of sympathetic magic to influence events in the physical world (i.e., hunting and reproductive magic). It also incorporates ideas by other mid-nineteenth-century French archaeologists such as Annette Lanning, Max Raphael, and André Leroi-Gourhan (1967, 1968) who, heavily influenced by Lévi-Strauss, used binary cultural concepts borrowed from Structuralism to interpret Paleolithic symbolism (Nelson 2004).

Today the fathers and the sons from the band go deep in the cave, deeper than Alahärmä had ever ventured. At sundown, they stop at the entrance of the cave and make drawings of the man's sex and some angular shapes he does not understand very well. Alahärmä's father, Perniö, explains that the drawing magic is powerful, that it increases the herds of food animals and wards off dangerous ones. Perniö tells the boy that long before he was born, the Ancestors of the families came to these particular caves and discovered that the different parts of the cavern and different drawings made the magic work in different ways. Perniö holds Alahärmä's hand as the older men lead them deeper and deeper. The cave is cold and wet and dark, the flickering tapir casting shadows of their trembling bodies on the walls. His father teaches him how to draw bears, cave lions, ibex, mammoths, rhinoceroses, deer, sea animals, owls, pregnant horses, handprints, water, and the life-giving parts of women. Before they left the camp, Alahärmä's mother, Salo, told him that the families make this type of magic to shape the future world. He is uncertain of what she meant but even more uncertain that he will be able to kill bison during the next hunting season with the older men, so Alahärmä redoubles his efforts at drawing the man's animals and the woman's animals with the black ash and red crayon. He is terrified that a bear or lion will find them. He whispers to his father, "There's no easy way to run out of this part of the cave." "It's okay, it's okay" Perniö says in a reassuring tone. Alahärmä is old enough to remember seeing several people die from starvation several winters ago. So he stifles his fear and scratches out the lines with Perniö and the others on the sand-colored walls. As he makes the magic, Alahärmä prays: he thinks about hunting with the men and returning with meat and hides. He prays that Salo's baby will be healthy and survive the winter and that he will soon have other brothers and sisters. The men can go no further and stop to rest. Here they may eat only raw foods, never cooked. His father shows him how to make a Venus figurine from a scrap of animal hide but doesn't let Alahärmä touch the delicate diamond-shaped woman with wide hips and large breasts he's carving out of a piece of mammoth tusk. They listen to the noises in the cave: dripping, the whispering of prayers and requests for help, the sound of paint-ing and carving. On the back wall of the cave Perniö and Alahärmä draw bison and the woman's sex over and over again, together. When they return to the entrance, it is once again light out.

(2) Paleoporn

Paleoporn (Paleolithic pornography) is the term used both seriously and in jest (Adovasio, Soffer, and Page 2007: 188) to refer to interpretations of depic-tions of Paleolithic women as explicitly sexual or erotic in nature. While the Venus figurines have long been referred to as pornography (Absolon 1949: 202) or "Paleolithic pin-up girls" (Eller 2000: 135–36; Kurtén 1986; Nelson 1990: 16), the best-known ideas on the subject come from zoologist-paleontologist R. Dale Guthrie (1984, 2006). Although Guthrie discusses many other impor-tant aspects of Paleolithic art in general (e.g., the inclusion of children in Paleolithic art making, the incredible naturalism of Paleolithic artists), many feminist archaeologists (see Eller 2000; Nelson 1990, 2004) have critiqued sexually charged interpretations, noting that they overemphasizes the erotic nature of Paleolithic art, impose modern conceptions of gender and sexuality on Paleolithic gender and sexuality—of which we know very little—and tend to be androcentric, excluding female-centered viewpoints or interpretations.

Inari's older brother, Raahe, wakes him, grabbing his wrist and pulling him out from under his hide. At dawn, they sneak away from camp with the other boys before most of the adults are awake. The boys love to go exploring, even if it's dangerous. Inari has already seen one boy killed by a lion last season, but he is confident that that won't happen to him. Deep in the woods they find the entrance to the caves. Raahe makes a fire, and the boys take out their lamps from their kits. The group moves from the entrance of the cave into the dark. Inari knows that at any moment they might

wake a bear or a cave lion, and he can feel his heartbeat throughout his entire body.
Completely alert, Inari feels his senses heighten. He hears every drop of water. In the
dim light, they can see their breath in the musty-smelling air. He trails his fingers
over the rough surface of the cave walls. The first mark Raaha makes is a red outline
of his hand by using a hollow bone to spit ochre at the wall. The rest of the boys follow
suit. With their lamps, they proceed into the cave's depths. Raahe and Inari scape a
section of a wall clean, turning it from a sandy color to white. He sees the oldest boys
drawing realistic horses, bears, lions, seals, birds, deer, mammoths, and bison—ani-
mals he cannot draw himself. Raahe instead draws a woman, her hips wide, large
breasts, and a clearly visible vulva. In some places, vulvas are all the boys draw,
scores of them. Inari fantasizes about the women they create. He's never been with
a woman, but today all he can think of is the chance to be paired with one when the
families meet up with his father's band next hunting season. Some of the boys aren't
particularly sure what they are making. Inari has seen naked girls and naked women
at the camp, but the inner workings of their bodies were still a mystery to him. Raahe
draws a figure wearing just a little bit of clothing, highlighting its nudity. They talk
about sex and the women's bodies. "No," he says, correcting Inari's work. "Draw her
lying down or maybe bent over from behind." Inari tries harder to impress his brother.
Raahe pulls some soft stones from his kit, along with some flakes and two knives. As
he begins to carve, Inari notices Raahe ignores the women's faces, hands, and feet,
whittling them away. Instead, his attention is focused on the middle of the woman's
body, resulting in a diamond-shaped figurine, full-figured and curvaceous, with her
vulva prominently displayed. Inari attempts to carve his in a similar fashion, but
the result doesn't look like much of anything. By the time the brothers return to the
entrance, the dark is settling in.

(3) FEMINIST PERSPECTIVES AND BEYOND

This narrative explores ideas about Paleolithic art following feminist archaeological critiques of androcentric biases in the discipline during the mid-1980s
and the 1990s. Specifically, it draws on Olga Soffer's (1993) article "The Case of
the Exploding Figurines," in which she uses both artifacts and experimental
archaeology to explore the production and consumption of Paleolithic figurines from the perspective of ritual performance. It also refers to Adovasio,
Soffer, and Page's (2007; also see Soffer, Adovasio, and Hyland 2000) work
on the link between technology and women's status among Paleolithic groups
that produced not only figurines but also woven baskets and many types of
textiles.

Today, my mother, Savonlinna, takes me deeper into the cave than I have ever ventured. I'm too short to reach the opening, so my mother's brother, Kajaani, lifts me and our baskets of food, fiber, ochre, beads and bits of shell, bone needles, and stone tools up to Savonlinna, who pops her head out of the entrance. My sister, Saarijärvi, scrambles up with her unnamed baby strapped to her. As I go inside, my loose ceremonial tunic catches on a rock, ripping the fibers apart a bit. My mother smiles and says, "Don't worry. We will sew it up later, after the ritual." On the walls of the cave I can see all types of animals, handprints of children and adults, woven nets, and many strange shapes. Is that a sign for rain? When we reach the back of the cave we can see that Kälviä, the shaman, is already in a trance. Her ivory jewelry rattles as she circles around the fire, passing through the group of people sitting at her feet. Her son, Kemi, hands her sticks of wood, with which she attacks the fire over and over again, drawing it upward and making clouds of sparks burst into the air. People lean their faces forward to blow air onto the coals and are momentarily illuminated, only to disappear back into the darkness. Kälviä is opening up the ritual for the group. She sings to them, exhorts them to come closer, driving both the fire and herself into a frenzy. She closes her eyes. When she opens them again, they are rolled back in her head, like a sick animal. Kälviä moves so fast that she's hyperventilating. Next to the hearth are two kilns partially dug into the ground. Thousands of pieces of white tusk and bone litter the ground surrounding them, standing out against the blackness. One at a time, each person in the group hands Kälviä a figurine. Earlier that day, they sat on the banks of the river, each fashioning one from clay. The figurines were still somewhat wet, clammy and cold to the touch. I am entranced by the dancing shadows of people cast on the wall and the flickering fires inside the kilns. Kälviä takes a figurine wearing a hat that is woven in the style of our baskets from someone with one hand and with the other grabs a handful of small, wet clay balls and throws them both into a kiln, and we all shield our faces. The sound of steam is followed by a terrific explosion and a bang! that makes everyone jump back. Kajaani fans the air toward the kiln and blows, reviving the fire. It's quiet and smoky. Kälviä pulls the fragments of the shattered figurines out of the fire and one by one consults the people at her feet. As soon as all the figurines have been destroyed and Kälviä's divinations have been given, she collapses into Kajaani's arms, exhausted by her performance. My mother and I stay by the fire, and the women show me how to weave the spiral hats. Mine has seven circles and two half-circles to cover part of my neck; my mother's looks more like a netted hood. She tells me stories about her mother, who once was the master weaver of our band, as she works on a ceremonial belt for when I become a woman. The other women sit next to us, working on both ceremonial clothes and more plain string skirts, shawls, hoods, and bandeaux. Kajaani keeps the fire going until my mother tells him it's time for the family to go home.

DENOUEMENT

> A good interpretation of anything—a poem, a person, a
> history, a ritual, an institution, a society—takes us into
> the heart of that of which it is the interpretation.
>
> —CLIFFORD GEERTZ (1973: 18)

Did I succeed in my endeavor? I think the jury is still out on this one. I still feel that the narratives I have attempted to write lack the specificity of well-written fiction. And I am still plagued by the specter of "hokeyness," a literary quality that is poison to the suspension of disbelief. Perhaps I am not a good enough fiction writer to completely pull it off. But this should not be taken as discouraging news: this discipline has plenty of brilliant people who are also excellent, engaging writers. Perhaps these narratives would have worked better at a larger (novelistic) scale, in which proper character development and narrative arcs would come into play and through which archaeological data could be incorporated more subtly. And perhaps it is a matter of literary taste. Have I produced narratives that I myself would read on a Sunday afternoon? No. But I have very specific tastes in my scientific and literary reading appetite. The fiction I enjoy reading is completely embedded in late-twentieth- and early-twenty-first-century culture. It is a type of fiction that is both self-aware and strictly emic: it comes from an understanding of an insider's view of the culture in which it is produced. As an archaeologist, I know that we can never really understand Upper Paleolithic tropes and cultural concepts from an emic perspective. However, this does not mean I should confuse my personal tastes with the validity of attempting to construct these types of narratives for the public's edification. To varying degrees, archaeologists are always constructing different types of narratives about the past, with differing degrees of success, as the archaeological record never "speaks for itself"—it must be organized and interpreted (and, indeed, the organization is itself a form of interpretation). If the insights of anthropology tell us anything, it is that we are all in some ways like the prisoners in Plato's allegory of the cave, trying again and again to interpret the flickering shadows the light of reality casts on its walls.

NOTES

1. I define these as fictional narratives based on the archaeological record and anthropological theory or as creative nonfiction essays or books that attempt to elucidate aspects of the archaeological record and anthropological theory.

2. Such works typically do not count toward tenure, perhaps discouraging non-tenured academics from writing them.

3. Ethnographers have been engaged with this problem for some time; see Heider (1988).

4. I think "hokeyness" is the primary obstacle to writing believable narratives about the archaeological record.

REFERENCES

Absolon, Karel. 1949. "The Diluvial Anthropomorphic Statuettes and Drawings, Especially the So-Called Venus Statuettes Discovered in Moravia." *Artibus Asiae* 12: 201–20.

Adovasio, James M., Olga Soffer, and Jake Page. 2007. *The Invisible Sex: Uncovering the True Roles of Women in Prehistory*. New York: HarperCollins.

Arnold, Bettina. 1990. "The Past as Propaganda: Totalitarian Archaeology in Nazi Germany." *Antiquity* 64 (244): 464–78.

Berenguer, Magin. 1973. *Prehistoric Man and His Art: The Caves of Ribadesella*. London: Souvenir.

Breuil, Henri. 1928. "Renseignements Inédits sur les Circonstances des Trouvailles des Statuettes Aurignaciennes des Baoussé-Roussé." *Archivio per l'Antropologia e la Etnologia* 58: 281–86.

Breuil, Henri. 1952. *Four Hundred Centuries of Cave Art*. Montignac, France: Centre d'Etudes et de Documentation Préhistoriques.

Breuil, Henri, and D. Peyrony. 1930. "Statuette Feminine Aurignacienne de Sireuil." *Revue Anthropologique* 40: 44–47.

Carmean, Kelli. 2010. *Creekside: An Archaeological Novel*. Tuscaloosa: University of Alabama Press.

Conkey, Margaret. 1997. "Mobilizing Ideologies: Paleolithic 'Art', Gender Trouble, and Thinking about Alternatives." In *Women in Human Evolution*, ed. L. Hager, 172–207. London: Routledge.

Delporte, Henri. 1987. *Edouard Piette, Pionnier de la Préhistoire*. Paris: Picard.

Delporte, Henri. 1993. *L'Image de la Femme dans l'art Préhistorique*. Paris: Picard.

Dominguez, Virginia. 2009. "Wiggle Room and Writing." *Iowa Journal of Cultural Studies* (November) Theme issue "Work." http://www.uiowa.edu/~ijcs/writing/wu_dominguez.htm., accessed May 23, 2013.

Eller, Cynthia. 2000. *The Myth of Matriarchal Prehistory: Why an Invented Past Won't Give Women a Future*. Boston: Beacon.

Fagan, Brian. 2006. *Writing Archaeology: Telling Stories about the Past*. Walnut Creek, CA: Left Coast.

Flannery, Kent. 1982. "The Golden Marshalltown: A Parable for the Archeology of the 1980s." *American Anthropologist* 84 (2): 265–78. http://dx.doi.org/10.1525/aa.1982 .84.2.02a00010.

Frazer, James. 1992. *The Golden Bough: A Study in Magic and Religion.* New York: Macmillan.

Geertz, Clifford. 1973. *The Interpretation of Cultures: Selected Essays.* New York: Basic Books.

Geertz, Clifford. 1988. *Works and Lives: The Anthropologist as Author.* Stanford: Stanford University Press.

Gimbutas, Marija. 1974. *Gods and Goddesses of Old Europe, 7000–3500 B.C.: Myths, Legends and Cult Images.* London: Thames and Hudson.

Gimbutas, Marija. 1989. *The Language of the Goddess.* London: Thames and Hudson.

Gimbutas, Marija. 1994. *The Civilization of the Goddess: The World of Old Europe.* New York: HarperCollins.

Guthrie, R. Dale. 1984. "Ethological Observations from Palaeolithic Art." In *La Contribution de la Zoologie et de L'ethologie à L'interpretation de L'art des Peuples Chaseurs Préhistoriques,* ed. H. G. Bandi, W. Huber, M. R. Sauter, and B. Sitter, 35–74. Fribourg, Switzerland: Editions Universitaires.

Guthrie, R. Dale. 2006. *The Nature of Paleolithic Art.* Chicago: University of Chicago Press.

Habermas, Jürgen. 1972. "Knowledge and Human Interests: A General Perspective." In *Knowledge and Human Interests.* Trans. Jeremy J. Shapiro, 301–17. Boston: Beacon.

Härke, Heinrich, ed. 1972. *Archaeology, Ideology and Society: The German Experience.* Frankfurt: Peter Lang.

Heider, Karl G. 1988. "The Rashomon Effect: When Ethnographers Disagree." *American Anthropologist* 90 (1): 73–81. http://dx.doi.org/10.1525/aa.1988.90.1 .02a00050.

Hitt, Jack. 2006. "Mighty White of You." In *The Best American Science Writing 2006,* ed. Atul Gawande, 237–71. New York: Harper Perennial.

Joyce, Rosemary, ed. 2002. *The Languages of Archaeology: Dialogue, Narrative, and Writing.* Malden, MA: Blackwell. http://dx.doi.org/10.1002/9780470693520.

King, Kathleen. 1983. *Cricket Sings: A Novel of Pre-Columbian Cahokia.* Athens: Ohio University Press.

Kurtén, Björn. 1986. *How to Deep-Freeze a Mammoth.* Trans. Erik J. Friis. New York: Columbia University Press.

Leroi-Gourhan, André. 1966. *Cronología del Arte Paleolítico.* Rome: Actas de VI Congreso internacional de Ciencias prehistóricas y protohistóricas.

Leroi-Gourhan, André. 1967. *Treasures of Prehistoric Art*. New York: Harry N. Abrams.

Leroi-Gourhan, André. 1968. *The Art of Prehistoric Man in Western Europe*. London: Thames and Hudson.

Marks, Jonathan. 2009. *Why I Am Not a Scientist: Anthropology and Modern Knowledge*. Los Angeles: University of California Press.

McCoid, Catherine H., and Leroy McDermott. 1996. "Toward Decolonizing Gender: Female Vision in the Upper Paleolithic." *American Anthropologist* 98 (2): 319–26. http://dx.doi.org/10.1525/aa.1996.98.2.02a00080.

McDermott, Leroy. 1996. "Self-Representation in Upper Paleolithic Female Figurines." *Current Anthropology* 37 (2): 227–75. http://dx.doi.org/10.1086/204491.

Meskell, Lynn. 1995. "Goddesses, Gimbutas and 'New Age' Archaeology." *Antiquity* 69: 74–86.

Mithen, Steven. 2004. *After the Ice: A Global Human History 20,000–5000 BC*. Boston: Harvard University Press.

Nelson, Sarah Milledge. 1990. "Diversity of the Upper Paleolithic 'Venus' Figurines and Archaeological Mythology." In *Powers of Observation: Alternative Views in Archaeology*, ed. Sarah Milledge Nelson and Alice B. Kehoe, 11–22. Archaeological Papers of the American Anthropological Association 2. N.p.: American Anthropological Association.

Nelson, Sarah Milledge. 2004. *Gender in Archaeology: Analyzing Power and Prestige*. Walnut Creek, CA: AltaMira.

Pauketat, Timothy. 2007. *Chiefdoms and Other Archaeological Delusions*. Walnut Creek, CA: AltaMira.

Piette, Eduoard. 1894a. *L'époque Éburnéene et les Races Humaines de la Periode Glyptique*. Saint-Quentin, France: Imprimerie, Ch. Poette.

Piette, Eduoard. 1894b. "Races Humaines de la Période Glypitque." *Bulletin de la Société d'Anthropologie de Paris, IVe série* 5: 381–94.

Piette, Eduoard. 1894c. "Race Glyptique." *Comptes Rendus de l'Académie des Sciences* 118: 825–26.

Piette, Eduoard. 1894d. "Nouvelles Fouilles á Brassempouy." *Association Française pour l'Avancement des Sciences, Congrés de Caen* 23: 675–83.

Piette, Eduoard. 1894e. "Sur de Nouvelles Figurines d'Ivoire Provenant de la Station de Brassempouy." *Comptes Rendus des Séances de l'Académie des Sciences* 19: 927–29.

Pluciennik, Mark. 1999. "Archaeological Narratives and Other Ways of Telling." *Current Anthropology* 40 (5): 653–78. http://dx.doi.org/10.1086/300085.

Soffer, Olga. 1993. "The Case of the Exploding Figurines." *Archaeology* 46 (1): 36–39.

Soffer, Olga, James M. Adovasio, and David C. Hyland. 2000. "The 'Venus' Figurines: Textiles, Basketry, Gender and Status in the Upper Paleolithic." *Current Anthropology* 41 (4): 511–37. http://dx.doi.org/10.1086/317381.

Spector, Janet. 1993. *What This Awl Means: Feminist Archaeology at a Wahpeton Village.* St. Paul: Minnesota Historical Society Press.

Sullivan, John Jeremiah. 2011. "Unnamed Caves." In *Pulphead: Essays*, 215–52. New York: Farrar, Strauss, and Giroux.

Sykes, Bryan. 2002. *The Seven Daughters of Eve: The Science That Reveals Our Genetic Ancestry.* New York: W. W. Norton.

Trinkaus, Eric. 2005. "The Adiposity Paradox in the Middle Danubian Gravettian." *L'Anthropologie* 43 (2-3): 263–71.

White, Randall. 2003. *Prehistoric Art: The Symbolic Journey of Humankind.* New York: Harry N. Abrams.

White, Randall. 2006. "The Women of Brassempouy: A Century of Research and Interpretation." *Journal of Archaeological Method and Theory* 13 (4): 250–304. http://dx.doi.org/10.1007/s10816-006-9023-z.

Whittaker, John. 2010. "Novels of Cahokia." *SAA Record* 10 (2): 34–36.

9

Eleven Minutes and Forty
Seconds in the Neolithic

Underneath Archaeological Time

Doug Bailey and
Melanie Simpkin

Do archaeologists work at the appropriate timescale? The work presented in this chapter asks that question and is part of a longer, broader, multimedia output that focuses on the present and past of the rural village of Măgura in south-central Romania (Jasmin 2011; Mills 2010). A core theme is the opening up of action, people, and behavior in the past and the ways archaeology represents, responds to, and constructs those pasts. The work in this chapter is linked to a film (*Twenty Minutes Inside Out: Landscape Transformation in Neolithic Southcentral Romania* [http://www.upcolorado.com/component/k2 /item/2712-subjects-and-narratives-in-archaeology -media]), which the lead author made in the summer of 2010 with the help of Peter Biella and Iván Drufovka and which was shown at the Society for American Archaeology 2011 session from which the current book has emerged (Biella and Drufovka 2010).

To make *Twenty Minutes Inside Out*, we set up a video camera on the corner of a street in Măgura and filmed for twenty-minute periods at four different times during one day. For the final film, as shown in Sacramento (and as available on this book's DVD), we positioned the four, twenty-minute clips as separate quadrants on one screen. At random places in the four films, we inserted the four words that represented the official themes (Landscape, Transformation, Art, Culture) of a larger European Union–funded project in which we were working at the time.[1]

The intention of the film was to use art to show that the transformation of both the landscape and culture

DOI: 10.5876/9781607323815.c009

occurs in real time, as people walk by, as carts or cars or bicycles wheel past, and as the slow, invisible processes of geomorphology, of rain and wind, of insects and dogs, create landscapes. The point was this: as archaeologists, we have been working at an inappropriate scale of time. The proposal was that the extraordinarily rich time (and timescale) is the scale at which life happens. One consequence is that archaeological fieldworkers and interpreters of the past must recognize as chronotypic fabrications the archaeological reductions of time we regularly carry out to produce site phasings and cultures, as well as the century-, millennia-, epoch-, and era-long units of prehistoric and historic reconstructions. Though useful for scientific simplifications, such temporal reductions do little more than fudge reality and only ever provide one, out-of-synch version of human action. In this sense, traditional archaeology misses the scale of lived action yet continues to talk grandly about agency, intention, belief, mentality, and the individual.

The intention of the film was to juxtapose the scales at which archaeologists work and at which other cultural producers, authors, and interpreters function. In our excavations of an Early and Middle Neolithic landscape (6000–5500 cal BC) on the outskirts of Măgura, we had grown frustrated that our engagement with the people of the past remained constrained within a coarse chronology of radiocarbon dates (even with AMS dates and Bayesian modeling) or through the relative, though more precise, sequencing of micro-morphological thin-sections of event sequences in any of the pit features at the site.

Where were the people we were studying who had dug that pit, held this pot, looked up to hear a hawk flying overhead? They were squashed in the collapse of time that institutions expect us to generate: the hypocritical time of archaeology. No matter the advances of excavation precision or dating refinement we employed, the techniques of our excavations at Măgura never put us in touch with the people whose past we had been spending substantial amounts of (our) time, funders' money, and everyone's efforts to study. In our excavations, not only were we kept at a distance, but (we started to realize) we were headed in the wrong direction. No increase in our efforts would get us any closer to the time of the prehistoric people we sought; if anything, when we moved from the chaos of soils, shards, and bones in the site trenches to the site records, reports, publications, and fifteen-minute conference presentations, we lost touch with the 8,000-year-old events and the people engaged in them. We had to try something else. The film and this chapter are first attempts at that "something else."[2]

The intention of this chapter (in its visual form) is to take the next step in the process started with the film. We invite the reader to bounce back and forth between the pages that follow and the videos; we invite the viewer of the videos to do the same. Alternatively, video and visual chapter invite individual viewing without reference to the other. There is no intractably correct way to experience either. To create this chapter, Melanie Simpkin and I translated the movements and activities recorded in one of the videos (the bottom left one when you watch the film) into a nontraditional (for archaeology at least) notation system: Benesh Movement Notation (BMN). Again, the aim was to disrupt the customary perception and standard representation of human action as recorded in the video (which itself had been a disruption of how we should think about the pace of archaeological and geomorphological change) and to elevate the significance of the slow, almost static pace of daily life.

BMN was developed in the 1950s by Rudolf and Joan Benesh as a three-dimensional language for recording choreographic works for a professional ballet company (Benesh and Benesh 1977; Hutchinson Guest 1989). The system records the choreographer's intentions, indicating with precision the steps to be taken, when to take them, and how to perform them. A BMN score gives specific instructions regarding dynamics, rhythm, and phrasing and provides a bird's-eye view of an individual dancer's location and direction of travel. The movement information is plotted in a series of notated frames on a five-line stave, similar to a musical stave. The depth of detail recorded can be adjusted, from simple walking to the complexities of partner work and the exact angle of a head or finger. Many levels of analysis are possible. The notation system is versatile and adaptable and has been applied beyond ballet and dance: in physiotherapy, as a research tool to record and assess a patient's progress; in work study, as a means of detailing the ways a machinist operates his or her equipment; and in anthropology, as a tool of analysis in different socio-cultural environments.

The BMN scores form the core of the work we offer in this chapter; on top of, around, underneath those scores we have juxtaposed objects, images, and texts from both the standard archaeological simplifications of people's pasts and more evocative references to a contemporary past (sensu Buchli [2009]; Buchli and Lucas [2001]; González-Ruibal [2008]; Harrison and Schofield [2009]; Lucas [2004]; Olivier [2011]; Shanks [1991, 1997], inter alia). As the reader/viewer moves through the twenty pages of the work, he or she will find patterns to the juxtapositions, and through it we have attempted to make our argument (sketched out in words in this introduction) in a nontextual manner.[3]

Part artwork, part archaeological conundrum, part provocation to think and to disagree, our position is that all of us (archaeologists, authors, photographers, artists) are working on the same project (the human condition through time); if we wish to make progress in that project, then we should dispense with current boundaries among disciplines, departments, media, practices, and outputs and venture out into difficult and uncertain territory, into disciplines and practices where the connection to a person's breath, scent, sound, and movement is more direct. The result may not (should not) fit within what we have been trained to understand as standard archaeology. This is as it should be, though there is no need to discard current traditional work on the past as accessed by the trowel and the calibration curve, since that work suits its purposes. However, there awaits a vast space in which new attachments to human behavior should be explored, attachments that will take novel and unimagined forms, attachments that will open our understanding of the past, of the present, and of our positions within both. We invite you into that uncertain territory.

ACKNOWLEDGMENTS (DB)

I am grateful for the help and advice from a number of notation specialists (Marion Bastien, Liz Cunliffe, Mary Deicher, Sally Ness, and Jo Tomalin), from colleagues at the Muzeul Județean Teleorman (Pavel Mirea), for friends in the village of Măgura, Romania, and from those who participated in the Southern Romania Archaeological Project or the Măgura: Past and Present project or who were part of both efforts (Amy Bogaard, Costel Haita, Christopher Knüsel, Mark Macklin, Richard MacPhail, Stephen Mills, Amelia Pannet, Laurens Thissen, Angela Walker). The original film on which this chapter is based would not have been possible without the work of Peter Biella and Iván Drufovka, to whom I owe a special debt of thanks. Extra-special appreciation is noted to Melanie Simpkin for her willingness to join in the work with enthusiasm (Melanie is an associate of the Institute of Choreology). Special thanks to friends and scholars who discussed the potential and challenges of alternative narratives with me or whose works have provided inspiration: Reinhard Bernbeck, Alfredo González-Ruibal, Meg Jordan, Bjørnar Olson, Mike Pearson, Heike Roms, John Schofield, Michael Shanks, Ruth Tringham, and Ruth Van Dyke.

Fragments of many different projects are included in this chapter, and I am grateful to these organizations for funding those projects: San Francisco State University (the Dean's Office of the College of Behavioral and Social Sciences), the British Academy, the Arts and Humanities Research Council (UK), and the European Union (the Landscape Transformation EC project

2007–4230, European Union Education, Audiovisual and Culture Executive Agency Culture Programme). None of these funders or any collaborator on the earlier unrelated projects is responsible for the work presented here.

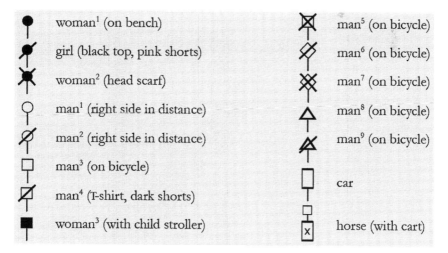

Legend showing Benesh symbols used in this chapter to identify individuals

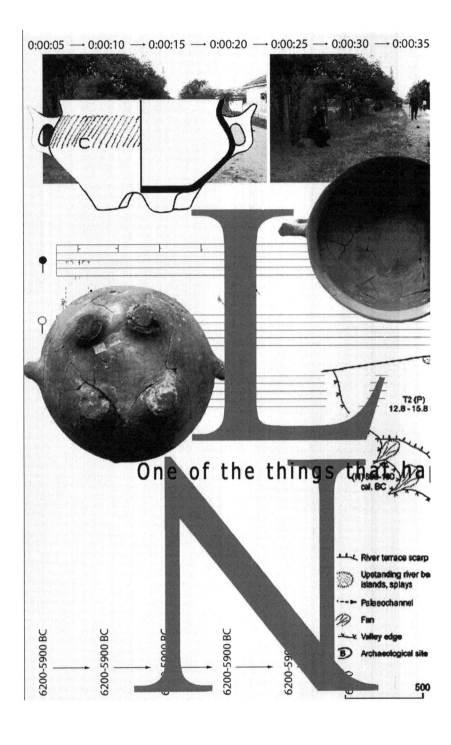

One of the things that ha

T2 (P)
12.8 - 15.8

(R)866-760
cal. BC

River terrace scarp

Upstanding river be
islands, splays

Palaeochannel

Fan

Valley edge

Archaeological site

6200–5900 BC → 6200–5900 BC → 6200-5900 BC → 6200–5900 BC → 6200-590

500

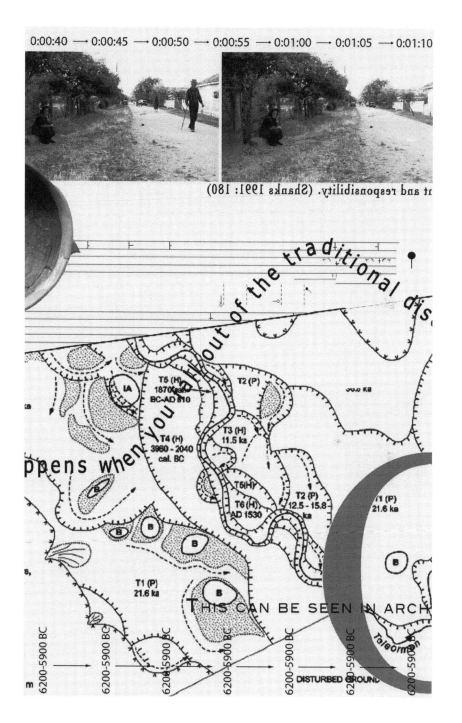

of the empirical reality of the past. This is the tension between experimen

ciplinary boundaries is that work becomes

AEOLOGY'S CONTINUED DILEMMA ABOUT THE F

6200–5900 BC → 6200–5900 BC → 6200–5900 BC → 6200–5900 BC → 6200–5900 BC → 6200–5900 BC → 6200–5900 BC

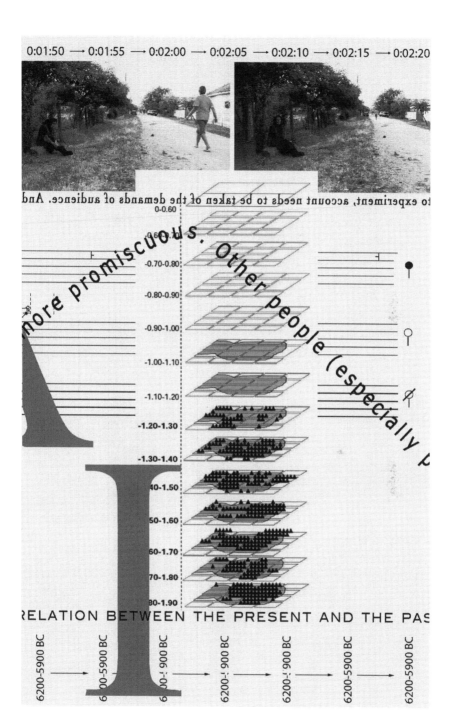

to experiment, account needs to be taken of the demands of audience. And

more promiscuous. Other people (especially p

0-0.60

-0.70-0.80

-0.80-0.90

-0.90-1.00

-1.00-1.10

-1.10-1.20

-1.20-1.30

-1.30-1.40

40-1.50

50-1.60

60-1.70

70-1.80

80-1.90

RELATION BETWEEN THE PRESENT AND THE PAS

6200-5900 BC → 6200-5900 BC → 6200-5900 BC → 6200-5900 BC → 6200-5900 BC → 6200-5900 BC → 6200-5900 BC

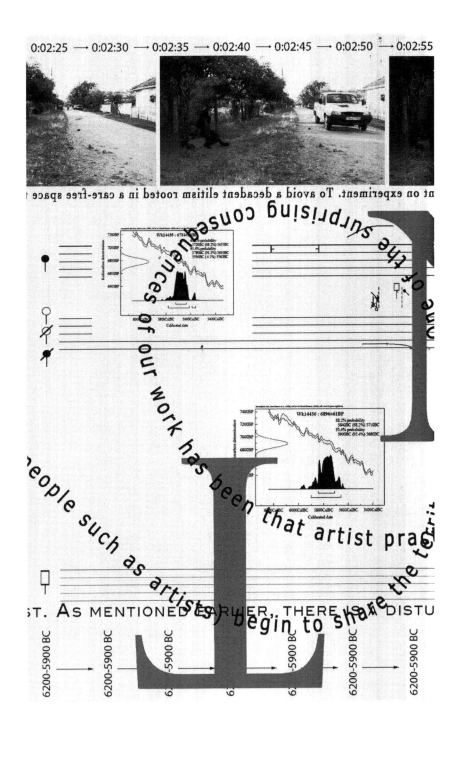

an excite and challenge accessibly. Audience matters. This is one constrai

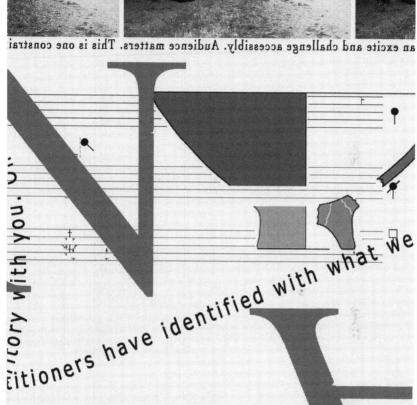

ory with you. O

tory with you. O

itioners have identified with what we

RBING QUESTION SURROUNDING OUR   OWL D

6200–5900 BC ⟶ 6200–5900 BC ⟶ 6200–5900 BC ⟶ 6200–5900 BC ⟶ 6200–5900 BC ⟶ 6200–5900 BC ⟶ 6200–5900 B

experimental energies drive the contemporary music scene. Experiment c

have been doing in relation to their

)GE OF PREHISTORY: ON THE ONE HAND, IT WA

not mean necessarily lapsing into an avant-garde obscurity; inventive and

own work The chronological terrain in which we work is up for grabs!

AS DEFINED AS A NEW PAST, A NEW TIME, BUT

6200-5900 BC → 6200-5900 BC → 6200-5900 BC → 6200-5900 BC → 6200-5900 BC → 6200-5900 BC

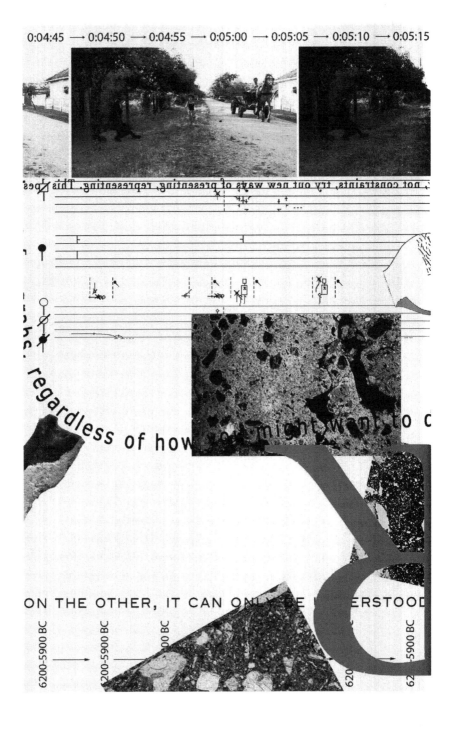

0:04:45 → 0:04:50 → 0:04:55 → 0:05:00 → 0:05:05 → 0:05:10 → 0:05:15

not constraints, try out new ways of presenting, representing. This does

regardless of how you might want to c

ON THE OTHER, IT CAN ONLY BE UNDERSTOOD

6200–5900 BC   6200–5900 BC   00 BC   5900 BC

riment. To put those disciplinary anxieties to one side and read possibility

lefine it (e.g., from the present all

(AND WAS CREATED) THROUGH ANALOGIES (D

6200–5900 BC → 6200–5900 BC → 6200–5900 → 6200–5900 BC → 6200–5900 BC → 6200–5900 BC

in archaeology and our inventive contribution to the past dare us to exper

the way back to the point when tra

(DIRECT OR INDIRECT) WITH THE PRESENT ... ARC

6200–5900 BC   6200–5900 BC   6200–5900 BC   6200–5900 BC   6200–5900 BC   6200–5900 BC   6200–5900

. A suggestive artifact, the lack of any final formulae or definitive method

5'18"   5'21"   5'25"   5'29"

ditional archaeology and heritage mai

HAEOLOGY CREATED ITS OWN MODEL OF TIME—

6200-5900 BC   6200-5900 BC   6200-5900 BC   6200-5900 BC   6200-5900 BC   6200-5900 BC   6200-5900 BC

0:07:05 → 0:07:10 → 0:07:15 → 0:07:20 → 0:07:25 → 0:07:30 → 0:07:35

...what archaeology and society does with them. Perceptive to suggestion...

A TEMPORALIZATION WHICH IS NOT NECESSARI

their work... A bit of think... can b

agement sta

6200-5900 B → 6200-5900 B → 6200-5900 B → 6200-5900 B → 6200-5900 B → 6200-5900 B → 62 -5900 B

th the artifacts as they come to light and are dispersed and transformed in

appen in this chronological terrain.

LY UNIQUE TO ARCHAEOLOGY (EXCEPT IN ITS D

6200- BC

6200-5900 BC

6200-5900 BC

6200-

6200-

6200-

6200-5900 BC

It has a great deal of political c

ave called throughout for a mobility of thought and perception, moving wi

6'51"   6'56"

DETAILS), BUT WHICH NONETHELESS SERVES TO

6200–5900 BC → 6200–5900 BC → 6200–5900 BC → 6200–5900 BC → 6200–5900 BC → 6200–5900 BC → 6200–5900 BC

s application for it, of factual past and the response or representation, I ha

pportunity and potential. When you beg

PLASTER OVER THE FRACTURE BETWEEN PRE

6200-5900 BC → 6200-5900 BC → 6200-5900 BC → 6200-5900 BC → 6200-5900 BC → 6200-5900 BC → 6200-5900 BC

with which I began this book, of developing theory and then finding some

gin to apply the archaeological met

SENT AND PAST BY CREATING A SPECIFIC TIME

6200-5900 BC → 6200-5900 BC → 6200-5900 BC → 6200-5900 BC → 6200-5900 BC → 6200-5900 BC → 6200-5900 BC →

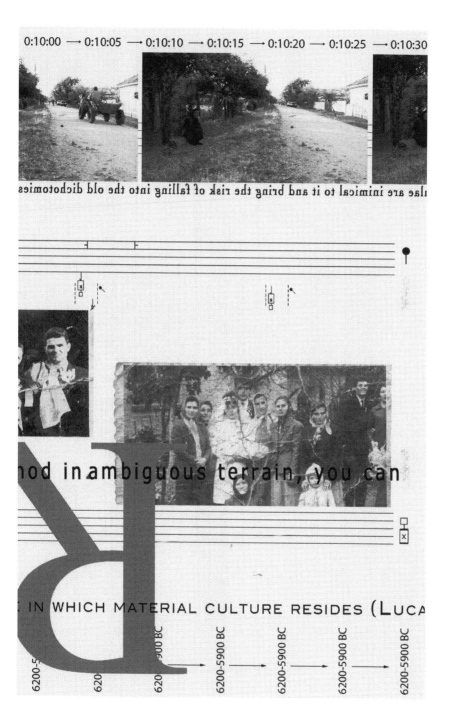

ılae are inimical to it and bring the risk of falling into the old dichotomies

ıod in ambiguous terrain, you can

: IN WHICH MATERIAL CULTURE RESIDES (LUCA

6200-5 620 620 6200-5900 BC ⟶ 6200-5900 BC ⟶ 6200-5900 BC ⟶ 6200-5900 BC

In writing of such a poetics I can only be suggestive. Form

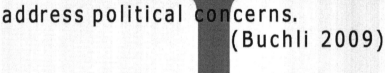

address political concerns.
(Buchli 2009)

s 2004: 112)

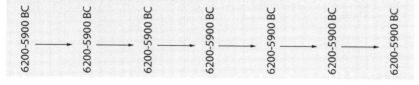

THE WASH-HOUSE WAS A VAST SHED WITH A FLAT ROOF, SUPPORTED BY VISIBLE BEAMS ON CAST-IRON PILLARS AND ENCLOSED BY WIDE CLEAR-GLASS WINDOWS, WHICH ADMITTED THE PALE DAYLIGHT SO THAT IT COULD PASS FREELY THROUGH THE HOT STEAM THAT HUNG LIKE A MILKY MIST. HERE AND THERE, WISPS OF SMOKE WERE RISING SPREADING OUT TO COVER THE BACK OF THE SHED WITH A BLUEISH VEIL. A HEAVY DAMPNESS RAINED DOWN, LADEN WITH THE SMELL OF SOAP – A MOIST, INSIPID, PERSISTENT SMELL, IN WHICH, FROM TIME TO TIME, STRONGER WHIFFS OF BLEACH WOULD DOMINATE. ALONG THE WASHING-BOARDS THAT LINED BOTH SIDES OF THE CENTRAL AISLE WERE ROWS OF WOMEN, THEIR ARMS NAKED TO THE SHOULDERS, THEIR NECKS BARE AND THEIR SKIRTS TUCKED IN TO REVEAL COLOURED STOCKINGS AND HEAVY, LACE-UP SHOES. THEY WERE BEATING FIERCE-LY, LAUGHING, THROWING THEIR HEADS BACK TO SHOUT SOMETHING THROUGH THE DIN OR LEANING FORWARD INTO THEIR TUBS, FOUL-MOUTHED, BRUTISH, UNGAINLY, SOAKED THROUGH, THEIR FLESH RED-DENED AND STEAMING. AROUND AND UNDERNEATH THEM, A GREAT STREAM COURSED BY, COMING FROM BUCKETS OF HOT WATER CARRIED ALONG AND TIPPED OUT IN A SINGLE MOVEMENT, OR ELSE FROM OPEN TAPS OF COLD WATER PISSING DOWN, THE SPLASHES OFF THE BEETLES, THE DRIPS FROM RINSED GARMENTS, ALL RUNNING OFF IN RIVULETS ACROSS THE SLOPING STONE FLOOR FROM THE PONDS IN WHICH THEIR FEET PADDLED. AND, IN THE MIDST OF THE CRIES, THE RHYTHMICAL BEATING NOISES AND THE MURMUROUS SOUND OF RAIN – THIS TEMPES-TUOUS CLAMOUR DEADENED BY THE DAMP ROOF – THE STEAM-ENGINE, OVER TO THE RIGHT, COMPLETELY WHITENED BY A FINE DEW, PANTED AND SNORED AWAY UNCEASINGLY, ITS FLYWHEEL SHIVERING AND DANCING, SEEMING TO REGULATE THIS MONSTROUS DIN (ZOLA 1876).

NOTES

1. For full details of the Măgura: Past and Present project, please visit http://www .magurapastpresent.eu/en/.

2. In a recent publication and exhibition project, I (DB) made a related attempt to rupture the way we understand and seek self-limiting definitions, interpretations, and meanings for one group of prehistoric artifacts from southeastern Europe and Japan (Bailey, Cochrane, and Zambelli 2010).

3. We recommend that interested readers experience works of similar format by Diller and Scofidio (1992); McLucas (2000).

REFERENCES

Bailey, Douglass, Andrew Cochrane, and Jean Zambelli. 2010. *Unearthed: A Comparative Study of Jōmon Dogū and Neolithic Figurines.* Norwich, UK: Sainsbury Centre for the Visual Arts.

Biella, Peter, and Iván Drufovka. 2010. *Eternity Was Born in the Village.* DVD. Philadelphia: Bilingual Media.

Benesh, Rudolf, and Joan Benesh. 1977. *Reading Dance: The Birth of Choreology.* London: Souvenir Press.

Buchli, Victor. 2009. "Interview with Victor Buchli." *Studii de Prehistorie* 6: 7–14.

Buchli, Victor, and Gavin Lucas, eds. 2001. *Archaeologies of the Contemporary Past.* London: UCL Press.

Diller, Elizabeth, and Ricardo Scofidio. 1992. "Case no. 00-17163." In *Zone 6: Incorporations,* ed. Jonathan Crary and Sanford Kwinter, 344–61. New York: Zone Books.

González-Ruibal, Alfredo. 2008. "Time to Destroy: An Archaeology of Super-modernity." *Current Anthropology* 49 (2): 247–79. http://dx.doi.org/10.1086 /526099.

Harrison, Rodney, and John Schofield. 2009. "Archae-ethnography, Auto-archaeology: Introducing Archaeologies of the Contemporary Past." *Archaeologies: Journal of the World Archaeological Congress* 5 (2): 185–209.

Hutchinson Guest, Ann. 1989. *Choreo-Graphics: A Comparison of Dance Notation Systems from the Fifteenth Century to the Present.* London: Gordon and Breach.

Jasmin, Michaël. 2011. *The Brain of the Archaeologist.* Paris: Deux-Points.

Lucas, Gavin. 2004. "Modern Disturbances: On the Ambiguities of Archaeology." *Modernism/Modernity* 11 (1): 109–20.

McLucas, Cliff. 2000. "Ten Feet and Three Quarters of an Inch of Theatre." In *Site-Specific Art: Performance, Place and Documentation,* ed. Nick Kaye, 125–38. London: Routledge.

Mills, Stephen, ed. 2010. *Interventions: Măgura Past and Present*. Cardiff: School of History and Archaeology.

Olivier, Laurent. 2011. *Dark Abyss of Time: Memory and Archaeology*. Lanham, MD: AltaMira.

Shanks, Michael. 1991. *Experiencing the Past*. London: Routledge.

Shanks, Michael. 1997. "Photography and Archaeology." In *The Cultural Life of Images: Visual Representation in Archaeology*, ed. Brian Molyneaux, 73–107. London: Routledge.

10

The Talking Potsherds
Archaeologists as Novelists

SARAH MILLEDGE NELSON

"Narrative is the Other, the alter-ego of a scientific archaeology," Christopher Tilley (1993: 1) proposed in his project to create space for interpretation in archaeology. He compared narratives in archaeology to theater performances: "Back stage is the space of theatrical machinery and direction. What is seen by the spectators on the stage is dependent on the complex support from this invisible beyond" (ibid.). The backstage analogy is particularly useful in thinking about archaeological fiction. To underpin any archaeological story, there must be actual excavations, studies of artifacts, knowledge of the environment, and much more. Putting the discoveries of the spade and the work of the laboratory into a fictional story requires engaging the public in the story without too many grubby details but without ignoring them, either. As I will argue, some of the "machinery" of archaeology can even enrich the story. A novel about an archaeological site or region is an attempt to apply "thick description" (Geertz 1973) to archaeology, as other chapters in this collections also note.

I suggest that writing novels with archaeological subjects does not objectify the people who lived at the sites any more than does a standard archaeological report—fiction is probably less likely to make the dwellers at the site objects. Living people created the objects and features described by archaeologists. They lived in the landscape and altered it. Making them the subject of fiction gives them a voice. At the same time, with the binocular vision created by combining a narrative with

DOI: 10.5876/9781607323815.c010

present archaeological activity and past inhabitants, the reader can become involved with both ancient life at the site or sites and the process by which we learn about ancient people and their activities. Such a double vision allows the reader to participate in the construction of the story in a different way. The voice of the fictional archaeologist explains what was discovered in sites and what is from written documents, as well as which events are created from those artifacts but have no other basis in the archaeological record.

Toward the beginning of the movement to objectivity in archaeology, Lewis Binford (1972) characterized James B. Griffin, his mentor at the University of Michigan, as appealing to "talking potsherds," asking "what does this potsherd say to you?" Binford said he hoped the time would come when the potsherds spoke to him, when pictures of potsherds "screamed forth self-evident truths from the past" (ibid.: 5). I had some sympathy for Griffin when I read this. No sherd can tell us the thoughts or emotions of the person who made it, but that wasn't Griffin's point. His potsherds "told" where and when they were made. More can be learned, however. This chapter is about listening to things, creating a story from them, and gently informing the interested reader how we know about the past, as well as what kinds of events and emotions a people at a particular time and place might have encountered. My stories contain recurrent reminders that they are stories.

The post-processual turn made more room for interpretation, and we have come to understand that all archaeology is interpretation. "The specific communications of archaeologists actually create and sustain the entire ecology of niches that we recognize as the discipline of archaeology," Mitchell Allen and Rosemary Joyce (2010: 272) noted. My novels are intended to be "specific communications of archaeology" because they are responsible to the archaeological data. But to make a story, it is necessary to go beyond data. Archaeologists can be responsible to the data in ways those who are primarily writers of fiction are not trained to be.

In pursuing a goal of understanding the daily lives of the people at a site, I first wrote stories just for myself, to help me think about the missing pieces and what effect how knowing what people wore, for example, or how their rituals were carried out might change my understanding of the sites. But not just any story can be told. The data of the dig require certain parameters to a story and not others. Alison Wylie (2002) calls these "evidential constraints." We cannot tell just any story.

My attempts at fiction writing were informed by interests in gendered archaeology, the nature of leadership in early societies, and ritual itself. None of these topics can be "read" directly from the data. I hoped if my fictional interpretation fit all the known data, the story would form a coherent whole. For example, if creating a woman leader as heroine made some data untenable, then it was a poor hypothesis.

Misia Landau (1991) shows that even in professional writing about human evolution, there are implicit stories. This work describes discussions of human evolution as narratives, with a hero and a goal. To suppose that archaeologists are *not* telling stories is ingenuous. Fiction does not disguise its goal to entertain, but it should not distort the archaeological record.

My novels are written as teaching novels, especially for archaeology students but also for the interested public. In an earlier paper (Nelson 2003) I considered the questions of whether novels are legitimate ways to write archaeology and what archaeologists can learn from writing novels. In this chapter I want to explore how to listen to things, those talking potsherds, and create a story from them while gently instructing the interested reader on how we know about the past, as well as what kinds of actions and emotions the people of a particular time and place might have experienced. While several stories might be equally "true" based on a given assemblage, or assortment of artifacts, such possible stories are few compared to those that could not be true.

This perspective provides an opportunity to approach questions of gender in the past (Nelson 2004a), since writing a story (unless it is science fiction) requires gendering the characters and the plot. In each of my novels, I problematize the notion that leaders are male, an assumption built into our standard words for leaders (e.g., "chief," "king"), by making the leaders female (Nelson 2008b). Anne Pyburn (2004) has eloquently addressed this problem, especially with regard to archaeological theories about the origin of the state, and I use her perspective in writing fiction. I am often challenged by someone in an audience to explain how I *know* the leaders are female. I reply that perhaps they can tell me why they believe they are male. If our present culture makes women leaders seem odd enough to create "surplus alienation," perhaps this is a favor to the readers. It makes them realize that, although we do not know the gender arrangements of the past, they do not have to mirror those of the present.

The same arguments can be made in regard to imagining the beliefs and rituals of the people whose archaeological remains I have studied. Beliefs are rarely obvious in prehistoric sites, so I use local ethnography to help fill in that gap. Shamanism is still practiced widely in most parts of East Asia—although there was an attempt to root it out in China—and it is a logical supposition that animistic beliefs and shamanist rituals supplied the ideological underpinning of their lives.

The specific question of whether novels "objectify" the people of the past, instead of taking them as subjects, is not the immediate concern of the novelist trying to write a story and engage readers in the details of life in some place and time in the archaeological past. But to approach this concern, I will weave together the ways I have worked on narrative and character with the thorny question of whether the real people whose fragmentary remains provide the building blocks for the story are "objectified" by the story.

I try to listen for the potsherds (and other artifacts and features) to "speak." If they do, I consider how I "heard" them by means of exploring my own novels, less from the point of view of an archaeologist explaining archaeological discoveries to students and the public and more to examine what each novel is built on and to question whether the result does objectify the novels' subjects. Brian Fagan's (2010: 17) dictum about the reason for writing archaeology for the public is useful here: "The challenge is to make the past come alive, using an archaeological record that is often, to put it mildly, unspectacular." The source materials for my first novel would certainly fit Fagan's description, and yet it is the best loved of all my novels.

THE CLARA ALDEN SERIES

Spirit Bird Journey takes place in Early Neolithic Korea. The data are sparse and have little that would interest an art historian—or a looter. But ethnic differences could be implied by those talking potsherds. To explain briefly, the pottery on the west side of the Korean peninsula is similar to pottery in sites in northeast China (Nelson 1990), while that on the east side resembles pottery in Japan. Since no texts pertain to this time period in Korea, ethnography and folklore had to be layered into the gap. At the same time, I made use of theory, including gender theory and theories of shamanism.

In my novel *Jade Dragon*, the Hongshan culture of northeast China is considerably more complex. To probe this culture with its similarly structured villages but impressive ceremonial space, I posited that this region would have had shamanistic leadership. A structure in which life-sized statues of a woman, a pig, and a bird (or dragon?) made it likely that leadership might have been female in Hongshan times.

For creating *The Jade Phoenix*, contemporaneous written material as well as extensive archaeology and later history was available, providing more material for a novel but presenting a new problem. I had to create a character whose name is known—Lady Hao of the Shang Dynasty and her husband, King Wu Ding.

My novels are unified by having an archaeologist—I named her Clara—narrate the stories. She not only experiences the prehistoric past through dreams or visions, she also has conversations in the present about the archaeology while she is actively pursuing new discoveries about those cultures. Through her explanations of what was found, how archaeologists work, and how they interpret their results, the reader has a glimpse of the archaeological enterprise.

In each of the first two novels, Clara is working at an archaeological site and dreams—or possibly visits—the past of that place and time. I wanted Clara to be physically present in some way and seen by the prehistoric characters but not able to bring knowledge from the present into the past. Thus, when she participates in the past in her dreams or visions, she flies into the past as a bird, a benign and helpful spirit who appears at moments of crisis or change. She isn't just any bird. She flies into the past as a yellow Spirit Bird, with a crest like a shaman's crown and a long, flashy tail.

The novels differ in the way they are framed, depending on the amount and variety of artifacts available around which to weave the story. *Spirit Bird Journey*, which takes place in Neolithic Korea (Nelson 1999), is based on artifacts and features for the details of the story. In *Jade Dragon* (Nelson 2004b), which takes place in the Hongshan culture of northeast China in the Late Neolithic, methods largely take the place of artifacts, although artifacts make many appearances in the story to clue the reader in to particular parts of the story.

In *Spirit Bird Journey*, Clara requests to use random sampling for her part of the dig. Her random excavation units then form part of the story, as a way to introduce archaeological methods to readers. Methods explored in *Jade Dragon* include ground-penetrating radar, the use of global positioning systems, and archaeoastronomy. The third novel, *The Jade Phoenix* (Nelson n.d.), is based on considerably more evidence than either of the prehistoric novels. The ancient heroine is a real person, Lady Hao, who was often mentioned by name in the oracle bones of the Shang Dynasty of China, and in her un-looted tomb her name was inscribed on many of her artifacts. This richness of detail makes it easy to insert archaeological theories into the story and demonstrate the constructed nature of what we know about the past.

Perhaps the use of artifacts and features, archaeological methods, and archaeological theories works to distance the reality of those who actually lived in the times we describe in novels. On the other hand, it may allow the reader the double vision of the archaeological practices and the individuals who left behind traces of their lives.

WRITING *SPIRIT BIRD JOURNEY*

When the culture the archaeologist describes is preliterate, artifacts have to carry the plot, with some help from ethnography. I first thought about the plot of *Spirit Bird Journey* in connection with the fact that the pottery on the west side of Korea has geometric incising and pointed bases, while east coast pottery has flat bases and is largely undecorated. I wondered if such regional differences could reflect cultural or even physical differences. I began by imagining a population on the east coast of the peninsula that was related to the Ainu of northern Japan and the central region and west coast of Korea as peopled by Mongolian groups. Building a story on the east coast sites, where the novel begins, I used ethnographic materials from the Ainu to invent the perishable material culture of the people of "Bird Mountain Village." My thought was that trying the concept out in a story might reveal the flaws of positing physically different people meeting each other (Nelson 2003). This is particularly important in the regions of East Asia, where ethnicity is often inferred from artifacts.

I wanted the story in the present to reflect the story in the past so it would not seem entirely gratuitous. Thus, I created a narrator whose culture didn't match her phenotype—a Korean girl adopted as an infant by American parents. Clara opens the book by commenting on feeling "at home" upon arriving in Korea and seeing only Korean faces like hers while at the same time being bewildered about how to act and react as a stranger to the culture. Before describing the sites and artifacts, I needed to find a plausible way to allow Clara her expeditions into the past. The solution was to introduce her right away to Korean shamanism. On the first page she is teased into wearing a shaman's costume and dancing at the end ceremony, or *kut* (as described by Laurel Kendall [1985]). The beat of the percussion and the movement of the dance cause Clara's yellow wings to sprout and fly her to Bird Mountain Village, where a baby is born to become the village leader. She is named for the yellow Spirit Bird who appeared at her birth. Her tribe is the Golden tribe, thus the prehistoric heroine is named Golden Flyingbird. Her whole life, including her lessons, her rituals, her travels, and her funeral, creates the action in the prehistoric story. The village of her birth is based on the site of Osanni on the west coast of Korea (Im 1982; Im and Kwon 1984).

Many events in Flyingbird's life are based on unusual artifacts. A shell that was altered to look like a face, with round holes for eyes and a mouth, becomes an evil object, brought to Bird Mountain Village by a marrying-in bride from the south where such shells are common. It is possible to trace animistic ideas in Korea from antiquity to the present (Nelson 1995). A small, poorly crafted jar becomes a burial gift from a child to her grandmother.

Not all artifacts were so obvious. Pointed objects that have been found at no other site were an interpretive problem. The excavators made no attempt to ascribe a function to these stone tools. The heavy granite artifacts were ground, with a knob on top and a groove that appears to have been used to tie or wind string around. It would have required time to grind them into their very specific shape. The only thing I could conceive of for a function would be a weight. They are too large to be loom weights or net sinkers. The site is on the edge of the sea. Perhaps they were used to measure depth with a cord, but why would the people have needed to know the ocean's depth? I surmised the inhabitants had boats for deep-sea fishing. With boats, they could have traveled up and down the coast visiting relatives in other villages. Thinking about objects in this way reveals that villages with a fishing subsistence are not necessarily simple—in fact, such villages continue to exist in the modern world (Nelson 2009).

Osanni, the site forming the basis for descriptions of Flyingbird's village, is a typical village of the east coast, with sub-rectangular, semi-subterranean house floors, each with a central hearth. However, one house clearly has two hearths. We often suppose that the largest house belongs to the leader. Since I had imagined a matrilineal society, it had to be Flyingbird's house. Why would there be two hearths? If there were a headman of the village, no one would have a problem supposing he had two wives. So if she was the leader, it follows that Flyingbird must have had two husbands. To emphasize the ethnicity theme, one of the men is from a nearby village, the other is a man with Asian eye-folds and high cheek bones from across the mountains. While we do not know much about the specific appearance of any of these Early Neolithic peoples, it can be inferred from present populations that both "Paleo-asiatic" and "Mongolian" people existed in this region in Neolithic times (Kim 2011).

WRITING *JADE DRAGON*

The novel *Jade Dragon* (Nelson 2004b) is based on the site of Niuheliang in northeast China (Barnes and Guo 1996; Fang and Wei 1986; Guo 1995; Guo and Ma 1985; LICRA 1986; Sun 1986). I was the first foreigner allowed to see the site. It was so unusual that it caught my imagination at first acquaintance. Chinese archaeologists, however, had already created an interesting scenario from their excavations. They called Niuheliang the "Goddess Temple" site and named it, along with similar sites, the Hongshan culture.

At the center of the site is a 22-meter-long building with an irregular shape, including a three-lobed projection in which were found fragments of life-sized statues of unbaked clay with painted surfaces. The most spectacular of these was a face with inset green jade eyes. The statues included several females of different sizes, the jaw and trotters of a pig/boar, and the claw-like foot, which could be interpreted as a dragon or a very large bird. Furthermore, the insides of the walls were decorated both with paint and three-dimensional patterns. Compared to other fragmentary buildings, this is clearly an important ceremonial building. Chinese archaeologists called it Nüshen Miao, the Goddess Temple (Fang and Wei 1986; Nelson 1991).

In addition to the possible ritual building, several large tombs were excavated containing skeletons accompanied only by jade objects, which were placed around the bodies in positions that suggested earrings, bracelets, hair ornaments, and jade pendants. The jades had been made in distinct shapes—several kinds of birds, clouds, fish, and circular shapes were carved from thin slabs of jade. A thicker open ring with a pig head on one end and a hole in the middle for suspension was often found in a central place on the chest. Another round shape with an animal head is twice as large but with a thinner ring. The head is long and thin, with almond-shaped eyes and a mane. It looks more like a horse than a pig, although it is also lumped with the pig-dragons. I interpret this type as representing horses.

About 25 kilometers away another ritual site was excavated, which was found to have low round and square constructions referred to as "altars" and other low walls leading between these platforms. Artifacts included more jade objects and both medium and small statues of female figures. Some of these statues wore rope belts and sat with crossed legs (Guo and Zhang 1984).

Yet another construction of unknown use was an earthen "pyramid" surrounded by a circle of marble-like stones set flat into the ground and two other such circles within the artificial mound, one about halfway up and the other near the top. Near the very top of the mounds were some crude, broken pottery cups with incrustations, which upon testing proved to be copper (Han 1993). What wonderful raw material for a story! The complexity of the Hongshan culture has led to speculation that it was a proto-state (Nelson 1996a, 2002; Sun 1986).

In my story, Clara flies into the site and becomes the Spirit Bird of Jade, the Late Neolithic heroine. Jade trains a piglet she names Piggy to do tricks and is learning from her mother to be a shaman and a leader. I have imagined that Jade and Piggy and Spirit Bird are the threesome represented in the Goddess Temple, commemorated after Jade has become a leader and a shaman.

It is clear from the archaeology that pigs are extremely important in the Hongshan culture (Nelson 1996b). Chinese folktales often include pigs as characters. The travels of a girl, a pig, and a bird are thus consonant with the culture, both archaeologically and ethnographically. Since there are other sites in the region, in my story Jade travels—with her pig and bird companions—to the east, south, north, and west, allowing me to describe those areas and their differences. Trade is clearly an important feature of Hongshan (Nelson 1993; Shelach 1999). The way the jade emblems were carved could be described based on various studies (e.g., Guo 1997), and meanings could be ascribed to them. Horses appear in the story, ridden by Central Asian explorers (Anthony and Brown 1991) seeking new sources of tin for their bronze industry.

The prehistoric story thus flowed from the artifacts and features of Hongshan sites. But needing a plot for Clara in the present, I used part of the framing story to discuss archaeological methods. I had made a beginning in this direction in *Spirit Bird Journey*, where Clara insists on trying random sampling and codes everything into a computer. For this story I used ground-penetrating radar (GPR), seeking evidence of earlier buildings. I also introduced an astronomer, who comes upon the GPR crew by chance. He joins them to make measurements of sun and moon risings and settings, using a global positioning system (GPS). He uses the artificial hill for a backsight, measuring angles over the hilltop burials, reasoning that there was no other obvious purpose for the hill to have been constructed where it was (Nelson et al. 2014).

More characters are brought into the story. A busload of Korean archaeologists has come to visit the site, and Clara (and perhaps the reader) has met some of them before on her Korean adventure. Korean Bronze Age archaeology and ancient Chinese texts suggest that some Korean ancestors came from northeast China in the Early Bronze Age. Therefore, Korean archaeologists were eager to see this site, with its square-based pyramidal tomb resembling those of an early Korean kingdom. This possible homeland of Korean culture is home to many ethnic Koreans in the present (Kim Il-Sung, the first ruler of North Korea, was born in Shenyang, which was then part of Manchuria, as named by the Japanese).

The prehistoric story didn't seem exciting enough for anyone but an East Asian archaeologist to want to read, so I arranged for another character to join the crew mysteriously. The problem of looting at archaeological sites is so serious in China that the penalty if convicted is death. This penalty still does not deter the destruction of archaeological sites at a breathtaking rate. It seemed worth integrating looting into the modern story.

Thus, looters appear at the site, and Clara and a young woman student go missing. They have been kidnapped by the men doing the looting and are bound and taken to Hong Kong in a van with the stolen artifacts. The Korean bus follows the van, and the chase is on. From then on the emphasis is on the problem of looting, and the denouement will not be revealed here.

WRITING *THE JADE PHOENIX*

My third archaeological foray into the world of novelists is called *The Jade Phoenix* (Nelson n.d.). *The Jade Phoenix* is the story of Fu (Lady) Hao of the Shang Dynasty of China around 1250 BCE. She was certainly the wife of King Wu Ding and probably his queen (or one of them). Many artifacts adorned her very rich and untouched tomb, and written texts supplement the artifacts. It is uncertain what being a queen meant in Shang China, but three extraordinary tombs of women have been excavated, and they are presumed to be those of queens (Linduff 2002). In the succeeding Zhou Dynasty, the king could have many wives but only one queen, but we do not know the rules for the Shang Dynasty.

Wu Ding inquired about Lady Hao's health in writing on oracle bones, as well as whether to send her to battle as a general, along with other questions to be answered by his ancestral spirits. These are the first contemporaneous texts in China to guide the understanding of archaeological discoveries (Keightley 1978, 1984).

The inclusion of texts provides constraints as well as opportunities for telling a story. While a full picture of Lady Hao's life does not emerge from the oracle bones, Fu Hao is mentioned on oracle bones at least 170 times (Keightley 1999). These references provide guideposts for describing the life of Lady Hao. We know she was a general; in one specific case, she led 13,000 troops to battle against one of Wu Ding's many adversaries. She must have been good at leading troops to war because she is mentioned as a war leader several times in the oracle bones, and many weapons were placed in her tomb. We know she bore at least three children, two of whom were "inauspicious" in David Keightley's (2000) translation—in other words, girls. Her son, Zu Jia, appears in a list of Shang kings.

The tomb itself, with its wealth of artifacts, provides more grist for the story. Lady Hao was outfitted to become a revered ancestor, with bronze vessels in large numbers for serving both food and meat. One group of bronzes is unique—a kind of bronze stove, with three holes into which bronze pots with pointed bases could be set. Based on this artifact, I imagined King Wu Ding and Lady Hao creating a drawing of the bronze stove to resemble the pottery stoves of Lady Hao's homeland. Wu Ding's main queen appears to have been Lady Jing (identification based on inscriptions from a looted tomb [Linduff

2003]). Her tomb contained the largest bronze *ding* ever found. I created another scene in which Lady Jing rages about Lady Hao's bronze stove and is placated with this giant ding.

Lady Hao's tomb included three decorated bronze axes, one showing open-mouthed tigers surrounding a human head. This ax would certainly have been suitable for chopping off human heads, and indeed many severed heads have been unearthed. Furthermore, Lady Hao's tomb includes sixteen human sacrifices placed in niches. One had been chopped through the waist. I joined the ax and the severed spine together in a vignette in which Lady Hao orders this cruel manner of execution. I imagined that the sacrificed person had been Lady Hao's handmaid, who did not want to go to the Spirit World with Lady Hao. Having been selected for death, the handmaid appeals to King Wu Ding, who finds her too beautiful to have her head chopped off. When Lady Hao hears this order from her husband, she gets around it by having the girl chopped in half. Although I portrayed Lady Hao as mostly a kind and generous person, this scene is the culmination of her acceptance of the violence of Shang and her awareness of Wu Ding's dalliance with her maid.

The physical site of the Late Shang capital is modern Anyang in Central China. A great deal of excavation has taken place, making it easy to describe the Shang city and its environs and buildings. Other archaeological finds include a U-shaped building open to the east, which has been interpreted as a temple, and a long narrow building thought to be the palace apartments. These attributes were helpful in describing Lady Hao's surroundings (Keightley 2000).

But what about the servants? Little is known of the ordinary people of Shang except for those who were sacrificed, and they were variously treated (buried without heads or in groups of heads only, jumbled in a group, or buried singly in rows, kneeling under the edge of a building, placed in niches in the burials of royalty). This is often a problem in state-level societies, where excavation is tilted toward the grandiose and the precious, especially things found in tombs and temples.

In Shang, a small jade of a kneeling female has been interpreted as a servant, but her clothing is embroidered. If she was a servant, she must have been a servant of royalty. Among the excavations are some dark pits with stairs leading down into them that have been interpreted as houses of the poor. In my story, Lady Hao asks to see where her lady's maid lives and is appalled when she sees the dark and dingy hovel.

The palaces are long and narrow, suggesting that perhaps each of Wu Ding's wives had her own set of rooms. Thus, a harem-like arrangement of royal children raised together does not seem to be the case. I have imagined therefore that Lady Hao and her children live together and that Wu Ding visits them when he has the time and inclination.

Oracle bone inscriptions are an excellent source for continuing on with my theme of female leadership. While there are no queens in the Shang king lists, Lady Hao clearly plays leadership roles. She is not only a general but also a landowner. She is sometimes the scribe on oracle bones, and there are hints that she performed as a shaman. In the story, she gains access to the king's mother through using her own shaman rites to calm the wind thought to be the cause of Lady Shang's illness.

I first became interested in Lady Hao because of the apparent connections with the Chinese northeast, where I had worked (Nelson 1991). Katheryn Linduff (2002) has seen the connection, too, and commented on it. Some non-Shang artifacts in her tomb suggest that Lady Hao was a stranger to Shang, and various places have been suggested as her homeland. I needed to tackle the question of where she came from. The most convincing location to me is northeast China. There is an archaeological reason and a logical reason for choosing this area. Artifacts in Lady Hao's coffin, placed as though they were personnel effects of importance to her, included knives and mirrors in the style of the "Northern Zone," the Dongbei and Inner Mongolia (Linduff 1997). Perhaps they were gifts from her family, brought with her to the Yellow River region. In addition, there is the sudden appearance of horses and chariots at the same time as Lady Hao. Horses and chariots must have come from the northeast or the northwest (Fitzgerald-Huber 1996) and may have come to Shang from Lady Hao's homeland (Linduff 1997). While there are northern bronzes besides those of Lady Hao at Anyang, they are only in the graves of charioteers.

Related to Lady Hao's homeland is the question of domesticated horses (Anthony 2007; Anthony and Brown 1991; Fitzgerald-Huber 1996; Linduff 1998). Horse bones were discovered in the Hongshan culture and also in Shandong China during the Longshan culture. The question of their domestication is largely unstudied. The steppe people probably rode horses to move their flocks. Therefore, I have supposed that Lady Hao's natal family also rode horses, although hard evidence is lacking. The horses used to pull chariots in the Late Shang were obviously domesticated. Certainly, the steppe peoples both rode and herded horses (Anthony 2007: chapter 10).

Clara and her bird flights to the past were still my vehicle for telling the prehistoric story, as well as explaining the archaeology to the reader. For this novel, the framing story includes Clara's sister Chama, an art historian, who has been sent by a museum to scout for artifacts to use in an exhibit about Fu Hao. Chama invites Clara to come with her to China as her archaeological assistant. This configuration allows me to discuss some theoretical ideas about early state formation as the sisters disagree from the perspectives of their different fields.

One of my interests in the novels is testing the idea of K. C. Chang (1983, 2005) that shamanism was a basis for state formation in China. Chang saw King Wu Ding as solely the shaman, as do others (Childs-Johnson 1989). Shamans were leaders elsewhere in Asia (Thomas and Humphrey 1994). But shamanism in East Asia is largely a female occupation (Ching 1997; Nelson 2008a; Tedlock 2005). In pursuing the idea of female leadership, I imagined that Lady Hao, obviously an important personage from the writing on oracle bones, might well have functioned as a shaman. Tiger decorations on bronzes appear with Lady Hao, so I have provided her with a real tiger that she raised from a cub. Bird representations are also common in her artifacts, so Clara as a bird is appropriate for Lady Hao's story.

The tale is largely told in first person by Clara, both in the present and in the past, but now and then some other human character in the present story is given a voice—including the archaeologists at the site—when the story requires a different voice. Lady Hao's voice is only heard when she speaks to the Spirit Bird.

For the story of the past I imagined twin daughters, Joy and Bliss, of a queen in a matrilineal society somewhere on the edge of the grasslands of Inner Mongolia. One of the twins will follow her mother as queen. Clara sees the birth of the twins, and she is seen as Joy's Spirit Bird.

When the girls become teenagers, Wu Ding is chosen as the future king of Shang. He travels to Shandong in the northeast to learn about horses of which he has heard rumors and goes further to the Chifeng region to learn about the chariots recently acquired from the steppe people. Joy seduces Wu Ding, and Bliss is left to become queen of her polity.

But Wu Ding has been promised to marry his cousin Pear Flower (later Lady Jing), the sweetheart of his older brother, who had been expected to be selected as the heir apparent. Joy doesn't know of this arrangement until they arrive in Shang. Joy finds herself in opposition to Pear Flower, herself a royal member of the Shang, as well as Wu Ding's mother, Lady Shang, the queen of the current king. Pear Flower's details are created from the only woman's tomb among the royal king's burials. I reasoned that for a woman to be buried with the kings, she had to be descended from kings on both sides—possibly a cousin of the king, as well as his formal queen.

By using her shamanic powers and her intelligence, Joy becomes Lady Hao, the second queen of Wu Ding but the one he loves best (she turns up most often on the oracle bones). From this point the story moves into the violence of the Shang, who fought nearly continuous battles and beheaded many (presumable) war captives in honor of the ancestors, royal buildings, and the deaths of kings. Headless bodies are found, as well as piles of skulls. The Shang ancestors were a bloodthirsty lot.

I wondered how a woman from a matrilineal society, who might herself have become queen of her polity, would deal with a culture that allowed three queens (based on what may be three royal female burials [Linduff 2003]) and perhaps multiple other wives (more than sixty possible "ladies" mentioned on oracle bones). When she arrives in Shang (in the story), she learns for the first time that Wu Ding must marry Pear Flower. Later, Joy/Lady Hao is present when other wives or concubines are offered to Wu Ding.

CONCLUSION

Many questions arise when producing fiction based on archaeology. Whether the individuals have been portrayed accurately and without "objectivizing" them is an important question but one for which there is no "objective" answer. It is necessary to use objects and other facets of archaeological discoveries, and texts if we have them, to make stories. No matter how careful the author may be to stick to the archaeological facts and how reasonable the explanations in an author's note at the end, some other archaeologists are sure to object to details of the story.

It is worth thinking out such stories because having to make a story sharpens both archaeological reasoning and archaeological observation. The novelist must look closely at the archaeology to create the people and the story and hope that both have not fallen too far from reality. There is no way to test for objectivity or to know how the ancient people might respond if they could read my stories.

REFERENCES

Allen, Mitchell, and Rosemary A. Joyce. 2010. "Communicating Archaeology in the 21st Century." In *Voices in American Archaeology*, ed. Wendy Ashmore, Dorothy T. Lippert, and Barbara J. Mills, 270–90. Washington, DC: SAA Press.

Anthony, David. 2007. *The Horse, the Wheel, and Language*. Princeton: Princeton University Press.

Anthony, David, and Dorcas R. Brown. 1991. "The Origins of Horseback Riding." *Antiquity* 65: 22–38.

Barnes, Gina L., with Dashun Guo. 1996. "The Ritual Landscape of 'Boar Mountain' Basin: The Niuheliang Site Complex of North-eastern China." *World Archaeology* 28 (2): 209–19. http://dx.doi.org/10.1080/00438243.1996.9980341.

Binford, Lewis. 1972. *An Archaeological Perspective*. New York: Seminar Press.

Chang, K. C. 1983. *Art, Myth and Ritual: The Path to Political Authority in Ancient China*. Cambridge: Harvard University Press.

Chang, K. C. 2005. "The Rise of Kings and the Formation of City-States." In *The Formation of Chinese Civilization: An Archaeological Perspective*, ed. K. C. Chang and P. Xu, 125–40. New Haven: Yale University Press.

Childs-Johnson, Elizabeth. 1989. "The Shang Bird: Intermediary to the Supernatural." *Orientations* 20 (1): 53–61.

Ching, Julia. 1997. *Mysticism and Kingship in China*. Cambridge: Cambridge University Press. http://dx.doi.org/10.1017/CBO9780511612046.

Fagan, Brian. 2010. *Writing Archaeology: Telling Stories about the Past*, 2nd ed. Walnut Creek, CA: Left Coast.

Fang, Dianchun, and Fan Wei. 1986. "Brief Report on the Excavation of Goddess Temple and Stone Graves of the Hongshan Culture at Niuheliang." *Liaohai Wenwu Xuegan* 1986 (8): 1–17.

Fitzgerald-Huber, Louisa G. 1996. "The First Horses on China's Northwest Border." *Newsletter of the Institute for Ancient Equestrian Studies* 2: 27.

Geertz, Clifford. 1973. *Interpretation of Cultures*. New York: Basic Books.

Guo, Dashun. 1995. "Hongshan and Related Cultures." In *The Archaeology of Northeast China*, ed. Sarah Milledge Nelson, 21–64. London: Routledge.

Guo, Dashun. 1997. "Understanding the Burial Rituals of the Hongshan Culture through Jade." In *Chinese Jades*, ed. Rosemary E. Scott, 27–36. London: Percival David Foundation.

Guo, Dashun, and Sha Ma. 1985. "Neolithic Cultures of the Liao River Valley and Its Vicinity." *Kaogu Xuebao* 1985 (4): 417–44.

Guo, Dashun, and Keju Zhang. 1984. "Brief Report on the Excavation of Hongshan Buildings at Dongshanzui in Kezuo County, Liaoning Province." *Wen Wu* 1984 (11): 1–11.

Han, Rubin. 1993. "Recent Archaeological and Metallurgical Achievements of the University of Science and Technology, Beijing." Paper presented at the International Congress, Chinese Archaeology Enters the 21st Century.

Im, Hyo-jai. 1982. "Osanni Summary Report." *Hanguk Kogohak* 9: 26–33.

Im, Hyo-jai, and Haksu Kwon. 1984. *Osanni Site: A Neolithic Village Site on the East Coast*. Archaeological and Anthropological Papers, vol. 9. Seoul: Seoul National University.

Keightley, David N. 1978. *Sources of Shang History: The Oracle Bone Inscriptions of Bronze Age China*. Berkeley: University of California Press.

Keightley, David N. 1984. "Late Shang Divination: The Magico-Religious Legacy." In *Explorations in Early Chinese Cosmology*, ed. Henry Rosemont Jr., 11–34. JAAR Thematic Studies. Chico, CA: Scholar's Press.

Keightley, David N. 1999. "At the Beginning: The Status of Women in Neolithic and Shang China." *Nan Nu* 1 (1): 1–63. http://dx.doi.org/10.1163/156852699X00054.

Keightley, David N. 2000. *The Ancestral Landscape: Time, Space and Community in Late Shang China*. Berkeley: Institute of East Asian Studies.

Kendall, Laurel. 1985. *Shamans, Housewives, and Other Restless Spirits*. Honolulu: University of Hawaii Press.

Kim Choong Soo. 2011. *Voices of Foreign Brides*. Lanham, MD: AltaMira.

Landau, Misia. 1991. *Narratives of Human Evolution*. New Haven: Yale University Press.

LICRA (Liaoning Institute of Cultural Relics and Archaeology). 1986. "Brief Report on the Excavation of the 'Goddess Temple' and the Stone Graves of the Hongshan Culture at Niuheliang in Liaoning Province." *Wen Wu* 1986 (8): 1–17.

Linduff, Katheryn M. 1997. "An Archaeological Overview." In *Ancient Bronzes of the Eastern Eurasian Steppes*, ed. Emma Bunker, 18–112. New York: Arthur M. Sackler Foundation.

Linduff, Katheryn M. 1998. "A Walk on the Wild Side: Late Shang Appropriation of Horses in China." In *Prehistoric Steppe Adaptations and the Horse*, ed. Marsha Levine, Colin Renfrew, and Katherine Boyle, 139–62. Cambridge: McDonald Institute Monographs.

Linduff, Katheryn M. 2002. "Women's Lives Memorialized in Burial in Ancient China at Anyang." In *In Pursuit of Gender: Worldwide Archaeological Perspectives*, ed. Sarah Milledge Nelson and Miriam Rosen-Ayalon, 257–88. Walnut Creek, CA: AltaMira.

Linduff, Katheryn M. 2003. "Many Wives, One Queen in Shang China." In *Ancient Queens: Archaeological Explorations*, ed. Sarah Milledge Nelson, 59–75. Walnut Creek, CA: AltaMira.

Nelson, Sarah Milledge. 1990. "Neolithic Sites in Northeastern China and Korea." *Antiquity* 64: 234–48.

Nelson, Sarah Milledge. 1991. "The Goddess Temple and the Status of Women at Niuheliang, China." In *The Archaeology of Gender*, ed. Dale Walde and Noreen D. Willows, 302–8. Calgary: Archaeological Association of the University of Calgary.

Nelson, Sarah Milledge. 1993. "The Development of Complexity in Prehistoric North China." *Sino-Platonic Papers* 631 (17): entire issue.

Nelson, Sarah Milledge. 1995. "The Roots of Animism in Korea, from the Earliest Inhabitants to the Silla Kingdom." In *Korean Cultural Roots*, ed. Hwan K. Kwon, 19–30. Chicago: North Park College and Theological Seminary.

Nelson, Sarah Milledge. 1996a. "Ideology and the Formation of an Early State in Northeast China." In *The Ideology of the Early State*, ed. Henri Claessen and Jarich von Oosten, 153–69. Leiden: E. J. Brill.

Nelson, Sarah Milledge. 1996b. "Ritualized Pigs and the Origins of Complex Society: Hypotheses Concerning the Hongshan Culture." *Early China* 20: 1–16.

Nelson, Sarah Milledge. 1999. *Spirit Bird Journey*. Littleton, CO: RKLOG Press.

Nelson, Sarah Milledge. 2002. "Ideology, Power, and Gender: Emergent Complex Society in Northeast China." In *In Pursuit of Gender: Worldwide Archaeological Perspectives*, ed. Sarah Milledge Nelson and Miriam Rosen-Ayalon, 73–80. Walnut Creek, CA: AltaMira.

Nelson, Sarah Milledge. 2003. "RKLOG: Archaeologists as Fiction Writers." In *Ancient Muses, Archaeology and the Arts*, ed. John H. Jameson, John E. Ehrenhard, and Christine A. Finn, 162–68. Tuscaloosa: University of Alabama Press.

Nelson, Sarah Milledge. 2004a. *Gender in Archaeology: Analyzing Power and Prestige*. Walnut Creek, CA: AltaMira.

Nelson, Sarah Milledge. 2004b. *Jade Dragon*. Littleton, CO: RKLOG Press.

Nelson, Sarah Milledge. 2008a. *Shamanism and the Origin of States: Spirit, Power and Gender in East Asia*. Walnut Creek, CA: AltaMira.

Nelson, Sarah Milledge. 2008b. "Feminist Theory, Leadership, and the Spirits of States in East Asia." *Archaeologies* 7 (1): 34–55. http://dx.doi.org/10.1007/s11759 -011-9165-9.

Nelson, Sarah Milledge. 2009. "Northeast Asia in Prehistory: Korean Coastal Sites." *North Pacific Prehistory* 3: 69–86.

Nelson, Sarah Milledge. n.d. The Jade Phoenix. MS in author's files.

Nelson, Sarah Milledge, Rachel Roberts, Rachel Matson, and Robert Stencel. 2014. *The Hongshan Papers*. BAR International Series 2618: 97–105.

Pyburn, K. Anne. 2004. "Rethinking Complex Society." In *Ungendering Civilization*, ed. K. Anne Pyburn, 1–46. New York: Routledge.

Shelach, Gideon. 1999. *Leadership Strategies, Economic Activity, and Interregional Interaction: Social Complexity in Northeast China*. New York: Kluwer/Plenum.

Sun, Shuodao. 1986. "Niuheliang in the Hongshan Culture." *Liaohai Wenwu Xuegan* 1986 (10): 53–56.

Tedlock, Barbara. 2005. *The Woman in the Shaman's Body*. New York: Bantam Books.

Thomas, Nicholas, and Caroline Humphrey. 1994. *Shamanism, History and the State.* Ann Arbor: University of Michigan Press.

Tilley, Christopher. 1993. *Interpretive Archaeology.* Providence: Berg.

Wylie, Alison. 2002. *Thinking from Things.* Berkeley: University of California Press.

---

11

*Limits of Archaeological
Emplotments from
the Perspective of
Excavating Nazi
Extermination Centers*

In 2006 a student in my department, Yoram Haimi, asked me to supervise his doctoral dissertation. He suggested excavating the Nazi extermination center of Sobibór in eastern Poland. As a prehistorian, my immediate reaction was to refuse, but since I was aware that nobody in Israel is formally qualified to supervise such a dissertation, I agreed. The reason I agreed is that members of my family, including my grandparents, were exterminated at Treblinka, another Nazi extermination center in eastern Poland. Until 2009 we carried out three short field seasons at Sobibór, two of them devoted to excavations and one to a geophysical survey.

In the summer of 2010 Reinhard Bernbeck invited me to participate in the Society for American Archaeology 2011 symposium Alternative Narratives in Archaeology, the subject of the current volume. He told me that his students found that our 2009 article on the archaeology of Nazi extermination centers (Gilead, Haimi, and Mazurek 2009) contains an "objectivist archaeological description." Although I first took this as a compliment, after reading the symposium abstract I realized that the organizers of the symposium probably refuted my objectivist approach since they were, as the symposium title indicated, "Against Objectivized Subjects" (Bernbeck, this volume).

I begin with a terminological note. Our research is based on archaeological sites and artifacts. These are our "objects," literally and ontologically. The objects and sites are conceived by us and influence us and thus

Isaac Gilead

DOI: 10.5876/9781607323815.c011

turn us into "subjects" (but also objectify us in certain aspects). In the session abstract, the organizers suggest that the traditional expository texts and images—that is, technical and scientific writing—treat the people of the past with disrespect, at a safe and unknowable distance. I have no intention of disregarding past subjects, be they Chalcolithic villagers or victims and survivors of Nazi extermination centers.

The archaeological sites and features recovered during excavations do not fully illuminate past realities; therefore, narration is not always possible, especially an objectivist one. At the 2011 Theoretical Archaeological Group meetings in Bristol, Milena Gošić and I delivered a paper titled "Telling the Story of Copper: Towards a Semi-Fictional Reconstruction of the Ghassulian Copper Working." The copper industry of the second half of the fifth millennium BC cal. is relatively well researched. However, the probable ritualized protocol of the actual smelting of copper has never been discussed. By attempting to write a semi-fictional reconstruction, we explicitly acknowledge the advantage, in certain circumstances, of activating our subjects by narration.

I admit that the article mentioned earlier (Gilead, Haimi, and Mazurek 2009) on the archaeology of extermination centers is to a considerable degree an "objectivist description." However, I understand "objectivist" and use it in this chapter as a term related to "empiricist," "positivist," "processualist," and the like. I think the objectivist approach is called for in dealing with at least some aspects of the archaeological record. Spatial and temporal organization of typological regularities and settlement patterns, for example, cannot be carried out without an objectivist procedure.

The archaeological background of my chapter is based on the brief overview, cited earlier, of the main results of the excavations carried out at the extermination centers of Chełmno, Bełżec, and Sobibór (ibid.). A point made in that overview has bearing on issues discussed in this chapter. I maintain that "the extermination of Jews at Sobibór and other centers in particular, is *a historically established truth* which does not need to be proven by archaeological excavations" (ibid.: 13; emphasis mine). This is relevant to issues of objectivity, historical relativism (e.g., Hayden White, and discussion below), and multivocality—issues dealt with in the current volume.

Truth, objectivism, representation, and alternative narratives are prominent in historical, ideological, and aesthetic studies devoted to the Holocaust (i.e., "Final Solution," "Shoah"), and some of them are pertinent here. A major issue in the representation and narration of the Holocaust revolves around the approach of Hayden White (1973) in his *Metahistory* and later publications.

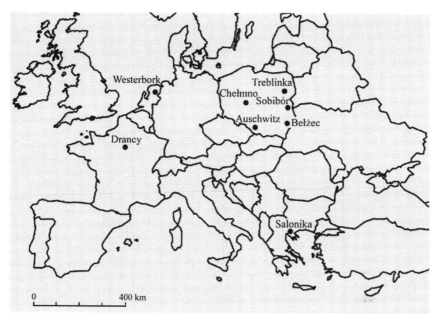

FIGURE II.I. *Map of Nazi extermination centers (from Gilead, Haimi, and Mazurek 2009: figure 1)*

THE ARCHAEOLOGY OF NAZI EXTERMINATION CENTERS

I summarize briefly a few aspects concerning the archaeology of the Nazi extermination centers (for details and references, see Gilead, Haimi, and Mazurek 2009; Sturdy Colls 2012). By the term *Nazi extermination centers* I mean sites constructed for the systematic elimination of humans, almost exclusively Jews. Victims from Eastern and Western Europe were transported to such places, murdered on arrival by carbon monoxide asphyxiation, and immediately cremated, buried, or both. During the first half of 1942, in the framework of the so-called Operation Reinhardt, the Nazis constructed three extermination centers in eastern Poland (Arad 1987)—Bełżec, Sobibór, and Treblinka—where the victims were murdered in gas chambers. At Chełmno in western Poland, the fourth extermination center, Jews were murdered in gas vans, mostly during 1942 (figure II.I).

From the archaeological perspective, in terms of layout, structures, and site formation processes, the four extermination centers clearly differ from Auschwitz-Birkenau and Majdanek—concentration and extermination centers. The latter were originally concentration camps, and forced labor was used

FIGURE 11.2. *Barracks at Majdanek (http://www.upcolorado.com/component/k2 /item/2712-subjects-and-narratives-in-archaeology-media; photo by author)*

there before, during, and after the systematic extermination of Jews took place. Since they were in use up to the arrival of the Red Army, their structures still stand today (figure 11.2). Other camps, such as Buchenwald and Dachau, to mention only two famous examples in Germany, were concentration centers, since there was no intention to murder the transportees upon their arrival. Here again, structures are still extant. The extermination centers were established solely for killing; when that task was accomplished during the second half of 1943, they were erased and no structural remains were left behind (figure 11.3).

It is estimated that more than 1.7 million Jews were exterminated during 1942–43 in the four extermination centers. In August and October 1943 slave workers in Treblinka and Sobibór, respectively, revolted and escaped, and about 100 of them survived the war. Their testimonies are an important source of information on the extermination process there.

Chełmno was the first extermination center to be excavated, in 1986. Bełżec and Sobibór were excavated in the late 1990s, and another excavation of Sobibór was begun in 2007 (most of Treblinka became a monument in the 1960s, and it has never been excavated). A survey of the main results has been published elsewhere (Gilead, Haimi, and Mazurek 2009), and in this chapter

FIGURE 11.3. *Sobibór, the Ash Monument (http://www.upcolorado.com/component/k2 /item/2712-subjects-and-narratives-in-archaeology-media; photo by author)*

I discuss just two aspects of the evidence. The most important point concerning the archaeology of extermination centers is that they were intentionally eliminated by the perpetrators a short time after their use terminated. Yitzhak Arad (1987: 373; emphasis added) described what happened: "He [the commandant of Treblinka] was responsible for *dismantling* the camp, *destroying the gas chambers, and erasing all signs of the extermination camp* . . . Bricks from the gas chambers were used for the farmhouse . . . As in Bełżec and Treblinka, all the buildings in Sobibór were destroyed and a farm was built."

The fact that the extermination centers were obliterated diminishes the possibility of recovering meaningful structural remains. This is significant if we consider John Moreland's (2001: 11) suggestion that by excavating gas chambers, archaeology, or its sub-discipline, historical archaeology, can fight what he calls the lie of the Holocaust deniers. Since the Nazis erased the gas chambers, not finding them is a reasonable possibility, a result that will undoubtedly be used to "support" the claims of Holocaust deniers. So far, no remains of gas chambers have been recovered in Bełżec, despite the excavator's claims (see Gilead, Haimi, and Mazurek 2009), and since the entire site has been covered and turned into a monument, no structural remains will be unearthed there in the foreseeable future. At Sobibór as well, no remains of gas chambers have been unearthed. If the Nazis left any remains, they are probably under the asphalt cover on which the two memorial monuments were erected, south of the ash hill (Gilbert 1997: 250).

Although the chances of recovering structural remains are limited, the possibility of their discovery is important because, to quote Raul Hilberg's (2001: 185) approach to historical texts, "any source may have significance." In addition to structures, the recovery of artifacts is also significant, as it has now been established that tens of thousands of artifacts can be discovered on the terrain of the former extermination centers (Gilead, Haimi, and Mazurek 2009). Artifacts that were used by both the perpetrators and the victims can shed light on many aspects of the extermination process and the everyday lives of the people involved. The case of the Lysol bottle described later illustrates this point. Moreover, artifacts not recovered by archaeologists will be looted by locals who have ravaged the terrain of extermination centers ever since they were erased by the Nazis in late 1943 (Gross and Grudzinska Gross 2012).

Archaeological excavations of extermination centers can also uncover written documents, similar to the known "Auschwitz Scrolls"—diaries and notes found near the crematoria at Birkenau (Cohen 1990, 1998), written in Yiddish by three members of the Sonderkommando, a unit of slave workers who burned the bodies of gassed victims. The "Auschwitz Scrolls," hidden in glass containers and recovered between 1945 and 1961, were partially damaged by moisture. Salman Gradowski wrote in the cover letter: "Dear finder, search everywhere, in every inch of soil. Tens of documents are buried under it" (cited in Gilbert 1986: 730). Thus, by means of archaeological excavations, such notebooks can be recovered from other extermination sites as well, although their state of preservation may be poor.

LIMITS OF REPRESENTATION

According to White (1973: 5–11), writing history consists of two major steps. The first is the arrangement of events in a sequence (chronicle), which is the basis for forming a story out of them, with a beginning, middle, and end. This is a technical phase that is followed by questions of a higher order, such as "what is the point of it all" (ibid.: 7) or how to explain it. Such questions can be answered in several ways. The most prominent among them is the one White calls "Explanation by Emplotment," that is, what kind of story is being told. He defines four modes of emplotment: Romance, Tragedy, Comedy, and Satire. Romance is a story of "triumph of good over evil," of "light over darkness," of redemption. Satire is the opposite—a drama of "diredemption" (ibid.:

8–9). An example of romance is the victory of democracy over fascism, and an example of a satire is the Nazis' "Final Solution" (Jenkins 1995: 165). In comedy, there are temporary triumphs, reconciliations, and festive occasions, and in tragedy the protagonists fall and there are no festive occasions (White 1973: 9).

White is regarded by most authorities as a historical relativist, since he asserts that the same historical chronicles/stories can be explained differently by working within the framework of distinct modes of emplotment. He clearly states: "When it is a matter of choosing among these alternative visions of history, the only grounds for preferring one over another are *moral* or *aesthetic* ones" (ibid.: 433; original emphasis), or "one must face the fact that when it comes to apprehending the historic record, there are no grounds to be found in the historical record itself for preferring one way of construing its meaning over another" (ibid.: 75). White was charged with "debilitating relativism," and his attempts to counter such charges (ibid.: 76) were unsuccessful (Kansteiner 1993). Thus, he is still considered a relativist who denies the possibility of objective knowledge. Richard Evans (1997: 100) suggests that for White, there is no difference between conducting research for writing a novel and conducting research for writing a history book.

White's scheme was discussed by archaeologists as well (e.g., Holtorf 2010; Joyce 2002; Pluciennik 1999). Although Mark Pluciennik (1999: 658) regards White's approach as stimulating, his insistence on literary forms over context is overdrawn. Rosemary Joyce (2002: 14, 36) praises White's concept of the historical narrative as a useful issue that archaeology must address but thinks his narrative forms are static. It is significant that Pluciennik does not consider the implication of White's relativism for archaeological narratives and that Joyce relates cursorily to this aspect. The editors of this volume suggest in their session abstract that we explore alternative forms of archaeological narratives, alternatives that "transcend the traditional limitations of expository prose and the linearity of language." No doubt those traditional narratives have limitations in terms of form and media, as well as in terms of content. The contributors to the current volume suggest an array of alternative narratives, ranging from creative nonfiction (Van Dyke, Nelson, Thomas) to playwriting/drama (Gibb, Mary and Adrian Praetzellis) and film (Bailey and Simpkin) to imaging (Phillip and Judy Tuwaletstiwa) and database narratives (Tringham). The traditional archaeological expository texts have limitations, and alternative archaeological narratives probably have limitations as well. From the perspective of the archaeology of the Holocaust, the most important question to ask is not what are the limitations of current narratives but rather, what are the limits of all present and future potential alternative narratives/presentations of archaeology?

Before we deal with limits of presentation, it is important to refer to Adorno's famous statement that writing poetry after Auschwitz would be barbarous. Whatever the exact meaning of the original statement, it is still controversial. It is commonly interpreted as suggesting that the Holocaust is indescribable, ineffable, that it cannot be represented in art and history (Lang 2000: 5). By describing Auschwitz as a star of ashes facing planet Earth, Ka-Tzetnik (Y. Dinur) in his Eichmann trial testimony (Eichmann Trial 1993: 1237) implied that the events of the Holocaust took place on another planet, "the planet of Auschwitz," and are therefore incomprehensible (Eaglestone 2004: 16–19). For Elie Wiesel (1977: 405) the Holocaust cannot be communicated: "A novel about Treblinka is either not a novel or not about Treblinka; for Treblinka means . . . death of language and imagination. The mystery is doomed to remain intact."

This radical position, probably a posttraumatic reaction, to use a notion of Dominick LaCapra (2001), is not prevalent. Numerous scholars, writers, and artists—today and in the past—treat every aspect of the Holocaust intensively. I am convinced that the academic study of the Holocaust, including the archaeological research, is to be carried out under the same principles and by the same methods as the study of other events in human history. Although the Holocaust can and should be studied and represented, scholars debate the limits of its representation.

During recent decades, the limits of representation have been a major subject of historical research concerning the Holocaust. A very important contribution to this subject is the volume *Probing the Limits of Presentation—Nazism and the "Final Solution,"* edited by Saul Friedlander and published in 1992. Friedlander refers mostly to limits concerning the previously described modes of historical emplotment, as detailed by White in his *Metahistory* and later works (White 1973, 1987, 1992).

In a nutshell, the question Friedlander (1992: 9–10) asks is whether the Holocaust can be emplotted in one of the modes White suggests, such as "comic" or "pastoral." His answer is that "there are limits to representation *which should not be but can easily be transgressed*" (ibid.: 3; original emphasis). White (1992), in reaction, partially agrees by suggesting that "the facts" concerning the events of the Third Reich justify removing the "comic" or "pastoral" modes of emplotment from the list of competing narratives.

The idea that the Holocaust is a kind of event for which limits to its representations should be set is challenging. It raises the question of whether limits should be set to representations of other historical events and what criteria differentiate between events that deserve unlimited representation and those that should be limited. Discussing such a question is beyond the scope of this chapter, but since we deal with aspects of alternative narratives in archaeology, limits of presentation pertaining to archaeological narratives are also relevant to us, as will be shown later.

ALTERNATIVE NARRATIVES—FICTION

The Holocaust involved millions of people—perpetrators, victims, and bystanders (Hilberg 1993); today it attracts the mass media and the public in general, as well as scholars, artists, and Holocaust deniers. Thus, the impact of the Holocaust on culture and scholarship is enormous, as clearly reflected in the intensity of intellectual, literary, and artistic output during recent decades. The Holocaust captures the interest and imagination of the public probably more than archaeology does. For example, the terms *Holocaust*, *Shoah*, and the combination *The Final Solution, World War* yield slightly more results in Google searches than the term *archaeology/archeology* (ca. 75.3 million vs. ca. 75 million, respectively). The fact than the term *Holocaust*, an event that lasted less than a decade, is marginally more frequent than the term *archaeology*, which covers hundreds of thousands of years, undoubtedly reflects the public's huge interest in the political, social, and ideological aspects of the Holocaust. This cannot yet be substantiated quantitatively, but it seems that the modes of representing the Holocaust, especially in literature, cinema, and art (Lang 2000; Vice 2000; Zelizer 2001), are more frequent than representations of the archaeological past.

The rich yield of Holocaust representations covers a wide range of works, beginning with literature (for example, *The Kindly Ones* [Littell 2010]) through cinema (for example, Lanzmann's 1985 *Shoah* and Syberberg's 1977 *Hitler, Ein Film aus Deutschland*) to art (for example, the paintings of Bak [1997] and Kiefer [Saltzman 2000]). The variety and nature of this abundance clearly indicate that setting limits to representation of the past is practically impossible. This is best illustrated by Roberto Benigni's (1997) *Life Is Beautiful*, a partially comic movie about the Holocaust that was produced several years after Friedlander's assertion that "comedy" is beyond the limit of Holocaust presentations (discussed earlier). Benigni's movie won a number of Academy Awards, on the one hand, and was heavily criticized, on the other hand (Niv 2003).

Another point of interest emanating from the numerous alternative narratives of the Holocaust is that certain narratives cannot be classified in a clear-cut category and that the distinctions between fiction and nonfiction are sometimes controversial (Lang 2000: 72–89). For decades, Wiesel's (1960) *Night* was registered as a work of fiction in the Library of Congress records until his literary agent demanded that it be reclassified as nonfiction. Art Spiegelman's (1986) *Maus*, classified as best-seller fiction in the *New York Times Book Review*, was moved into the nonfiction list at the author's request (Lang 2000: 74).

The dichotomy between fiction and nonfiction is more complex than the problem of where to draw the formal dividing line between the two. Jorge Semprún, a Buchenwald survivor and a writer, thinks the "facts" of the Holocaust cannot be narrated faithfully because of the unreal nature of the camps and the events. Such events can only be transmitted through art and imagination. Thus, his narration is based on "Autofiction," an autobiography based on a mixture of real and imagined events (Munté 2011).

Turning to archaeology, the question to ask is, what, if any, are the limits of archaeological narratives, be they expository or storytelling, filmmaking, and the like? For example, does a narrative by Holocaust deniers based on archaeology (expository or nor) belong within the limits? Since our sites and artifacts are meaningfully related and since as such they are our *facts* and represent *events* or a *chronicle* (whatever their potential emplotment, to use White's term), they should be described properly. This, as far as I understand it, is what Ruth Van Dyke refers to as the "archaeological information," the archaeological facts, data on sites and artifacts, in which works of creative alternative narratives should be grounded. I fully agree that any representations—a novel or a story, a computer program or a play—must be grounded in archaeological information when carried out by archaeologists.

The question to ask here is, what are the limits of such alternative narratives? For example, can archaeologists invent artifacts, people, or events to create a better story? Sarah Pollock's advice (this volume) is very relevant: "If an author [archaeologist] departs from what is understood to be archaeology, it is important to instruct the 'reader' on how to read the text." I suggest that those of us who have the gift of creative writing may use it to create alternative narratives that do "allow the past subaltern to speak" and "leave the imagination of past subjects open"—as long as they are grounded in archaeological information and the reader knows how to distinguish between imagination and information. For them, expository texts with an objectivist gist are a legitimate alternative that may be opted for. An explicitly objectivist approach has the advantage of bringing to the forefront aspects that tend to be obscured in a non-objectivist approach.

Beyond limiting alternative narratives to cases that can be grounded in archaeological information, there should be no other limits, neither scientific nor ideological or aesthetic. This is my conviction, in spite of the fact that

Holocaust deniers (described, for example, by Lang [2010]; Lipstadt [1994]; Shermer and Grobman [2009]) make extensive use of archaeological materials and argumentation in their attempts to deny the existence of the extermination centers, including the results of our recent work at Sobibór (e.g., Graf, Kues, and Mattogno 2010: 162–67). They do so by presenting alternative narratives of Nazi policies and activities. Holocaust denial is a social and political problem and is dealt with in many countries by laws against genocide denial (Kahn 2004). Intellectually and scientifically, I think we should follow Richard Evans (2002: 237), who suggests that professors of geography (and of archaeology) should not waste time debating with people who think the earth is flat. Thus, I stress the point made in the introductory note: the reality of the Holocaust is firmly established by historical research, and archaeology cannot either prove or dispute it.

Once our representations are grounded in archaeological information, we can move to the broader issues concerning the alternative narratives. Creative nonfiction writing, filmmaking, and the like are very efficient ways to transmit our findings and conclusions to non-specialists. However, the potential contribution of alternative narratives and the various modes of representing them to the intra-scientific discourse remains to be proven. What worries me more is the question of talent. Creative writing, playing, and movie making are generated by inner drives and by abilities people are born with and develop during their lifetimes. The drives and talents that "make" archaeologists are of a different order, and very few can excel in both archaeology and the arts. We are indeed interested in *Things*, but do we have the talent of Georges Perec (1965)? Can archaeologists acquire such skills? I doubt it. If not, why should the public read books or watch movies created by unprofessional authors or directors? Thus, the most serious limit of alternative narratives is not related to science, politics, and ideology—the main limit is that most of us are not creative writers, directors, or performers. Having said that, I do not imply that there are no individuals among us who have the talent to write fiction creatively or make movies. François Bordes, the famous French prehistorian, is only one example of a scientist and a writer. Under the penname Francis Carsac, he wrote science fiction novels that were translated into a number of languages and are still very popular in Russia and other East European countries.

ALTERNATIVE NARRATIVES—NONFICTION

Alternative narratives depend on archaeological information, and as archaeologists we cannot emancipate ourselves from data. Thus, a mode of simultaneous or almost simultaneous presentation of data and narrative is called for. The principle behind such a presentation is centuries old and is best exemplified by the layout of a Talmud page (figure 11.4). The format of the Talmud page shown and discussed here is the standard page of what is known as the *Vilna Shas*, first printed in the late nineteenth century (Heller 1995: 49–50).

The Talmud is a major collection of Jewish Rabbinical texts that consist of two elements: the Mishnah and the Talmud (or Gemarah). The Mishnah is a collection of texts in Hebrew, mainly of a legal nature (Halakhah), that was codified in about 200 CE. The Talmud consists of a collection of texts in Aramaic (ca. 200 CE to 550–600 CE) that explains and expands on the Mishnah (Steinsaltz 2006: 3–4). The Midrash literature discussed by Mary and Adrian Praetzellis in this volume is a distinct literary corpus that is not part of the Talmud, although both are broadly contemporaneous and share a number of similar attributes.

The text block that forms the core of a Talmud page (figure 11.4) consists of both the Mishnah and the Gemarah, which date back to late antiquity. This block of text is surrounded at its margins and below by assorted commentaries, cross-references, and glosses written mainly in the Middle Ages. A single Talmud page thus consists of a variety of distinct texts that represent different periods in a time span of more than 1,000 years. During recent decades the entire Talmud (ca. 2,700 pages) was translated into Hebrew within the traditional page format (the *Steinsaltz Talmud*), and a new layer of commentaries was added. I do not suggest that we present our information and narratives in Talmud-like paper pages; rather, I am pointing out that HTML and the format of Internet pages is a modern and highly sophisticated version of a simultaneous presentation of different types of data, levels of narration, and interpretations.

The page layout of the Talmud represents an open, multilayer dialogue that is of a nonlinear, non-expository nature. Recently, Mikhal Rozenberg and colleagues (2006) suggested that a Talmud page may be regarded as a metaphor for a scientific text. They see such a page as a model of interpretative discussion arranged in a multivocal, multiple-meaning set of narratives, a "polyphony of voices" (ibid.: 16). In this context, Thomas Mann's (1948) well-known dichotomy in *Doctor Faustus* between "subjective harmony" vs. "objective polyphony" comes to mind. The literal and musical meaning of the term *polyphony*, "having many sounds or voices" (*Oxford English Dictionary*), perfectly describes the "multivocality" we are dealing with in the current volume. Using Mann's terms implies that the representation of our subjects in multivocal narratives objectivizes rather than subjectivizes them.

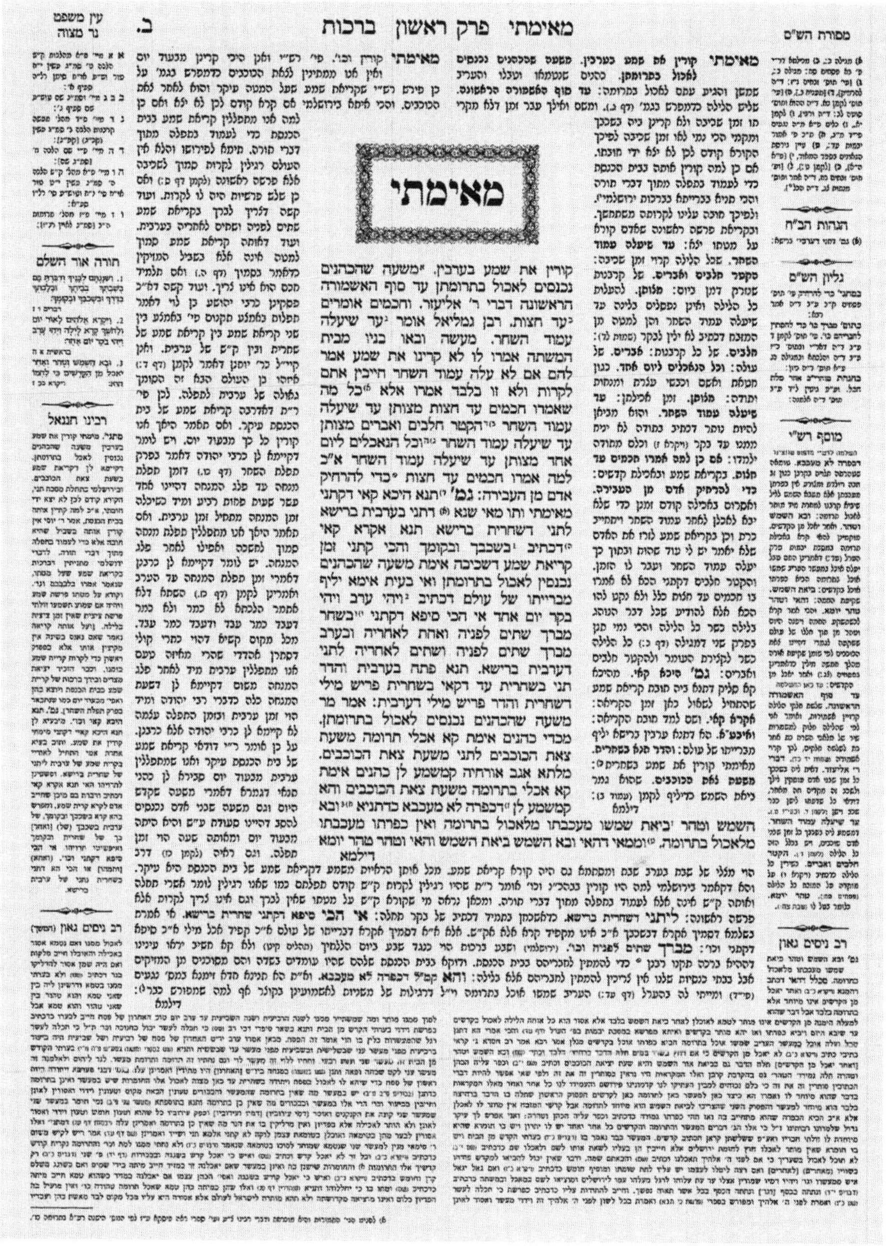
מאימתי פרק ראשון ברכות ב.

מסורת הש״ס

עין משפט נר מצוה

מאימתי

מאימתי קורין את שמע בערבין. משעה שהכהנים נכנסים לאכול בתרומתן עד סוף האשמורה הראשונה דברי ר׳ אליעזר. וחכמים אומרים עד חצות. רבן גמליאל אומר עד שיעלה עמוד השחר. מעשה ובאו בניו מבית המשתה אמרו לו לא קרינו את שמע אמר להם אם לא עלה עמוד השחר חייבין אתם לקרות ולא זו בלבד אמרו אלא כל מה שאמרו חכמים עד חצות מצותן עד שיעלה עמוד השחר הקטר חלבים ואברים מצותן עד שיעלה עמוד השחר וכל הנאכלים ליום אחד מצותן עד שיעלה עמוד השחר א״כ למה אמרו חכמים עד חצות כדי להרחיק אדם מן העבירה: גמ׳ תנא היכא קאי דקתני מאימתי ותו מאי שנא דתני בערבית ברישא לתני דשחרית ברישא תנא אקרא קאי דכתיב בשכבך ובקומך והכי קתני זמן קריאת שמע דשכיבה אימת משעה שהכהנים נכנסין לאכול בתרומתן ואי בעית אימא יליף מברייתו של עולם דכתיב ויהי ערב ויהי בקר יום אחד אי הכי סיפא דקתני בשחר מברך שתים לפניה ואחת לאחריה ובערב מברך שתים לפניה ושתים לאחריה לתני דערבית ברישא. תנא פתח בערבית והדר תני בשחרית עד דקאי בשחרית פריש מילי דשחרית והדר פריש מילי דערבית: אמר מר משעה שהכהנים נכנסים לאכול בתרומתן. מכדי כהנים אימת קא אכלי תרומה משעת צאת הכוכבים לתני משעת צאת הכוכבים. מלתא אגב אורחיה קמשמע לן כהנים אימת קא אכלי בתרומה משעת צאת הכוכבים והא קמשמע לן דכפרה לא מעכבא כדתניא ובא השמש וטהר ביאת שמשו מעכבתו מלאכול בתרומה ואין כפרתו מעכבתו מלאכול בתרומה. וממאי דהאי ובא השמש ביאת השמש והאי וטהר טהר יומא דילמא

הגהות הב״ח

גליון הש״ס

מוסף רש״י

תורה אור השלם

רבינו חננאל

רב ניסים גאון

FIGURE 11.4. *Talmud page—Pesahim Tractate (http://www.hebrewbooks.org/shas)*

The Geertz-Ryle notion of "thick description" (Geertz 1973: 3–30), applied to artifacts *sensu lato*, is another version of non-artistic alternative narrative to be considered (discussed by Thomas, this volume). A "thick description" of artifacts found in a dig often turns archaeologists into storytellers, as illustrated in the case of the Lysol bottle discussed next.

Glass bottles of many shapes, sizes, and functions comprise one of the most common categories found in Nazi death centers (e.g., Kola 2000: figures 90–91). During the 2009 season at Sobibór we uncovered in Camp 3 a base fragment of a bottle made of brown glass, the standard type of glass used for Lysol. Lysol is the brand name of a liquid disinfectant produced since the 1890s by Schülke and Mayr, a company established in 1889 in Hamburg and still active today. The bottom of the bottle clearly indicates that it was a product of Schülke and Mayr (figure 11.5). Lysol was originally made of cresol and soap solutions, and it became internationally known because it was considered effective against the Spanish influenza at the end of World War I. It was used mainly as a disinfectant for private houses, hospitals, and similar structures. It is also known to have been used to disinfect places and humans at the Nazi concentration and extermination camps. Ada Lichtmann, a survivor of Sobibór, mentions in her testimony that slave workers at the camp had to clean dirty clothes first with Lysol and then with water (Novitch 1980). The Germans undoubtedly brought large quantities of Lysol to Sobibór in bulky containers. The possibility that the German perpetrators disinfected clothes or places with Lysol from bottles as small as the ones we uncovered seems implausible.

Beyond a general-purpose detergent and disinfectant, in the early twentieth century women used Lysol as a contraceptive. In her 1914 booklet on birth control, Margaret Sanger described a vaginal douche as most important in cleansing a woman after sex. She advised that "one teaspoon of lysol to 2 quarts of water (warm) makes a good solution for douching" (quoted in Jensen 1981: 560). The reaction of Marie Stopes (1922: 48–51), the English paleobotanist and pioneer of family planning, was more reserved. Although she acknowledged that women widely used douching for birth control, she warned that Lysol and other strong fluids are destructive rather than healing. Thus, in the 1920s and 1930s the "Lysol douche" had economic, social, and cultural significance (Sarch 1997; Tone 1996). It was still used in the 1960s, and other varieties of vaginal douching are practiced today (Martino, Youngpairoj, and Vermund 2004). The producers of the TV series *Boardwalk Empire* recently brought the Lysol douche back to public attention. Episode 6 of the series, "Family Limitation," shows Margaret Schroeder, one of the main characters, following Sangers's advice and using a Lysol douche after sex.

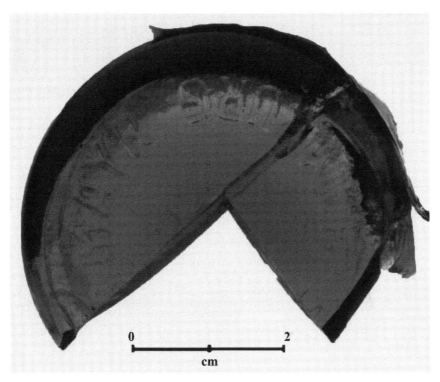

FIGURE 11.5. *Fragment of a Lysol bottle produced by Schülke and Mayr, found at Sobibór*

The bottle fragment we uncovered has a base about 5 centimeters in diameter; it was probably about 9 centimeters high and contained about 300–400 milliliters of Lysol. Brown Lysol bottles are currently traded in the antique bottle market and online (e.g., eBay, Antique Bottles website). Such a bottle, dated to the beginning of the twentieth century and produced by Schülke and Mayr in Hamburg, has been reported from the excavations of Scott Farmstead in New Zealand (Furey 2011: 109). Similar types of Lysol bottles were advertised in the pre–World War II years by Lehn and Fink, Inc., which bought Lysol from Schülke and Mayr in 1922. The ads use the euphemism "feminine hygiene" (Sarch 1997); one of them mentions, for example, that in Berlin, Paris, Vienna, and London, "*die eleganten Damen*" use Lysol for "feminine hygiene" (figure 11.6).

Given this background, the bottle we found was not likely introduced to the site by the perpetrators. This artifact was probably brought by a Jewish victim, perhaps a woman, who left all her belongings at Sobibór before being

In brilliant BERLIN
"die eleganten Damen" use
"LYSOL" for feminine hygiene

A type of German beauty one sees in exclusive meeting places of Berlin.

TONIGHT, in the most exclusive cafés of Berlin—on the Kurfürsten Damm and the Potsdamer Platz—will gather "die eleganten Damen" of the gay German capital. Smart women of society, the stage and the screen, envied for their immaculate beauty and rare charm.

Brilliant women! Like their fashionable sisters of Paris and Vienna and London, they rely on feminine hygiene to help protect their health and retain that assurance of true cleanliness. And like them, they use "Lysol" Disinfectant for this intimate purpose.

Everywhere "Lysol" is the standard antiseptic for feminine hygiene among women who *know*. It penetrates. It is non-poisonous when diluted and used according to directions. For forty years doctors and hospitals the world over have depended on "Lysol" at the most critical time of all—childbirth—when disinfection *must* be thorough and without possible risk of injury.

What greater assurance could *you* have that "Lysol" is safest and surest for personal cleansing?

Know more about feminine hygiene and the protection "Lysol" affords. A prominent woman physician will give you professional advice and specific rules in the booklet offered below. It is reliable, it is enlightening. It is free. Send for your copy today. In the meantime, get a bottle of "Lysol" at your druggist's and follow the directions on the circular enclosed. Being a *concentrated* germicide, "Lysol" gives you many times more for your money.

Be careful! *Counterfeits of "Lysol" are being sold.* Genuine "Lysol" is in the brown bottle and yellow carton marked "Lysol."

LEHN & FINK, Inc., *Sole distributors*
Dept. 443, Bloomfield, N. J.
Please send me, free, your booklet, "The Facts about Feminine Hygiene"

Name ....
Street ....
City ....
State ....

© 1930,
L. & F., Inc.

In Canada, address Lehn & Fink (Canada) Limited, 7 Davies Ave., Toronto 8

FIGURE 11.6.
Advertisement for using Lysol for "feminine hygiene" (http://www.flickr.com/photos/mrbill/37804459/in/set-834100)

murdered. I do not claim that this brief account is a "thick description" in the Geertzian meaning of the word, but it suggests that even a sketchy attempt to tell the story of a single artifact discloses its socio-cultural background and highlights the people behind major historical events. Paraphrasing Browning (1992: 35), this Alltagsgeschichte approach to artifacts reveals the deeper layers of the events and human faces behind them, be they perpetrators, victims, or bystanders.

Saul Friedlander (1997, 2007) uses another way of integrating linear-expository texts with alternatives narratives in his comprehensive study *Nazi Germany and the Jews*. Friedlander describes the actions and policies of the Nazi perpetrators, along with the reactions of the victims and bystanders. He creates a contrapuntal mixture by interweaving standard scientific, archival history with personal memories recorded in the victims' diaries. He fuses the standard expository text with alternative voices that represent what he calls "different levels of reality" (Eaglestone 2004: 188–89). According to Alon Confino (2009), by means of a discontinuous, broken narrative, Friedlander creates a "historical sensation" that allows readers to conceive and imagine the Holocaust.

In archaeology, we have no memories or diaries of our subjects, but such narratives can be invented as long as they are grounded in the archaeological data. Archaeological expository texts with additional voices embedded in them have been known in the archaeological literature for decades. In *After the Ice Age*, Mithen (2003: 5) mentions the risk of turning the archaeological evidence into lists of cultures, sites, and artifacts. Therefore, he invents a modern person he calls John Lubbock, the famous author of the 1865 book *Pre-Historic Times*, and sends him to the prehistoric past to see and experience ways of life and the way they change over thousands of years. Kent Flannery (1976) uses another way to add voices to expository texts in *The Early Mesoamerican Village*. Instead of inventing narratives of past events or accounts of past subjects, he uses fictional voices of colleagues and students that self-reflect on the problems and prospects of studying past societies.

CONCLUSIONS

The Holocaust is an event of recent history that attracts unparalleled attention and captivates the thinking, imagination, and feelings of millions of people. This event has been and still is looked at from many perspectives: from the point of view of the perpetrators, the victims, the bystanders, the descendants of each of the above, of laymen, past and present-day scholars, deniers, and similar groups. The resulting output of this thinking, imagining, and feeling is vast, both in terms of the individual items and of the variety of modes and media used by survivors and witnesses, scientists, writers, and artists of all kinds.

This profusion raise the question of limits, most clearly stated in the framework of the Friedlander-White controversy. Although the idea that certain limits should be set in representing the Holocaust may be ethically justified, the extent of the limits and the qualifications of the people who set them are issues that remain unresolved. Concerning archaeology, on a general level it seems there are no limits to the variety of alternative narratives and the modes and media to create them. At the more specific level of professional archaeologists, two limits should be considered.

The first is that alternative narratives created by archaeologists have to be grounded in archaeological information, in actual sites and artifacts. Moreover, the relations between fictional narratives, on the one hand, and sites and artifacts, on the other hand, should be made clear to readers, as Pollock recommends (this volume). The second limit results from the simple truth that most people, including many professional archaeologists, are not endowed with creative talents, and the array of their potential alternative narratives will always be within or close to the range of expository texts. The idea of a Talmud page, of HTML formats or "thick description," can facilitate the presentation of different voices and opinions concerning the archaeological record.

Archaeology can contribute to Holocaust studies the "down-to-earth" dimension that characterizes an essential aspect of our discipline. By "down to earth" I mean we should view the Holocaust as an event carried out by Homo sapiens; as such, it falls within the range of the potential behavior of our species. In addition to aspects of the Holocaust that are extensively studied currently, such as politics, ethics, and ideology from the perspectives of the nineteenth and twentieth centuries and modernism, attention should also be devoted to aspects of the anthropology of genocide and the Holocaust within the framework of general human behavior (Hinton 1998, 2002; Lewin 1992; Moses 2004).

In Hans-Jürgen Syberberg's (1977) *Hitler, Ein Film aus Deutschland*, Hitler's spirit utters these lines on Wagner's grave: "I am a human being with two eyes and ears, like you, and if you prick me, do I not bleed? I, too, I am one of you, too." I regard this to be an objectivistic anthropological statement in a work of art. Such an approach is to be retained in the archaeological study of the Nazi extermination centers, *mutatis mutandis*, in the archaeological research of other phenomena.

ACKNOWLEDGMENTS

I would like to thank Reinhard Bernbeck and Ruth Van Dyke, who kindly invited me to deliver the oral version of this chapter at the 2011 SAA meetings in Sacramento. Their comments on a draft of the chapter are greatly appreciated. Steve Rosen and Milena Gošić read parts of the manuscript and made important comments. Any mistakes, however, are mine.

REFERENCES

Arad, Yitzhak. 1987. *Belzec, Sobibor, Treblinka: The Operation Reinhard Death Camps.* Bloomington: Indiana University Press.

Bak, Samuel. 1997. *Landscapes of Jewish Experience/Paintings by Samuel Bak.* Boston: Pucker Gallery, in association with Brandeis University Press.

Browning, Christopher. 1992. "German Memory, Judicial Interrogation, and Historical Reconstruction: Writing Perpetrator History from Postwar Testimony." In *Probing the Limits of Representation—Nazism and the "Final Solution,"* ed. Saul Friedlander, 54–65. Cambridge: Harvard University Press.

Cohen, Nathan. 1990. "Diaries of the *Sonderkommando* in Auschwitz: Coping with Fate and Reality." *Yad Vashem Studies* 20: 273–312.

Cohen, Nathan. 1998. "Diaries of the Sonderkommando." In *Anatomy of the Auschwitz Death Camp,* ed. Yisrael Gutman and Michael Berenbaum, 522–34. Bloomington: Indiana University Press.

Confino, Alon. 2009. "Narrative Form and Historical Sensation: On Saul Friedländer's *The Years of Extermination.*" *Theory and History* 48 (3): 199–219. http://dx.doi.org/10.1111/j.1468-2303.2009.00504.x.

Eaglestone, Robert. 2004. *The Holocaust and the Postmodern.* Oxford: Oxford University Press. http://dx.doi.org/10.1093/acprof:oso/9780199265930.001.0001.

Eichmann Trial. 1993. *The Trial of Adolf Eichmann: Records of Proceedings in the District Court of Jerusalem,* vol. 3. Jerusalem: State of Israel Ministry of Justice.

Evans, Richard J. 1997. *In Defense of History.* London: Granta Books.

Evans, Richard J. 2002. *Telling Lies about Hitler.* London: Verso.

Flannery, Kent V. 1976. *The Early Mesoamerican Village.* New York: Studies in Archeology. Academic Press.

Friedlander, Saul. 1992. "Introduction." In *Probing the Limits of Representation—Nazism and the "Final Solution,"* ed. Saul Friedlander, 1–21. Cambridge: Harvard University Press.

Friedlander, Saul. 1997. *Nazi Germany and the Jews: The Years of Persecution, 1933–1939.* New York: HarperCollins.

Friedlander, Saul. 2007. *Nazi Germany and the Jews: The Years of Extermination, 1939–1945*. New York: HarperCollins.

Furey, Louise. 2011. *Excavations at Scott's Farmstead, Ihumatao*. Oakland: CFG Heritage.

Geertz, Clifford. 1973. *The Interpretation of Cultures*. New York: Basic Books.

Gilbert, Martin. 1986. *The Holocaust: The Jewish Tragedy*. London: Collins.

Gilbert, Martin. 1997. *Holocaust Journey: Travelling in Search of the Past*. London: Phoenix.

Gilead, Isaac, Yoram Haimi, and Wojciech Mazurek. 2009. "Excavating Nazi Extermination Centres." *Present Pasts* 1: 10–30.

Graf, Jürgen, Thomas Kues, and Carlo Mattogno. 2010. *Sobibór Holocaust Propaganda and Reality*. Washington, DC: Barnes Review.

Gross, Ian Thomasz, and Irena Grudzinska Gross. 2012. *Golden Harvest: Events at the Periphery of the Holocaust*. Oxford: Oxford University Press.

Heller, Marvin J. 1995. "Designing the Talmud: The Origins of the Printed Talmudic Page." *Traditions* 29 (3): 40–51.

Hilberg, Raul. 1993. *Perpetrators, Victims, Bystanders: The Jewish Catastrophe 1933–1945*. New York: HarperPerennial.

Hilberg, Raul. 2001. *Sources of Holocaust Research: An Analysis*. Chicago: Ivan R. Dee.

Hinton, Alex. 1998. "Why Did the Nazis Kill? Anthropology, Genocide and the Goldhagen Controversy." *Anthropology Today* 14 (5): 9–15. http://dx.doi.org/10.2307/2783388.

Hinton, Alex, ed. 2002. *Annihilating Difference: The Anthropology of Genocide*. Berkeley: University of California Press.

Holtorf, Cornelius. 2010. "Meta-Histories of Archaeology." *World Archaeology* 42 (3): 381–93. http://dx.doi.org/10.1080/00438243.2010.497382.

Jenkins, Keith. 1995. *On "What Is History?" from Carr and Elton to Rorty and White*. London: Routledge.

Jensen, Joan M. 1981. "The Evolution of Margaret Sanger's 'Family Limitation' Pamphlet, 1914–1921." *Sign* 6 (3): 548–67. http://dx.doi.org/10.1086/493834.

Joyce, Rosemary A. 2002. *The Languages of Archaeology: Dialogue, Narrative, and Writing*. Oxford: Blackwell. http://dx.doi.org/10.1002/9780470693520.

Kahn, Robert A. 2004. *Holocaust Denial and Law*. New York: Palgrave Macmillan. http://dx.doi.org/10.1057/9781403980502.

Kansteiner, Wulf. 1993. "Hayden White's Critique of the Writing of History." *History and Theory* 32 (3): 273–95. http://dx.doi.org/10.2307/2505526.

Kola, Andrej. 2000. *Bełżec: The Nazi Camp for Jews in Light of Archaeological Sources: Excavations 1997–1999*. Warsaw, WA: Council for the Protection of Memory of Combat and Martyrdom and the United States Holocaust Memorial Museum.

LaCapra, Dominick. 2001. *Writing History, Writing Trauma*. Baltimore: Johns Hopkins University Press.

Lang, Berel. 2000. *Holocaust Representation: Art within the Limits of History and Ethics*. Baltimore: Johns Hopkins University Press.

Lang, Berel. 2010. "Six Questions on (or about) Holocaust Denial." *History and Theory* 49 (2): 157–68. http://dx.doi.org/10.1111/j.1468-2303.2010.00537.x.

Lewin, Carol McC. 1992. "The Holocaust: Anthropological Possibilities and the Dilemma of Representation." *American Anthropologist* 94: 161–66.

Lipstadt, Deborah E. 1994. *Denying the Holocaust: The Growing Assault on Truth and Memory*. New York: Plume.

Littell, Jonathan. 2010. *The Kindly Ones*. London: Vintage Books.

Mann, Thomas. 1948. *Doctor Faustus*. New York: Alfred A. Knopf.

Martino, Jenny L., Surasak Youngpairoj, and Sten H. Vermund. 2004. "Vaginal Douching: Personal Practices and Public Policies." *Journal of Women's Health* 13 (9): 1048–65. http://dx.doi.org/10.1089/jwh.2004.13.1048.

Mithen, Steven. 2003. *After the Ice Age: A Global Human History 20,000–5,000 BC*. London: Weidenfeld and Nicolson.

Moreland, John. 2001. *Archaeology and Text*. London: Duckworth.

Moses, A. Derek. 2004. "The Holocaust and Genocide." In *The Historiography of the Holocaust*, ed. Dan Stone, 533–55. London: Palgrave Macmillan.

Munté, Rosa-Auria. 2011. "The Convergence of Historical Facts and Literary Fiction: Jorge Semprún's Autofiction on the Holocaust." In *Forum: Qualitative Social Research*, part 14, vol. 12, at http://www.qualitative-research.net/index.php/fqs/article/view/1754/3261.

Niv, Kobi. 2003. *Life Is Beautiful, but Not for Jews: Another View of the Film by Benigni*. Filmmakers Series 107. Lanham, MD: Scarecrow.

Novitch, Miriam. 1980. *Sobibor: Martyrdom and Revolt*. New York: Holocaust Library.

Perec, Georges. 1965. *Les choses: Une histoire des années 60*. Paris: Julliard.

Pluciennik, Mark. 1999. "Archaeological Narratives and Other Ways of Telling." *Current Anthropology* 40 (5): 653–78. http://dx.doi.org/10.1086/300085.

Rozenberg, Michal, Miri Munk, and Anat Kainan. 2006. "A Talmud Page as a Metaphor of a Scientific Text." *International Journal of Qualitative Methods* 5 (4): 1–17.

Saltzman, Lisa. 2000. *Anselm Kiefer and Art after Auschwitz*. Cambridge Studies in New Art History and Criticism. Cambridge: Cambridge University Press.

Sarch, Amy. 1997. "Those Dirty Ads! Birth Control Advertising in the 1920s and 1930s." *Critical Studies in Mass Communication* 14 (1): 31–48. http://dx.doi.org/10.1080/15295039709366995.

Shermer, Michael, and Alex Grobman. 2009. *Denying History: Who Says the Holocaust Never Happened and Why Do They Say So?* Berkeley: University of California Press.

Spiegelman, Art. 1986. *Maus: A Survivor's Tale.* New York: Pantheon Books.

Steinsaltz, Adin. 2006. *The Essential Talmud.* Thirtieth anniversary ed. New York: Basic Books.

Stopes, Marie C. 1922. *Wise Parenthood: The Treatise on Birth Control for Married People: A Practical Sequel to Married Love,* 8th ed. London: Putnam.

Sturdy Colls, Caroline. 2012 "Holocaust Archaeology: Archaeological Approaches to Landscapes of Nazi Genocide and Persecution." *Journal of Conflict Archaeology* 7 (2): 70–104. http://dx.doi.org/10.1179/1574077312Z.0000000005.

Syberberg, Hans-Jürgen. 1977. *Hitler, Ein Film aus Deutschland.* Produced by TMS Film/Bernd Echinger.

Tone, Andrea. 1996. "Contraceptive Consumers: Gender and the Political Economy of Birth Control in the 1930s." *Journal of Social History* 29 (3): 485–506. http://dx.doi.org/10.1353/jsh/29.3.485.

Vice, Sue. 2000. *Holocaust Fiction.* London: Routledge.

White, Hayden. 1973. *Metahistory.* Baltimore: Johns Hopkins University Press.

White, Hayden. 1987. *The Content of the Form: Narrative Discourse and Historical Representation.* Baltimore: Johns Hopkins University Press.

White, Hayden. 1992. "Historical Emplotment and the Problem of Truth." In *Probing the Limits of Representation—Nazism and the "Final Solution,"* ed. Saul Friedlander, 54–65. Cambridge: Harvard University Press.

Wiesel, Elie. 1960. *Night.* New York: Hill and Wang.

Wiesel, Elie. 1977. "Art and Culture after the Holocaust." In *Auschwitz: Beginning of a New Era? Reflections on the Holocaust,* ed. Eva Fleischner, 403–15. New York: KTAV Publishing House.

Zelizer, Barbie, ed. 2001. *Visual Culture and the Holocaust.* London: Athlone.

12

*From Imaginations
of a Peopled Past to a
Recognition of Past People*

Reinhard Bernbeck

NARRATIONS IN ARCHAEOLOGY: FROM SYSTEMS TO PEOPLE

Different paradigms in archaeology have resulted in specific narrative styles. When Kent Flannery (1967: 120) remarked that archaeologists should not search for "the Indian behind the artifact" but rather for "the system behind both the Indian and the artifact," it was more than a statement about the content of archaeological research. It was a legitimation of processualist narratives whose human figures could remain shadowy to the point of nonexistence. The more abstract and general, the better, for two reasons. First, large-scale historical and other processes, researched by archaeology, anthropology, and history, were assumed by processualists to occur largely without the explicit and intentional contributions of people. Archaeologists following a processualist tradition conceptualized historical change that is of relevance as beyond the reach and motivations of individuals and collectives. Second, abstract renderings of the past were seen (and still are seen) by many archaeologists as more "scientific" than personalized representations. Flannery himself must have felt uneasy with the stale and depopulated texts of an "explicitly scientific" archaeology. He invented funny and often profound dialogues that made the *Early Mesoamerican Village* famous (Flannery 1976; for a related approach, see Pauketat 2007). Interestingly, however, the fictionalized elements in Flannery's work all remained in the present, while the past was

DOI: 10.5876/9781607323815.c012

described either in empirical detail or in objectivist and often quantifying language.

Post-processual archaeology, with its focus on meaning and representation (e.g., Hodder 1989), attempted to reverse this objectivizing trend. The rediscovery of hermeneutics (Hodder 1986: 118–46; Shanks and Tilley 1992: 103–12) led to a problematizing of author-text relations that became typical of early post-processualism. However, it was feminist archaeologists who had the greatest impact on a reconsideration of narrative forms. Two fundamental texts are Ruth Tringham's (1991) contribution to *Engendering Archaeology* (Gero and Conkey 1991), in which she invents dialogues among archaeologists, and Janet Spector's (1993) *What This Awl Means*. The latter is a story woven around one particular artifact, a carved wooden awl handle recovered during excavations in the mid-1980s at Little Rapids, Wisconsin. Since then, a steady stream of feminist archaeologists has attempted to include credible subjects in their writings, often by adopting literary forms. This book is an outgrowth of such attempts. The main argument in favor of an insertion of subjects into our writing is to make clear that people in the past were not machine-like entities who passively submitted to an optimization of means-ends relations, as proposed by many science-oriented accounts and especially the hard-core scientific models such as Darwinian archaeology (e.g., Cochrane 2011; Yesner 2008: 46–47), systems analysis, or, more recently, agent-based modeling (e.g., Bentley and Maschner 2008: 260–61; Kohler and Gumerman 2000).

NARRATORS, AUTHORS, AND THE PAST

These fundamental differences in approach have led to sometimes bitter disputes about the content of archaeological research. What has gone partly unrecognized is that the texts of the advocates for hermeneutics versus science also have a formally different character. To understand these differences to their full extent, one needs to distinguish between the author and narrator of a text. Any time we start writing, we do not do so as full subjects but rather in a role that is at best a series of subconsciously chosen aspects of an author's personality (see Stanzel 2001). When we produce a text,[1] we always create at the same time the subject who relates the text—the narrator—and we set this figure willingly or not apart from ourselves, the authors. Academic writing produces specific author-narrator differences (Bernbeck 2005). Scientific texts regularly hide emotions, particular individual dispositions, specific parts of our own knowledge about the world, and much of our own cultural setting. The attempted de-personalization of the scientific writing self produces an auctorial, omniscient writing style that has been variously theorized, most poignantly by Edmund Husserl (1992) with his notion of "epoché."The necessity to reflect on the writing subject is itself based in part on anthropological insights into the naive ethnocentrism of early travel writings and imperialist forms of anthropology in the nineteenth century. The result has been an almost uniform tendency toward self-effacement in the service of a presumed greater truth. The author hides behind a god-like narrator. A good case in point is Bronislaw Malinowski, well-known for his detailed and insightful Trobriand ethnography and for the establishment of the standard ethnographic method of "participant observation." When his diary was published posthumously (Malinowski 1967), it showed a person whose academic claims to be an empathetic but external observer were reduced to a caricature (Geertz 1974).

Analyses in the vein of processual archaeology almost uniformly display all the characteristics of an omniscient narrator. Until recently, this was also a masculine self, as male pronouns were used generically.[2] Otherwise, the grammatical structure avoids specific positions and prefers passive verbal constructions. The fact that an author changed his or her opinions over time can only be admitted in a brief introduction to a text or in acknowledgments but not by creatively mobilizing narrator functions. When teachers explicitly tell students not to use the first-person singular in their papers and theses, this is an unreflected instruction to construct a writing self with qualities almost identical to narrators of such academic texts. The under-theorized assumption here is that linguistic commonalities among narrators make mutual communication of content unproblematic. The paradox of a self-effacing but omniscient writer is believed to ensure the reliable transmission of information. This kind of formal logic comes at a high price. The difference between the neutralized, omniscient academic author and personal experience (such as social, individual, gendered) is implicitly taken to be identical for all academics. To put it otherwise: the academic world either assumes that the relationship between author and narrator is closely similar for all writers or that the variability in this relationship is irrelevant.

It is perhaps obvious that this disregard for "the content of the form" (White 1987) and a narrator who was a priori supposed to be male, dominant, white, and truth-seeking led feminist scholars to insist on including author experience in archaeological and other writing (see Joyce et al. 2002).[3] The consequence of such reflections is, among others, the loss of an underlying formal comparability of narrators across a discipline's textual production. In archaeology, we currently witness not only a multiplication of different pasts, sometimes subsumed under a "new pragmatism" (Preucel and Mrozowski

2010), but also a growing variability of narrators. This latter process is often equated with the "literary turn" and the influence of *Writing Culture* (Clifford and Marcus 1986), leading to manifold reflections on academic positionality (e.g., Herausgeberinnen-Kollektiv des FKA 2012: 184–86; Narayan 1993). Resulting writing styles sometimes border on the confessional and have led to a new problem. The attempts at making the personal visible in academic writing assume a coincidence of the author and the narrator of a text. As discussed, first-person singular accounts cannot avoid constructing a narrator whose subjectivity will always and necessarily be different from the author's. If processual archaeological narratives tend to maximize the author-narrator difference by denying the author's presence, many feminist and post-processual accounts deny altogether any distance between the two.

Formal problems with such relations at the basis of archaeological texts would not matter were they not intricately interwoven with another dimension. In academic writing, both narrator and author are clearly situated in the present, but their main interests lie in the past. Writing always fabricates a relation between a text and its subject or theme. In archaeological texts, this relation is diachronic. The fundamental structure of all archaeological representation therefore consists of a double relationship: a synchronous author-narrator relation and a diachronic one established between this synchronous relation and past subjects, whether they are real people, systems, or cultures. In my view, some aspects of this diachronic textual relation have hitherto been neglected. I will discuss two of these issues here. One is a question of ethics and the possibilities for recognition of an Other. The second concerns the conceptual potential of finding meaning in the past.

PAST OTHERS AND DIACHRONIC VIOLENCE

The relation between us and past Others is not only a matter of content but also of the forms of our knowledge production. I am concerned above all with the political-ethical dimension of this relation. The inclusion of "real subjects" with "lived experiences," emotional depth, and sensuousness in archaeological texts is in most instances based on a dearth of evidence that is astounding to outsiders (Tarlow 2001). Janet Spector's (1993) well-known work, in which she invents a central person who owns a particular thing (an awl with a bone handle), displays a deep concern with this problem. This is remarkable, since the archaeological period she treats is quite recent: the nineteenth century. To bolster her construction of a girl she names "Mazaokiyewin," she includes the voices of Native Americans, drawings of the village from the nineteenth century, and a chapter that clearly frames her account as invented. Thus, already when we talk about periods of dozens, not to mention hundreds or thousands, of years ago, the material drawn on must be carefully handled to meet the requirements for inventing credible subjects. The author who aims to include flesh-and-blood people in an archaeological narrative is forced to fictionalize the past.

The invention of fictionalized subjects, however well meant the empathetic effort, implies a certain disrespect for past people. An attempted Geertzian "thick description" of the past that focuses on personalities and characters is an imposition on past people's rights to self-determination. As social scientists, we mostly do not reflect enough about our relations with those people with whom we claim to be so preoccupied. As a means to further our own goals, especially the explicitly political goals pursued by a Marxist, feminist, postcolonial, and even an indigenous archaeology, constructed subjects become (too) closely related to our present interests. We do not know exactly what motivated people to act against repression or to pursue one practice rather than another, even when we are dealing with time periods very close to our own.

Not knowing the motivations for past practices and actions, we project political desires back in time, carrying out in the process an act of colonization. We deny past peoples the right to speak for themselves, simply because they are the ultimate Other, one who will never be able to talk back. At the root of this problem is a structural paradox inherent in all archaeological and historical production. It may be common sense that the disciplines occupied with the past produce "knowledge." The field of knowledge is external to the author/narrator because of temporal differences between the object of writing and its producer. The relation of externality remains unproblematic as long as archaeology is a discipline interested in past systems, cultures, materiality, and the like. If, however, the main interest is in past people, a stark imbalance of power emerges. We no longer write as spectators of a play but rather become enmeshed in the play of the past as witnesses who talk for others, or, as Gayatri Chakravorti Spivak (1988: 276) puts it, we move from the production of a "portrait" to becoming a "proxy," making the implicit claim that one is able to fully stand in for someone else.

Postcolonial scholars such as Spivak (ibid.) and Dipesh Chakrabarty (2000: 97–116) have radically questioned the outcome of speaking for (past) others that is typical for anthropology but also for postcolonial approaches such as the Indian "subaltern studies group" (e.g., Guha 1988); the attempt at a translation of interests, the lending of a voice to the subaltern's plight, ends up in a reproduction of the position of the author. Giorgio Agamben (2002) exposes

a similar problem in the last chapter of his *Remnants of Auschwitz* by remind-
ing us that a true testimony for total de-subjectivation in Nazi concentration camps is impossible, albeit necessary. Inmates themselves differentiated
between those doomed to die (whom they called "Muselmann") and all others.
Being witness for the fey is the impossible task of the survivors who suffered
under this moral imperative (Levi 1986).

One does not need to delve into these extreme cases to realize that the
transition from knowing past peoples' lives to an acknowledgment of them as
dialogic partners is extremely difficult, if not impossible, to achieve. Should
we therefore continue to write "objectively," as if past subjects did not matter? I do not think so. Or should we follow Sherry Ortner, who seems to
sidestep the issue of a possible colonization of past/Other life-worlds: "The
anthropologist and the historian are charged with representing the lives of
living or once-living people, and as we attempt to push these people into the
molds of our texts *they push back.* The final text is a product of our pushing and
their back-pushing, and no text, however 'dominant,' lacks the traces of this
counterforce" (Ortner 1996: 298; original emphasis). Applied to archaeological
objects from colonial times, this would mean that the content of a museum
of colonialism never lacks traces of the colonized that militate against any
one-sided script of an exhibit. In my view, this is an unacceptably apologetic
dialectic, since the dominant discourse will always and invariably be that of
the present. An example from the Pergamon Museum in Berlin demonstrates
the problem clearly, despite the fact that past people in this case are not even
from a subaltern position. The exhibit of the reconstructed tomb of the ninth-
century BCE Assyrian king Assurnasirpal II was accompanied by a tablet
that read: "May the person who finds this coffin not take it for themselves, but
leave it alone in its place. Whoever reads this and does not disregard it, may
their good deed be rewarded" (Herausgeberinnen-Kollektiv des FKA 2012:
194). To exhibit such an assemblage deliberately can be interpreted as an honest attempt to elucidate the "pushing back" that Ortner refers to. But it can
also be interpreted as the outcome of cynical reason, a position that asserts the
unchangeable power of the present over the past, of the living in all their often
cruelly unequal conditions of life over the dead.

For the latter reasons, we need to remain aware that the transition from
"cognition to recognition" (Honneth 2007), from an objectivized to a subjec-
tivized past, is a paradoxical undertaking. By "peopling the past," we substitute disrespect for the Other—their reification—with a respect for the Other
that is a mirror of our (present) Self. Such instrumentalization of past peoples'
subjectivities amounts to *diachronic violence.* Instead of such approaches to

enlivening the past, I advocate a form of writing that takes us away from pure description and its vain claims to truth but also a form that escapes the creation of a relation to the past that has the trappings of Orientalism (Said 1978).

SUBJECTS, HISTORY, AND COHERENCE

If the insertion of past subjects into narratives amounts to more than silencing, namely a repression of the Other, we need to add another dimension to this critique. Historical narrations generally have a structure of closure and coherence (Pluciennik 2010: 57–59) that results from the task of constructing temporal continuity. To ease the agreement between narrator and listener/reader, the formal character of a story also needs to adhere to a single perspective (Röttgers 1982: 40). This pertains to all the narrator types I have discussed, whether they are omniscient or individuals with personal experiences and attendant limits. We encounter coherence in two forms: the meaningfulness of a narration's content and the formal aspect of the narrator's unitary subjectivity.

Roland Barthes (1984) strongly objected to the notion of narrators' unitary subjectivity. Mastery of the self, implying a coherent subjectivity, has been questioned since the Freudian psychological thesis of an internal personality division into Ego, Super-Ego, and Id and has been discussed in cultural anthropology (Sökefeld 1999; Strathern 1988: 13–14) and even archaeology (Fowler 2004). Louis Althusser (1971: 171–77) famously claimed that subjects are the product of ideological systems, while Michel Foucault (2002: 422) predicted an end to modern unitary subjects in his well-known last sentence of *The Order of Things*.[4] Since then, the "decentered subject" has become commonplace in post-structuralist philosophy. The political dimension of this tendency is most clearly shown by Ernesto Laclau and Chantal Mouffe (2001: 115–16) as a transition from a coherent and stable subjectivity characteristic of modernity, a construct that emerged around the turn of the nineteenth century in Europe, to one of shifting subject positions. The coherent subject as a unifying background for human beings needs to be historicized (Meißner 2010). If the notion is disappearing in our world, it is possible that past worlds did not have such personality constructs either.

This has fundamental consequences for the post hoc creation of past peoples, whether a girl such as Spector's Mazaokiyewin or other subjects we encounter in standard historical and archaeological narrations. But the historicity of unitary subjects needs also to be taken into account for the author-narrator couple. Barthes (1982, 1984) denounces as bourgeois the overvaluation of the author as an autonomous and coherent subject-source of text production. Authors' ideological functions are almost imperceptible, as they push an audience toward a subcutaneous, purely formal consensus with a class- and culture-specific world through a narrative formality.

Coherence of content is expressed by the meaningfulness of the past. Most historians—and all indications suggest that this is also true for archaeologists—do not insist explicitly on meaningfulness as part of their business because a meaning of the past is an unquestionable basis of the discipline. What is at stake is only how to unravel meaning and what it might consist of (see Burckhardt 1905: 1–2). More perceptive scholars explicitly address meaningfulness as a *conditio sine qua non* of any historiography (Hobsbawm 1997: 192–200; Stone 1979), often with the explicit idea that the task of representations of the past is "orientation" in and for the present (Rüsen 1994, 2011: 486–87).[5] But what about the potential that the past lacks a coherent meaning? What if the "real past" as opposed to the narrated past was a chaotic jumble, a rhizomatic entity of contingent events? The background for the strong general interest in meaningfulness is human suffering. Neither Greek, Roman, nor US slavery can ever be undone. Still, the cruelty committed produces a strong desire to "make sense" of these injustices. To a certain extent, all history is driven by a search for justice, an idea that itself depends on stringent, coherent criteria (Koselleck 2000: 349).

However, the ultimate collective crime of a sequence of events that borders on the morally unthinkable—the Holocaust—defies a search for coherent meaning and sense (Levi 1986: 11–19). The Holocaust was not only a caesura in world history; it also marks a break in historiography as a narration with emplotment. Still, the desire for an orientational function of past experiences for the construction of expectations about a future (Koselleck 1979: 349–75) is so overwhelming that even the Holocaust has been turned into a (negative) foundation on which to build (see Leggewie and Lang 2011).

A starkly different position was advocated by Theodor Lessing (1919), who wrote that all historical narratives are creations of "meaning out of meaninglessness." The past's first characteristic is its "Uneinholbarkeit," its "uncatchability." Alexander Kluge's (1978) *Schlachtbeschreibung* is an excellent textual realization of Lessing's theories. Kluge's book includes a host of short chapters consisting of letters, documents, official announcements, photographs, simple narratives from unknown narrators, and more. The locations of the various producers of this collage of texts range from Stalingrad and Berlin to many other places in Europe. All those small text fragments sound as if they are archival documents, but which ones and how many really are remains unknown to the reader. Furious critics objected to this mixing of the factual and fictional. They found the lack of a clear narrative line objectionable and resented the cold and a-personal, bureaucratic tone of the text (e.g., Hillgruber 1964; Reich-Ranicki 1964). But Kluge's goal was not to render the battle of Stalingrad understandable, to allow empathy with specific actor(s), but rather the opposite: to make the reader aware of the *un-understandability*, the irreducible complexity of this (and other) historical event(s). If we follow this line of argument, our production of any meaningful and coherent narrative about the past, whether literary-fictional or academic, is nothing other than an ideology based on reductionism (see also Wagner 2001: 8–9). This does not mean we should abandon archaeology and the construction of narrations. It implies, however, that we need to look for new forms of rendering the past, forms that allow us to cast doubt on the assumption of historical coherence, unified meanings, and attendant reductionist forms of representation. Traditional writing, filming, virtuality, and other media representations are efforts to reproduce subjects who believe in the meaningfulness of the past, so it can be abused accordingly by institutions and powers-that-be.

SOME CHARACTERISTICS OF ARCHAEOLOGICAL NARRATIVES

The consequences of such reflections for archaeological narratives are situated in three areas. (1) The recognition of a non-identity between author and narrator frees authors to create a kind of narrator that does not follow the model of the unitary subject; narrators can occupy shifting subject positions and thus produce variable relations between present and past on the level of textual form. This dynamic and shifting narrator avoids the naturalization and de-historicization of the modern subject. (2) We should engage with past people in a relation of recognition (*Anerkennung*) that respects the potential for fundamentally different constructions of the self. Unless the material and textual archives provide clear indications thereof, the inclusion of coherent subjects in narratives about the past should be avoided. (3) The more encompassing our narratives try to be, the less they should be coherent. With increasing scales investigated, the degree of reductionism and thus of a hidden tendency toward fictionalizing increases. Works such as Ian Morris's (2010) *Why the West Rules* or Jared Diamond's (1997) *Guns, Germs and Steel* are cases in point. Such global histories (see also Toynbee 1934–61) were and are popular because they read meaning into long-term changes. But even the small-scale search for a coherent "story" can be misguided when it is driven by an attempt to find relief from the threat of meaninglessness. Jacques Lacan (1978: 22; Zizek 1989:

169–73) has called this threatening sphere the "Real," a world that completely withstands symbolization and representation by linguistic or other means. To find a way through these problems, I propose an alternative narrative strategy that relies on three fundamental tenets of archaeological narratives (see also Bernbeck 2010).

The sources at our disposition for constructing narratives are fragmented and, to put it mildly, incomplete. A major characteristic of archaeology is its primordial void (Bernbeck 2007). One of the main, albeit undervalued, fascinations of archaeology is this fundamental lack, which in turn creates the desire for replenishment. Our discipline systematizes methods for the fulfillment of this desire. Archaeology is ultimately nothing other than a huge machine that churns out reasoned ways to bridge gaps in knowledge, to mend the fragments of past worlds with the glue of images, texts, and graphs. It is not a positive process of *Sichtbarmachung*, a "making visible," that is at the core of our discipline; rather, every one of the much-touted discoveries entails a further mystery of the undiscovered and undiscoverable. If we follow the fashionable metaphor of "weaving" texts, then the archaeological narrative should not resemble a densely woven cloth but rather lace.

Whether we are concerned with historical periods or prehistory, the bulk of our sources do not allow us to address individuals. This has become increasingly problematic with the post-processual turn and the ensuing interest in quotidian practices of non-elite people. However, archaeologists start by necessity from a position that prevents them from telling credible stories of characters in all their complexities, internal contradictions, hopes, desires, and disappointments, unless we invent them (see above). In that case, we step over the boundaries of our sources. This also implies that the constructed intersubjective relations are our own fantasies. On the other hand, if we don't impose our imagination on the evidential world, it remains stale. Naming people in the past is an even more insurmountable problem, with the exception of a few whom we know through textual sources.

Finally, we have a very detailed, sensual knowledge of fragments of the material past. This stands in stark contrast to our lack of knowledge about past peoples and their selves, as well as the material world in its erstwhile complete state. We tend to describe the fragmentary world in extraordinary detail, from color to haptic characteristics, from the state of preservation to the materials out of which broken objects were made. We insist on noticing the microscopically tiny scars that remain as traces of use. Consistency, hardness, feel, shape, and scratches are all observed and described in painstaking detail, pressed into cartographies, graphics, tables, websites, and textual renderings that produce an aesthetic all their own. This symbolic realm is obsessed with the smallest observable units, often to the point of forgetting the larger picture.

A NARRATIVE MODEL FOR ARCHAEOLOGY:
THE *NOUVEAU ROMAN*

I have argued that the idea of a "thick description" is inappropriate when applied to past subjects because we cannot know them, and if we pretended to do so, we would do injustice to their lives. However, thick description is not just about subjectivities and intersubjective relations but can be equally successfully applied to material culture. It is in this realm that I find potential inspiration in the French writers around Alain Robbe-Grillet and his ideas of the *nouveau roman* (Robbe-Grillet 1963). The principles of the nouveau roman provide a path toward new ways of narrating an archaeologically preserved past.

Writers of the nouveau roman were particularly active in the 1950s and 1960s. Other than Robbe-Grillet, the group included many well-known novelists such as Nathalie Sarraute and Michel Butor. Robbe-Grillet was the spiritus rector of this loose group and also authored most of the programmatic statements about how ways of narrating need to change to leave behind the bourgeois structure of a literary form based on a stable and coherent subject (see also Barthes 1968). Four elements of the nouveau roman seem to me to have a particularly close relationship to archaeology—namely, a fractured reality, a complex and often ruptured chronological system, the importance of a world of things, and the deliberate avoidance of protagonists with whom a reader might empathize.

The nouveau roman starts from the premise that we can only grasp fractions of the reality around us. Bourgeois realism of the nineteenth century is inadequate not only for attempts at narrating twentieth- or twenty-first-century conditions but also for accounts of a deep past of which we surely have nothing but a few pieces in our hands. Robbe-Grillet's (1989) analysis of Flaubert's *Madame Bovary* points out that the substance of French novels in the nineteenth century tends to become more and more structured around gaps and voids when compared with the exemplary writer of the French bourgeoisie, Balzac.

Chronologically ordered narrations with a plot structure have become so ubiquitous as to give the impression of naturalness. Their harmonized form runs counter to the broken, ruptured reality of modernities (Barthes 1968; Morrissette 1963). But—and here we return to Lessing—was coherence ever part of reality? Isn't this one of the desires that drives us to pursue archaeology, read literature, watch movies? Meaning-making, the bundling of past events, texts, material items, practices, and institutions into a coherent re-presentation, is an absurd endeavor, a paradox: while past processes likely were to a large extent devoid of "meaning-fullness," we as humans seem to be dependent on it to survive. The nouveau roman revolts against literature as a means to forget one's own historical situated-ness. It abolishes not just omniscient views of the world but also those based on the existence of autonomous subjects with a linear life history. The world can be seen simultaneously from many different angles and points in time, and reality does not fit into linear chronological sequences. Rather, it tacks back and forth between various moments. In the works of the nouveau roman, this manifests itself in repetitions, reversals of time, and other effects that destroy the feeling of an underlying "progressive" narrative structure. The dimension of space manifests itself in the recurrence of one and the same material item described in different ways from various angles. Such novels are difficult to read. Not just the content needs to be captured, but the form requires reflection.

For archaeologists, the most interesting element of such literary forms is the importance of a "thing world." According to Robbe-Grillet, objects do not have meaning; they are simply there. It is only humans who are obsessed with reading meaning into them. The use of adjectives in the description of the material world is driven by the desire to "make sense" of an unrecognized reality that exists just as well without ascribed symbolic qualities. Here, the novelists' principles merge with those of Lacan's Real (discussed earlier).

Such insights lead the nouveau roman authors to favor a cold, analytical gaze that refrains from flowery language and stays as descriptive and technical as possible (Morrissette 1963: 69). Presaging tenets of postmodern thought, proponents of the nouveau roman insisted on the surface of the object world in their narrations, to the point of using language to empty meaning out of things (Barthes 1963: 10). However, the reason for superficiality is very different from that of postmodernism. Where Jean Baudrillard (1972) and others suggest that in the present the signifier prevails over the signified, Robbe-Grillet and colleagues made the political argument that the search for deep meaning is a typically bourgeois, reactionary endeavor, a relation to the world that sets the bourgeois class apart from workers.

A good example of the style that abandons traditional principles of narration can be found in the opening sentences of Robbe-Grillet's (1994: 39) novel *Jealousy*: "Now the shadow of the column—the column which supports the southwest corner of the roof—divides the corresponding corner of the veranda into two equal parts. This veranda is a wide, covered gallery surrounding the house on three sides. Since its width is the same for the central portion as for the sides, the line of shadow cast by the column extends precisely to the corner of the house."

Such descriptions abstain from assigning meaning, not to speak of agency, to observable objects and even people. There is no symbolism in material culture. This approach, called *chosiste* or thing-obsessed by critics, led to accusations that it was banal (Boisdeffre 1967), that it is not literature but "high art at its unpalatably highest" (Marche 2008), even that the books should be burned (see quotes in Lindwedel 2005: footnote 5).

The last point, the abstention from any engagement with people's emotions and feelings, is the result of a setting with rather vague figures, none of whom can serve as a "protagonist" with whom a reader might empathize. Reading such texts can be just as (positively) irritating as regarding a cubist painting.[6] The narration is segmented into multiple, often contradictory elements. This way of rendering reality accords well with the dissolution of modernity's Cartesian subject (Leenhardt 1973: 32–36), replacing it with Laclau and Mouffe's mere subject positions. The goal of the *nouveau roman* is political: the coherent subject is a bourgeois ideal of a past to which we cannot and should not return. Consequently, there is no account of harmonious experiences and expectations, disappointments and hopes in such books. Rather, subject states mostly circle around specific mental conditions that are typical for an ephemeral subject position.

ARCHAEOLOGY AND AN APPROPRIATE NARRATIVE FORM

I contend that we can learn a lot from such styles of narration, since subjectivities of Others, whether in recent or distant pasts, remain foreign to us. Past people's alterities resist our attempts at empathy. The latter approach is the only one that can even claim to approach the issue of recognition of the subjectivity of past Others. At the same time, empathy runs into the problem of assuming an unwarranted inner coherence of subjects. Giving Tringham's "faceless blobs" a real face is nothing other than a colonizing project that turns past Others, who likely had a fundamentally different kind of self, into peoples whose emotions, desires, and rationalities are close to our own.

I suggest that fictionalizing the past in the way of the *nouveau roman* is a better solution. Instead of creating coherent individuals, we should restrict ourselves to transient subject positions we can derive from past material remains and elaborate on those ephemeral positions. This would also make the gap between our knowledge and the lack of it more apparent. A brief vignette provides an insight into the kind of thick description I have in mind.

The Sherd Site

They will follow at some point into this bare landscape whose main superfluities seem to be a nimble lizard rushing around—and the bluster of the wind. No tree or shrub counters its power. Protective shade, which could weaken the burning of the sun, has never made its presence felt here. A few small thorny bushes dot the glaring emptiness with their twisted shapes. Unprotected are not only people but all those animals that do not have a propensity to crawl into self-dug holes in the ground. Only flight, the unrest that saves one's own life, could drive people into this flat, dusty area abraded by constant gusts of wind. Whoever comes here has had no choice when, where, and how to do so.

In this confusing endlessness, a bond to someone else is delivered by the signs of a predecessor. At arm's length, a slightly bent rim of a beaker sits in a small depression in the fine, hot sand that continues to the north in thousands of tiny parallel waves. The waves are complexly structured. The wind must have driven the sand toward the east, down a slight slope, so that without moving one's glance, one can count thirty-eight small steps, each of which ends after a slow eastward lifting with a sudden escarpment about one inch in height. Perhaps the gusts of the harsh wind have created small bulges that merge on the horizon into parallel lines. The sherd is of a monotonous dull black on its left side's surface. Abruptly and without any transition, the rest of the object changes to a slightly yellow color with russet sprinklings. Only this lighter part reveals the grooves from a fast-turning wheel. Three lines, exactly parallel, set apart by a distance no more than a fingernail's thickness, embrace the lower neck. The potter must have left them inadvertently when shaping this beaker, before setting it aside where it petrified in a drying sun and then in a fire. Taking these straight lines as a back-sight, they cut diagonally through the waves of sand in the west, the direction from which the apprehenders will come: the Provincia Palaestina. The sherd's sooted part signals a violent fire that caught up with the vessel, which at the time must have been half covered so that part of the surface was left unscathed by flames. But from excessive heat, the beaker burst into sharply edged pieces.

Next to the sherd, the sand is broken by a spiny shrub of an ell's height. The half-withered plant has featherweight spherical hollow pods at the ends of the bent twigs. Three body lengths farther, another ceramic sherd is stuck in the sandy soil. A cylindrical extension with the diameter of a thumb sticks out of the base of a gray, coarse bowl fragment—it looks strange and archaic, on careful consideration an impractical vessel. Maybe it was also a drinking cup? Who would have brought it to a waterless plain such as this one? It is a meager message about the temporally pulsing, unwilling

attraction of the desert. This lifeless reservoir of broken traces accommodates only shat-
tered things.

Afar on the right hand, some faint bluish hills are barely visible to the tired eye.
Behind them, a flourishing irrigated plain may be hidden—or again only the merci-
lessly sun-drenched, smoothly abraded flat landscape, broken up by a few insistent
shrubs that ultimately cannot withstand the relentless winds. Like fugitives, they are
driven away by the wind into the distance, where they will never again take root.

ACKNOWLEDGMENTS

I thank Ruth Van Dyke for her patience with my finishing this chapter under strenuous circumstances and for pushing me to "practice what I preach" by writing the vignette at the end. Two anonymous reviewers provided important input. Susan Pollock was, as always, a constructive critic. Another German version of my thoughts, albeit with a different orientation, has appeared in the journal *Ethnographisch-Archäologische Zeitschrift* (Bernbeck 2010).

NOTES

1. I use the word *text* here as a stand-in for a variety of representational forms, including film, photography, and other (multi)media.

2. In Germany, where I reside, this is still the dominant mode of talking and writing about archaeology.

3. A similar challenge to the traditional narrative form is posed by Homi Bhabha's notion of "third space" (Bhabha and Rutherford 1990). A postcolonial migrant position from which the world is accounted for, narrated, and evaluated must be decidedly uncertain, a space in motion that makes the traditional Hegelian fixed positions of master or serf, as well as the concomitant possibility for academic critique, difficult.

4. "One can certainly wager that man [l'homme' in the original] would be erased, like a face drawn in the sand at the edge of the sea."

5. Even Hayden White's (1973) *Metahistory* fits into this mold (see also Ankersmit 2001: 254–57).

6. Marche's (2008) obituary ends thus: "The relief I felt when I heard about Robbe-Grillet's death was also partly hope. Now we can go on, I was thinking."

REFERENCES

Agamben, Giorgio. 2002. *Remnants of Auschwitz: The Witness and the Archive.* New York: Zone Books.

Althusser, Louis. 1971. *Lenin and Philosophy*. Trans. Ben Brewster. New York: Monthly Review Press.

Ankersmit, Frank R. 2001. *Historical Representation*. Stanford: Stanford University Press.

Barthes, Roland. 1963. "Préface." In *Les romans de Robbe-Grillet*, by Bruce Morrissette, 7–16. Paris: Éditions de Minuit.

Barthes, Roland. 1968. *Writing Degree Zero*. Trans. Annette Lavers and Colin Smith. New York: Hill and Wang.

Barthes, Roland. 1982. "Le discours de l'histoire." *Poétique* 13: 13–21.

Barthes, Roland. 1984. "La mort de l'auteur." In *Le bruissement de la langue: Essais critiques IV*, by Roland Barthes, 61–67. Paris: Éditions du Seuil.

Baudrillard, Jean. 1972. *Pour une critique de l'économie politique du signe*. Paris: Gallimard.

Bentley, R. Alexander, and Herbert D.G. Maschner. 2008. "Complexity Theory." In *Handbook of Archaeological Theories*, ed. R. Alexander Bentley, Herbert D.G. Maschner, and Christopher Chippindale, 245–72. Lanham, MD: AltaMira.

Bernbeck, Reinhard. 2005. "The Past as Fact and Fiction: From Historical Novels to Novel Histories." In *Archaeologies of the Middle East: Critical Perspectives*, ed. Susan Pollock and Reinhard Bernbeck, 97–122. Oxford: Blackwell.

Bernbeck, Reinhard. 2007. "From the Search for Meaning to the Recognition of Ignorance." *Cambridge Archaeological Journal* 17 (2): 207–10.

Bernbeck, Reinhard. 2010. "'La Jalousie' und Archäologie: Plädoyer für ein subjektloses Erzählen." *Ethnographisch-Archäologische Zeitschrift* 51 (1-2): 64–86.

Bhabha, Homi, and Johnathan Rutherford. 1990. "The Third Space: Interview with Homi Bhabha." In *Identity: Community, Culture, Difference*, ed. Jonathan Rutherford, 207–21. London: Lawrence and Wishart.

Boisdeffre, Pierre de. 1967. *La cafetière est sur la table, ou contre le "Nouveau Roman."* Paris: La Table Ronde.

Burckhardt, Jacob. 1905. *Weltgeschichtliche Betrachtungen*. Berlin: W. Spemann.

Chakrabarty, Dipesh. 2000. *Provincializing Europe: Postcolonial Thought and Historical Difference*. Princeton: Princeton University Press.

Clifford, James, and George E. Marcus, eds. 1986. *Writing Culture: The Poetics and Politics of Ethnography*. Berkeley: University of California Press.

Cochrane, Ethan E. 2011. "Units of Transmission in Evolutionary Archaeology and the Role of Memetics." In *Evolutionary and Interpretive Archaeologies: A Dialogue*, ed. Ethan E. Cochrane and Andrew Gardner, 31–62. Walnut Creek, CA: Left Coast.

Diamond, Jared. 1997. *Guns, Germs and Steel: The Fate of Human Societies*. New York: W. W. Norton.

Flannery, Kent V. 1967. "Culture History vs. Cultural Process: A Debate in American Archaeology." *Scientific American* 217: 119–22.

Flannery, Kent V. 1976. *The Early Mesoamerican Village*. New York: Academic Press.

Foucault, Michel. 2002. *The Order of Things: An Archaeology of the Human Sciences*. New York: Routledge Classics.

Fowler, Chris. 2004. *The Archaeology of Personhood: An Anthropological Approach*. New York: Routledge.

Geertz, Clifford. 1974. "'From the Native's Point of View': On the Nature of Anthropological Understanding." *Bulletin of the American Academy of Arts and Sciences* 28 (1): 26–45.

Gero, Joan M., and Margaret W. Conkey, eds. 1991. *Engendering Archaeology: Women and Prehistory*. Oxford: Blackwell.

Guha, Ranajit. 1988. "The Prose of Counterinsurgency." In *Selected Subaltern Studies*, ed. Ranajit Guha and Gayatri Chakravorti Spivak, 45–88. Oxford: Oxford University Press.

Herausgeberinnen-Kollektiv des FKA. 2012. "Beyond Affirmation: Perspectives for Critical Archaeologies." *Forum Kritische Archaeologie* 1: 167–96. http://www.kritischearchaeologie.de/fka/article/view/22, accessed January 2, 2013.

Hillgruber, Andreas. 1964. "Beschreibung der unbeschreibbaren Schlacht von Stalingrad: Protest eines Historikers." *Die Welt der Literatur* (May 28): 189.

Hobsbawm, Eric. 1997. *On History*. New York: New Press.

Hodder, Ian. 1986. *Reading the Past*. Cambridge: Cambridge University Press.

Hodder, Ian, ed. 1989. *The Meaning of Things*. London: Unwin Hyman.

Honneth, Axel. 2007. *Reification: A New Look at an Old Idea*. Oxford: Oxford University Press.

Husserl, Edmund. 1992 [1909–10]. *Grundprobleme der Phänomenologie: 1910/11*. Hamburg: Meiners.

Joyce, Rosemary, Robert Preucel, Jeanne Lopiparo, Carolyn Guyer, and Michael Joyce. 2002. *The Languages of Archaeology*. Oxford: Blackwell.

Kluge, Alexander. 1978. *Schlachtbeschreibung: Der organisatorische Aufbau eines Unglücks*. Munich: Wilhelm Goldmann.

Kohler, Timothy A., and George J. Gumerman, eds. 2000. *Dynamics in Human and Primate Societies: Agent-Based Modeling of Social and Spatial Processes*. New York: Oxford University Press.

Koselleck, Reinhart. 1979. *Vergangene Zukunft*. Frankfurt: Suhrkamp.

Koselleck, Reinhart. 2000. *Zeitschichten*. Frankfurt: Suhrkamp.

Lacan, Jacques. 1978. *Le séminaire de Jacques Lacan, Book II: Le Moi dans la théorie de Freud et dans la technique de la psychanalyse, 1954–1955*. Paris: Éditions du Seuil.

Laclau, Ernesto, and Chantal Moutte. 2001. *Hegemony and Socialist Strategy: Towards a Radical Democratic Politics*, 2nd ed. London: Verso.

Leenhardt, Jacques. 1973. *Lecture politique du roman "La Jalousie" d'Alain Robbe-Grillet*. Paris: Éditions de Minuit.

Leggewie, Klaus, and Anne Lang. 2011. *Der Kampf um europäische Erinnerung: Ein Schlachtfeld wird besichtigt*. Munich: C. H. Beck.

Lessing, Theodor. 1919. *Geschichte als Sinngebung des Sinnlosen*. Munich: C. H. Beck.

Levi, Primo. 1986. *The Drowned and the Saved*. Trans. Raymond Rosenthal. New York: Summit Books.

Lindwedel, Martin. 2005. "Alain Robbe-Grillets intermediale Ästhetik des Bildes." PhD diss., Hannover University, Hannover, Germany.

Malinowski, Bronislaw. 1967. *A Diary in the Strict Sense of the Word*. New York: Harcourt, Brace and World.

Marche, Stephen. 2008. "The Man Who Ruined the Novel." Salon, March 6, 2008. http://www.salon.com/2008/03/06/robbe_grillet/, accessed January 2, 2013.

Meißner, Hanna. 2010. Jenseits des autonomen Subjekts: Zur gesellschaftlichen Konstitution von Handlungsfähigkeit im Anschluss an Butler, Foucault und Marx. Bielefeld, Germany: transcript.

Morris, Ian. 2010. *Why the West Rules—for Now: The Patterns of History, and What They Reveal about the Future*. New York: Farrar, Straus and Giroux.

Morrissette, Bruce. 1963. *Les romans de Robbe-Grillet*. Paris: Éditions de Minuit.

Narayan, Kirin. 1993. "How 'Native' Is a Native Anthropologist?" *American Anthropologist* 95 (3): 671–86.

Ortner, Sherry. 1996. "Resistance and the Problem of Ethnographic Refusal." In *The Historic Turn in the Human Sciences*, ed. Terrence J. McDonald, 281–304. Ann Arbor: University of Michigan Press.

Pauketat, Timothy R. 2007. *Chiefdoms and Other Archaeological Delusions*. Lanham, MD: AltaMira.

Pluciennik, Mark. 2010. "Is Narrative Necessary?" *Ethnographisch-Archäologische Zeitschrift* 51 (1-2): 48–63.

Preucel, Robert W., and Stephen A. Mrozowski. 2010. "The New Pragmatism." In *Contemporary Archaeology in Theory: The New Pragmatism*, ed. Robert W. Preucel and Stephen A. Mrozowski, 3–49. Malden, MA: Wiley-Blackwell.

Reich-Ranicki, Marcel. 1964. "Autor Klu. scheitert bei St. Ein Buch, das nicht nur sein Verfasser verschuldet hat." *Die Zeit* 1964 (24). http://www.zeit.de/1964/24 /autor-klu-scheitert-bei-st, accessed January 2, 2013.

Robbe-Grillet, Alain. 1963. *Pour un Nouveau Roman*. Paris: Éditions de Minuit.

Robbe-Grillet, Alain. 1989. *Vom Anlaß des Schreibens*. Tübingen, Germany: Rive Gauche.

Robbe-Grillet, Alain. 1994. *Jealousy and In the Labyrinth*. Trans. Richard Howard. New York: Grove/Atlantic.

Röttgers, Kurt. 1982. "Geschichtserzählung als kommunikativer Text." In *Historisches Erzählen*, ed. Siegfried Quandt and Hans Süssmuth, 29–48. Göttingen, Germany: Vandenhoeck and Ruprecht.

Rüsen, Jörn. 1994. *Historische Orientierung*. Cologne, Germany: Böhlau.

Rüsen, Jörn. 2011. "Historik: Umriss einer Theorie der Geschichtswissenschaft." *Erwägen-Wissen-Ethik* 22 (4): 477–619.

Said, Edward. 1978. *Orientalism*. New York: Pantheon Books.

Shanks, Michael, and Christopher Tilley. 1992. *Re-Constructing Archaeology: Theory and Practice*. London: Routledge.

Sökefeld, Martin. 1999. "Debating Self, Identity and Culture in Anthropology." *Current Anthropology* 40 (4): 417–48.

Spector, Janet. 1993. *What This Awl Means: Feminist Archaeology at a Wahpeton Dakota Village*. St. Paul: Minnesota Historical Society Press.

Spivak, Gayatri Chakravorti. 1988. "Can the Subaltern Speak?" In *Marxism and the Interpretation of Culture*, ed. Cary Nelson and Lawrence Grossberg, 271–315. Urbana: University of Illinois Press.

Stanzel, Franz K. 2001. *Theorie des Erzählens*, 7th ed. Göttingen, Germany: Vandenhoeck and Ruprecht.

Stone, Lawrence. 1979. "The Revival of Narrative: Reflections on a New Old History." *Past and Present* 85 (1): 3–24.

Strathern, Marilyn. 1988. *The Gender of the Gift: Problems with Women and Problems with Society in Melanesia*. Berkeley: University of California Press.

Tarlow, Sarah. 2001. "The Responsibility of Representation." In *The Responsibilities of Archaeologists: Archaeology and Ethics*, ed. Mark Pluciennik, 57–64. Oxford: Archaeopress.

Toynbee, Arnold J. 1934–61. *A Study of History*, 12 vols. Oxford: Oxford University Press.

Tringham, Ruth. 1996. "But Gordon, Where Are the People? Some Comments on the Topic of Craft Specialization and Social Evolution." In *Craft Specialization and Social Evolution: In Commemoration of V. Gordon Childe*, ed. Bernard Wailes, 233–39. Philadelphia: MASCA Press, University of Pennsylvania.

Wagner, Roy. 2001. *An Anthropology of the Subject: Holographic Worldview in New Guinea and Its Meaning and Significance for the World of Anthropology*. Berkeley: University of California Press.

White, Hayden. 1973. *Metahistory: The Historical Imagination in Nineteenth Century Europe*. Baltimore: Johns Hopkins University Press.

White, Hayden. 1987. *The Content of the Form: Narrative Discourse and Historical Representation*. Baltimore: Johns Hopkins University Press.

Yesner, David R. 2008. "Ecology in Archaeology." In *Handbook of Archaeological Theories*, ed. R. Alexander Bentley, Herbert D.G. Maschner, and Christopher Chippindale, 39–56. Lanham, MD: AltaMira.

Zizek, Slavoj. 1989. *The Sublime Object of Ideology*. London: Verso.

13

Wrestling with Truth

Possibilities and Peril in Alternative Narrative Forms

Sarah Pollock

In fall of 2010, Binghamton University archaeologist Ruth M. Van Dyke emailed me with a curious invitation. A group of her colleagues were engaged in experimental methods of telling their research stories—"challenging the prevalence of the passive, expository style," as she put it—and intended to present their work at the 76th meeting of the Society for American Archaeology (SAA). Would I be willing to join their presentation and offer a critique of their work? At first I was somewhat flummoxed—I am, after all, a journalist and a professor of nonfiction writing—and it wasn't clear to me what I had to offer. But as I reflected on the invitation and we discussed the group's goals, it became clear to me that Van Dyke had presented an engaging challenge, one that complemented my own abiding concerns about the value of fact-based writing in works of nonfiction.

Is it possible to write creatively and to acknowledge the slipperiness of truth and facts while still staying true to what we commonly understand to be nonfiction? If not, what do we mean when we present a piece of writing as nonfiction? And how does the public understand the term? In recent years, these questions have gripped the field of creative nonfiction (as it is known in MFA writing programs), pitting the established ethical values of journalism against a literary license that has increasingly been claimed by writers who assume the mantle of nonfiction but who challenge our notion of what is true. It became clear to me that these archaeologists

DOI: 10.5876/9781607323815.c013

were entering the conversation from a different disciplinary foundation, and it could be illuminating for us to talk across disciplines.

The archaeological narratives included in this anthology (first presented at the 76th SAA conference) wrestle with questions of truth and invention in a variety of ways. Many deliberately blur the boundary between science and artistic invention, many employ a nonlinear approach to tell stories, some express a desire to share authorship of archaeological interpretation with the readers of texts, and a few experiment with new technologies to achieve these ends. Alternatively, some of the included essays challenge aspects of the experimentation and caution against it.

The motivations articulated for such narrative experimentation are various. Some argue that there's a growing consensus that most archaeological interpretations are as much art as science or social science, and they say that creative interpretations are useful in making archaeology more relevant to those outside the discipline. They propose narrative invention on a continuum that may even include making up details or elements to speak to an emotional or historical "truth" that does not (by virtue of being made up) reflect factual reporting. Some express a strong commitment to giving voice to long-passed peoples whose lives are excavated in, while others caution that fabricating imagined voices may be another form of appropriation.

Reinhard Bernbeck, a professor at Freie Universität Berlin and Van Dyke's co-editor for this volume, underscores some of these risks and raises pivotal ethical concerns about what invented narratives mean to the discipline of archaeology. "The invention of subjects, however well meant the empathetic effort is, implies a certain disrespect for past people," he writes (see Bernbeck, this volume). "Not knowing the motivations for past practices and actions, we project political desires back in time, carrying out in the process an act of colonization."

Similar ethical issues to those raised in this volume have gripped the broader nonfiction-writing community for the past decade or so. On one extreme, you have traditional journalism with strict standards for fact-checking and a clear notion that if you call a piece of writing nonfiction, it had better be as close as you can get to factually true. At the other extreme, you have proponents of a nonfiction that claims an artistic license to write *as though* something happened but with liberty to invent subjects and adjust (or invent) facts as seems useful to the author. The argument made by those advocating this position is that such artistry gets at a more true truth than strict adherence to fact can achieve and is also perhaps more engaging.

Even as this anthology was being edited, the issue surfaced anew in the literary world with the publication of a book by John d'Agata and Jim Fingal

(2012), *The Lifespan of a Fact*. The book purported to be an accurate account-
ing of the correspondence between a writer (d'Agata) and a magazine fact-
checker (Fingal) in which they engage in "a fascinating and dramatic power
struggle over the intriguing question of what nonfiction should, or can, be"
(d'Agata and Fingal 2012: jacket cover). Fingal was fact-checking an essay for
publication, much of which was later adapted nearly verbatim for inclusion
in d'Agata's (2010) much-acclaimed book about the Yucca Mountain nuclear
waste dump, *About a Mountain*. D'Agata, who argues that he can change even
the most verifiable facts (the name and location of a bar [d'Agata and Fingal
2012: 32), the content of people's quotes, what sights can be viewed from a
particular vantage point [ibid.: 84], even the color of a fleet of vans, from
pink to purple) to suit his artistic inclination, was pilloried (McDonald 2012).
Then it turned out that the *Lifespan* book itself was a fabrication, an after-the-
fact dramatization intended to heighten the ethical conflict and make it more
marketable.

Arguments ensued at the 2012 annual professional meeting of creative writing programs (Associated Writers and Writing Programs), with panelists and
writers both challenging and supporting d'Agata's transgressive approach. (For
the flavor of the discussion, see commentary and reports in Dzieza 2012; Farrar
2012; Moore 2012; Nester 2012; Read 2012; Stuckey-French 2012.) I agree with
the comments in an essay by *Brevity* editor Dinty W. Moore, who expressed
distress about what he called d'Agata's disrespect for his colleagues and readers. Moore also pointed out that d'Agata was playing into the hands of those
who would undermine the entire field of nonfiction, including "those on the
political right who criticize journalists for 'just making everything up,'" as well
as "those who want to discount the entire memoir category as baloney because
memory is not a perfect tool" (Moore 2012).

For another example, consider the quagmire in which author and actor
Mike Daisey found himself after his theatrical monologue, *The Agony and
Ecstasy of Steve Jobs*, hit the big time. The public radio program *This American
Life* aired the show, which detailed purportedly truthful facts about how workers in China were exploited to create products for Apple. Much of the material
was well documented, but when it turned out that parts of Daisey's account
were fabricated, *This American Life* ran a full-episode retraction on March 16,
2012. After ten days of criticism in the press and blogosphere, Daisey wrote
an anguished apology on his blog. "When I said onstage that I had personally
experienced things I in fact did not, I failed to honor the contract I'd established with my audiences over many years and many shows," he wrote. "In
doing so, I not only violated their trust, I also made worse art" (Daisey 2012).

The core issue in both examples is whether one can credibly label outright inventions nonfiction. It is clear that creative, imagined literary and theatrical expression can achieve true and beautiful renderings of our common world. And it is clear that great artistry has been achieved in accurate and creative reporting of events. The ethical trouble surfaces when a writer assumes the mantle of authenticity associated with nonfiction as he or she simultaneously subverts the common understanding of what that label means.

~ ~ ~

I am not alone in arguing that the stakes here are high: if a work pretends to be factually true and is not, it then becomes a lie, and such lies are dangerous to a society in which we depend upon evidence-based arguments to make social and political choices. Though the literary provocateurs would dismiss such an allegiance to facts as outré and unachievable, I echo the position of literary scholar Marilyn Chandler McEntyre, who argues that writers and scholars in particular have a moral responsibility to resist "the tidal wave of contaminated information" that threatens to drown us (McEntyre 2009: 62). While acknowledging that truth is ambiguous and complex, she says, our response should be neither cynicism nor naïveté; nor should we fall into the existential abyss. In other words, while we may agree that positionality, memory, and the very nature of language preclude some Platonic absolute conception of one fixed universal truth, to acknowledge the slipperiness of narrative or presentation does not equate to giving up adherence to empirical facts.

We come to this confusing juncture for a variety of reasons, some of which also are driving the experimental narratives included in this anthology. Literary theorists and philosophers have long been dismantling our notions of truth and raising important and provocative questions about its definition. Objectivity is now widely agreed to be unattainable. And yet, if we are to present a work as nonfiction, there is something critically important about our fidelity to the effort to *get it right*, to tell the truth as best we can, to adhere to the facts as we are best able to establish them, a fidelity that is essential to the social contract. Because when the theoretical argument is transported out of the halls of academia and into our common culture, a great deal is at stake. We can no longer say that what happens in Vegas stays in Vegas.

While it may be important to challenge the notion of truth in texts—historical accounts and laws that pretend to lack bias are, for example, dangerous indeed—that position becomes corrosive when taken to an extreme and then translated into the larger realm of social discourse. If we can't agree on what is true—if, in fact, we have no common agreement that it's even possible or necessary to agree on a truth—we have a society in which politicians can lie to us without consequence, in which "news" programs can freely distort the events of the day to suit their political agendas, in which even the Holocaust can be discounted as merely a rumor.

You may say we've already come to that. Indeed, McEntyre asserts that great damage to the social contract has been inflicted by the subversion of the value of truth: "The generation of students coming through high schools and universities now expect to be lied to. They know about 'spin' and about the profiteering agendas of corporate advertising. They have grown used to the flippant, incessantly ironic banter that passes for conversation," she writes. "I don't know how many times over the past year I've heard students, trying to make sense of the news, lament, 'I don't know how to tell what to believe!' 'How do I tell what's reliable?' 'How do I distinguish what's true?'" (McEntyre 2009: 7).

These questions are good ones for all of us, and they are critical catalysts for these experimental archaeological narratives. Some of the authors herein suggest that to deliver an account in the passive, fact-driven authoritative voice of science may imply a degree of objective, unbiased knowledge that is often false. In other words, the form itself can render its content false. They are looking for a way to challenge the conventional way of presenting "truth" and to chart a new, more imaginative path to tell their stories. So how do they decide what is "true"? The same question has entangled many of us trying to tell nonfiction stories in creative ways, to get at truths that would otherwise remain unexpressed.

In pursuit of some answers, author Bonnie Rough (2007) decided to interview scientific artists when she set out to articulate clearer boundary lines for the creative nonfiction genre, particularly memoir. Ironically, she turned to a paleontological reconstructionist and a forensic reconstructionist. Rough articulates the boundary between fiction and creative nonfiction as follows: "The difference comes with intent. Nonfiction writers imagine. Fiction writers invent. These are fundamentally different acts, performed to different ends" (ibid.: 66). The scientists she interviewed described a careful process in which they first gather all the data points available and then, "in very good faith," use what paleontological reconstructionist Robert Walters calls *disciplined imagination* to fill in what is missing. They trust their experience and build on what is known, and then they add details to create the most likely story: they take conservative leaps to decide, for example, what colors to use in painting dinosaurs for the Smithsonian Institution in Washington, DC, and the Carnegie Museum of Natural History in Pittsburgh.

The challenge for many of the authors in this collection is to determine exactly how disciplined, or conservative, their imaginative leaps must be. Many of them feel enchained by what they call academic subjectivization, and they resist a policing effort that would discount their narrative contributions. And the best of this work falls more within the realm of Walters's *disciplined imagination* than the creative process described by d'Agata, who claims artistic license to turn a pink van purple to achieve a certain rhythm in his sentence. Or Daisey, who invented characters and events and thus transformed his work from documentation to untrustworthy propaganda (albeit for a worthy cause).

~ ~ ~

The porosity of the boundary between fact-based imagination and invention is not the only experimental aspect of the narratives in this anthology. The archaeologists experimenting here also share a narrative playfulness and invention that is percolating throughout the literary world. Like other nonfiction (and fiction) writers, they are experimenting with multiple strands of narration, the use of hypertext, and stories in which the reader directs the outcome (see Tringham, this volume). The two most revolutionary aspects of the new technologies, in my view, are the de-prioritization of the traditional linear narrative and the increasingly interactive engagement of the reader, so that the line between author and reader is softened. All these choices raise fascinating questions about the nature of narrative and the parameters of nonfiction and fiction (or, for archaeologists, of science versus art).

When Van Dyke asked me to comment on these experimental essays, she proposed that I offer guidelines and insight from outside the discipline. Given the battles being fought in the world of literary nonfiction, I cannot provide unequivocal directives about how to navigate this new, occasionally perilous terrain. But I can offer some suggestions.

First, be respectful of your audience, which means be clear with them about what you are doing. My graduate students, who had been reading d'Agata's book *About a Mountain* as part of their course work, felt betrayed to find out that his "facts" were unreliable. (The book created a simulacrum of facticity by including 193 endnotes that seemed to clarify what material was reshaped, what is imagined, and what were the sources for the factual assertions he made.) What had once appeared to be a beautifully and persuasively rendered portrait of the cultural context of Las Vegas—a city that had embraced a massive nuclear waste dump—lost much of its credibility when the readers could no longer be sure of the facts. Among other things, students thought d'Agata had made a powerful case against the pro-nuke propaganda disseminated in support of the waste dump (d'Agata 2010: 51–79), but the case collapsed if his "facts" were no more reliable than those proffered by the other side. When the conversation veered from the content of his narrative to the trustworthiness of his account, the book became substantially less valuable.

The problem is that we read a narrative differently if we believe it to be *true* vs. imagined. In nonfiction, it is the *actuality* of the experience that touches us. While fiction may touch us equally, for different reasons, part of what compels us in nonfiction is that the events actually happened. I believe we undermine our authority as writers of nonfiction if we include fiction *disguised as fact* in our narratives. Why label it nonfiction if it is not? But that does *not* mean we cannot be creative, poetic, and experimental with our material. It means we need to keep track of what we know and what we do not know and provide the reader with signposts that distinguish those elements.

Take, for example, Van Dyke's Chaco Canyon narrative (see Van Dyke, this volume). It is clear that much of the first-person material must be invented, and I wanted to know, as a reader, which details were known data points and which were extrapolated. Van Dyke explains that she has grounded the material in empirical data and offers examples and specifics about what that distinction means. It is very helpful to understand where her imagination steps in, and I found it enlightening to read about how and why she constructed the imagined narrative of a ten-year-old girl. Van Dyke's contextualization provides an excellent rationale for the value of such imagined narratives.

However, some of these experimental narratives may make the assumption that one of the characters in the Praetzellis narrative (see Praetzellis and Praetzellis, this volume) articulates. The "character," Adrian, says that "some archaeology may be science; some may be art; some may even be psychotherapy. And most thinking people are pretty clear which is which ... We have to provide technical reports that document our methods and findings. But at that point it is anyone's game for interpretation."

My editorial question is: *is* everyone clear about which is which? Is the public clear? Are there signposts in the narrative you are creating that establish those distinctions? If not, why not?

One of the places where I had no trouble making those distinctions is in what I have seen of the multimedia work of Ruth Tringham (see Tringham, this volume), which I find exciting. As a journalist, part of what I respond to in her work is the way she is clear about what material is hard data and what is imaginative. She is not *inventing facts*, but she is acknowledging through her multimedia approach that facts are limited and have limitations. She is building on her expertise to *imagine* what the data might mean and to offer readers their own ability to create stories. In her work, narrative is open-ended and definitely not linear.

This narrative structure and openness resonates with the comments of Isaac Gilead (see Gilead, this volume), who cautions that "as archaeologists, we cannot emancipate ourselves from data." Yet he references the multiple strands of text and commentary in the Talmud as "a mode of simultaneous or almost simultaneous presentation of data and narrative"—an analogy that has come up similarly in some of my colleagues' creative nonfiction essays that use multiple narrative tracks on the same page (e.g., *Finding Faith* by Faith Adiele).

Tringham's multimedia work also capitalizes on the explosion of cross-genre publishing work taking place in multimedia formats. Writers and publishers are just beginning to imagine how tablets and portable reading devices will change the nature of reading and how the new technology will more easily permit the exploration of nonlinear narratives. Writers have been imagining and experimenting with these ideas on the printed page and also on websites, CD-roms, and DVDs, but the new portable reading devices are making hypertext and nonlinear visual displays far more accessible to the common reader and are already changing the nature of publishing.

Overall, I think fascinating, innovative work is being created by these archaeologists, who are engaging in a conversation that extends far beyond their discipline. I believe they are correct in asserting that the most effective narrative is not necessarily linear, that stories may more accurately be represented by an accretion of fragments rather than a traditionally structured "arc," and that truth is more elusive than a simple recounting of the "facts" would suggest.

But as scientists experimenting with new narrative forms, the authors would be wise to maintain an awareness of risk and a commitment to disclosure. A nonfiction writer who claims artistic license to invent facts and pretend they are true loses the authority granted to work believed to be nonfiction. Likewise, a scientist who fills in gaps between evidence-based knowledge with imaginative leaps is not, then, delivering a fully scientific account. The narratives can reach beyond the discipline's boundaries and make archaeology more relevant—and even, arguably, more *true* to what is likely to have happened. They can give voice to long-passed peoples. But while such stories may be science-*based*, they are not, in and of themselves, science.

In this invention of something new, I recommend a few editorial guidelines:

- The authors should keep it clear to themselves (and to their readers) what is the implicit contract of their work and honor that contract.

- If an author departs from what is understood to be archaeology, it is important to instruct the "reader" how to read the text.
- Consider what is lost (or gained) by fictionalizing research. Are there ways to construct alternative narratives that include the imagined world without commingling it with the more data-driven material of traditional archaeology?

The presenters in this anthology are serious archaeologists, and they want the experimental work included here to represent them as such. The work is inventive, but in embracing the subjectivity of archaeological interpretation, they may sometimes confuse audiences about where scientific inquiry ends and disciplined imagination begins—especially when the audience is outside the field. Unless the authors of such texts are very clear to their readers about the parameters of their experimentation, they run the risk of sabotaging their discipline's scientific standards—and with that the discipline stands to lose essential value. Of course, all scientific inquiry involves the imagination, but if part of the agenda for creating these narratives is to reach an audience beyond the academy, then discursive framing is critical because it matters a great deal *how* that audience understands the material to be *true*.

REFERENCES

d'Agata, John. 2010. *About a Mountain*. New York: W. W. Norton.

d'Agata, John, and Jim Fingal. 2012. *The Lifespan of a Fact*. New York: W. W. Norton.

Daisey, Mike. 2012. "His Secret Fortress on the Web." http://mikedaisey.blogspot.ca /2012/03/some-thoughts-after-storm.html, accessed March 25, 2012.

Dzieza, Josh. 2012. "John d'Agata's Fact-Checking Battle." *The Daily Beast*. http:// www.thedailybeast.com/articles/2012/02/21/john-d-agata-s-fact-checking-battle .html, accessed June 19, 2012.

Farrar, Julie. 2012. "All Nonfiction Employs Art in Service to Facts." *Brevity's Nonfiction Blog*. http://brevity.wordpress.com/2012/03/07/awp-2012-all-nonfiction -employs-art-in-service-to-facts/, accessed June 19, 2012.

McDonald, Jennifer B. 2012. "In the Details." *New York Times*, February 21, BR1.

McEntyre, Marilyn Chandler. 2009. *Caring for Words in a Culture of Lies*. Grand Rapids, MI: William B. Eerdmans.

Moore, Dinty W. 2012. "D'Agata's Trickery and Manipulations." *Brevity's Nonfiction Blog*. http://brevity.wordpress.com/2012/02/27/dagatas-trickery/, accessed June 17, 2012.

Nester, Daniel. 2012. "Ned Stuckey-French's Dear John [d'Agata] Letter." *We Who Are about to Die*. http://wewhoareabouttodie.com/2012/03/08/ned-stuckey-frenchs -dear-john-dagata-letter/, accessed June 19, 2012. Accessed Nov. 1, 2014

Read, Katy. 2012. "AWP no. 13: Amidst the Gentility of Writers, Some Heated Controversy." *Minneapolis Star Tribune* online. http://www.startribune.com /entertainment/blogs/141347663.html, accessed June 19, 2012.

Rough, Bonnie J. 2007. "Writing Lost Stories: When Bones Are All We Have." *Iron Horse Literary Review* (Spring).

Stuckey-French, Ned. 2012. *Dear John, I'm Afraid It Is Over. Brevity's Nonfiction Blog*. http://brevity.wordpress.com/2012/03/08/dear-john-im-afraid-it-is-over/, accessed November 1, 2014.

DOUG BAILEY is professor of visual archaeology in the Department of Anthropology at San Francisco State University. His major monographs include *Unearthed* (2010) and
Prehistoric Figurines: Representation and Corporeality (2005).
He is an expert on the prehistory of Eastern Europe and
ancient art, and his most recent work focuses on nontraditional presentations of archaeological thought and the juxtapositions of past and present objects, thoughts, and output. His current project is a radical treatment of prehistoric
pit-houses in terms of twentieth-century artistic production
and performance. Doug's work pushes uncomfortably in the
tender spaces beyond and between the disciplines of art and
archaeology.

REINHARD BERNBECK is a professor at the Institute of Western Asian Archaeology at the Freie Universität Berlin. He in-
vestigates conditions surrounding the emergence of inequality, drawing on his fieldwork in Iran, Turkey, Jordan, and, at
present, Turkmenistan. From 2012 to 2014, he co-directed
excavations of Nazi forced labor camps and a short-lived
concentration camp at Tempelhof Airport in the middle of
Berlin. His latest co-edited volumes are *Ideologies in Archaeology* (2011) and *Interpreting the Late Neolithic in Northern
Mesopotamia* (2013).

JAMES G. GIBB operates his own archaeological consulting
business and holds appointments as research associate at
the Smithsonian Environmental Research Center in Maryland, USA, and as adjunct faculty at Stevenson University
and Anne Arundel Community College. He authored *The
Archaeology of Wealth: Consumer Behavior in English America*
and a number of journal articles on issues in Native American and EuroAmerican history and co-edited *The Archaeology of Institutional Life* with April M. Beisaw. Jim also has

written two plays that were produced at a local history site, marrying his interests in theater, history, and archaeology.

ISAAC GILEAD is a professor of prehistoric archaeology at the Department of Bible Archaeology and the Ancient Near East in Ben-Gurion University of the Negev, Israel. He is the author of "Grar: A Chalcolithic Site in the Northern Negev, Israel" in the *Journal of Field Archaeology*. He studies the Palaeolithic to Chalcolithic archaeology of the southern Levant and the archaeology of extermination centers.

SARAH MILLEDGE NELSON is an East Asian archaeologist who works mostly in South Korea and China. She has published 11 scholarly books and three novels about archaeology. Her most recent books are *The Hongshan Papers: Collected Studies in the Archaeology of Northeast China* (2014) and *Shamans, Queens, and Figurines: The Development of Gender in Archaeology* (2015). Currently she is writing a book on Kyongju in South Korea, a new edition of *The Archaeology of Korea* (co-authored with Rachel Lee), and a novel about an East Asian queen. She is John Evans Distinguished Professor Emeritus at the University of Denver.

MARK PLUCIENNIK is a University Fellow at the University of Leicester in the UK. Current field research involves Sicilian landscapes, as well as archaeological theory and philosophy. Publications include "Hunter-Gatherers in the History of Alterity," "Is Narrative Necessary?," and "Theory, Culture, Fashion." He is editor of *The Responsibilities of Archaeologists: Archaeology and Ethics* and co-editor of *Thinking through the Body: Archaeologies of Corporeality*. He is currently working with colleagues on a book exploring histories of central Sicily from the Bronze Age until the modern day.

SARAH POLLOCK directs the undergraduate journalism program at Mills College, where she also teaches nonfiction writing in the MFA program. She has worked as an editor, writer, and teacher for 30 years, including stints as senior editor at *Mother Jones* magazine and editor-in-chief at the California Academy of Sciences' natural history magazine (then called *Pacific Discovery*). She began her writing career as a daily newspaper reporter and has written many articles, essays, and book reviews for magazines and newspapers.

ADRIAN PRAETZELLIS has been professor of anthropology and director of the Anthropological Studies Center at Sonoma State University since 1992. His latest book, *Archaeological Theory in a Nutshell* (2015), is part of a continuing effort to get archaeologists to lighten up.

MARY PRAETZELLIS is associate director of the Anthropological Studies Center at Sonoma State University in California. There she works tirelessly to keep a dozen or so archaeologists employed full-time doing legally mandated archaeology in advance of development and training the next generation in a methodologically sound, ethically driven, research-focused archaeological practice. The team works throughout the West, and their work can be found in edited journals and publications and on the Center's website: http://www.sonoma.edu/asc/.

MELANIE SIMPKIN is a freelance choreologist and tutor at the Royal Academy of Dance in London. She is the author of original Benesh notation scores for ballets choreographed for the Royal Ballet and the Royal Opera (London) and American Repertory Ensemble (University of Texas). She is also co-editor of existing Benesh notation scores for the Royal Ballet and the Royal Academy of Dance.

JONATHAN T. THOMAS received his PhD from the University of Iowa's Department of Anthropology in May 2014 and works as a medical anthropologist and research scientist for the US federal government. He has published articles on the production and meaning of beads and pendants in Late Neolithic and Copper Age Iberia, the emergence of novel lithic technologies and symbolic objects during the transition from the Middle to the Late Stone Age in the Namib Desert, and archaeological epistemology. His most recent work, an interview with sociocultural anthropologist Sidney Mintz, appeared in *American Anthropologist* in September 2014. He is currently completing a book about the use of personal adornment to construct new types of social identities during the Neolithic.

RUTH TRINGHAM is professor in the Graduate School (anthropology) at the University of California, Berkeley. She is also the president and creative director of recently established nonprofit organization the Center for Digital Archaeology (CoDA). She has directed archaeological excavations in Southeast Europe and Turkey, most recently the BACH project at Çatalhöyük, whose final report was published in print as *The Last House on the Hill* in 2012 and its web edition in 2013. Her current research focuses on using digital primary archaeological data to create database narratives about the life-histories of people, places, and things and the multisensorial construction of prehistoric places.

JUDY TUWALETSTIWA is a visual artist and writer. Her books include *The Canyon Poem* (1997) and *Mapping Water* (2007). Her next book, on transformation in art, will be published by Radius in 2016. With her husband, Phillip, she is collaborating on a novel, *The Laughing Spiders*. She has served art residencies at University of Hawai'i, the Lannan Foundation, Pilchuck Glass School, and Bullseye Glass Company. William Siegal Gallery in Santa Fe represents her mixed media paintings.

PHILLIP TUWALETSTIWA is a member of the Hopi Tribe. He served for 24 years in the National Oceanic and Atmospheric Administration's Commissioned Corps, retiring as a captain. He and Judy lived on the Hopi Reservation for 12 years. During that time, he created the Hopi Land Information Office, mapping Hopi cultural and natural resources. He has done extensive work in archeo-astronomy in Chaco Canyon with the Solstice Project and is presently working with Mike Marshall on an archaeological alignment west of Chaco while collaborating with Judy on *The Laughing Spiders*.

RUTH M. VAN DYKE is a professor of anthropology at Binghamton University, SUNY. Her archaeological research addresses landscape, memory, representation, power, and phenomenology in the ancient North American Southwest. She is the author of *The Chaco Experience*, editor of *Practicing Materiality*, co-editor of *Archaeologies of Memory*, and author of numerous articles on Chaco Canyon and the ancient Southwest. She directs archaeological projects on the Chaco landscape in northwest New Mexico and on historic Alsatian immigration in Texas.

Page numbers in italics indicate illustrations.

authorship: archaeological, 56, 57–58, 59; role of, 60–67, 264
autofiction, 244
axes, Shang Dynasty, 227

Babi Yar massacre, 10
BACH project, 33, 51
Bak, Samuel, Holocaust paintings, 243
Baltimore, Lord, 147–48
Barthes, Roland: on death of the author, 62–63; on narrator subjectivity, 263–64
basketry, in Çatalhöyük Burial 634, 38–40
Beard, James, in Port Tobacco play, 155–57, 160
beliefs, imagining, 219
Bełżec, 17, 236, 237; excavation of, 238, 239
Benesh, Joan, 191
Benesh, Rudolf, 191
Benesh Movement Notation (BMN), 16, 191; of *Twenty Minutes Inside Out*, 193–213
Benigni, Roberto, *Life Is Beautiful*, 243
Binford, Lewis, 218; on post-processual archaeology, 129, 133
binocular vision, 16–17
BMN. *See* Benesh Movement Notation
Boardwalk Empire, 248
Bordes, François, 245
Bosnia, "Pyramids" in, 63, 64, 76–77(n1)
Brain, The, as Dead Women Do Tell Tales interface, 42
Breuil, Henri, 178, 179
Bronze Age, Korea, 225
Buchenwald, 238
burials: Çatalhöyük, 12, 38–40; Neolithic, 36–37

Cahokia, novels of, 172
California, Victorian era, 127
Calverts, 148
Carmean, Kelli, *Creekside*, 172, 175
Carsac, Francis, 245
Casa del Rio, 86, 87
Çatalhöyük, 6, 12, 33, 36
Çatalhöyük Research Project, 33, 51, 59
center place, symbolic visual and written language about, *103*, *104*, *120–21*
ceremonialism: Chacoan, 84–85; imagined narratives of, 86–88; Pueblo, 13–14
Chacoan outliers, 86, 89, 92–93

Chaco Canyon, 13; imagined narratives and, 86–88, 92–93, 283; landscape, 88–89; ritual at, 84–85, 90–92
Chakrabarty, Dipesh, on postcolonialism, 261
Chang, K. C., on shamansim and state formation, 229
character, for micro-histories, 37–38
chariots, Shang Dynasty, 228, 229
Chelmno, 17, 236, 237
Chesapeake Bay, European colonization of, 146–48
Chesapeake region, sedimentation in, 148–50, 151, 157–60, 161–63
Chiefdoms and Other Archaeological Delusions (Pauketat), 175
Childs, Craig, *House of Rain*, 172
Chimera Web, 6; constructing, 29–30
China: Late Neolithic, 17, 220, 221, 223–26; state formation in, 228–29
choreography, BMN notation system, 16, *193–213*
chronicle, Holocaust, 244
chronocentrism, 4
chronology: archaeological, 190; real time, 16, 189–90
civic engagement, through archaeology, 126–27
clarity, 14
Clifford, James, *Writing Culture*, 260
coherence, 9; in archaeological knowledge, 92–93
collaboration, 8, 68–69
colonialism, 72, 74
Colonial period (American), Chesapeake Bay, 146–48
comedy, 240, 241, 243
communities of interest, 68–69
concentration camps, Nazi, 237–38, 248
consequences, 8; of archaeological knowledge, 92, 93
constituencies: authority in, 66–67; Port Tobacco Archaeological Project, 160–61
context(s), 8, 71, 93
contextualization, of artifacts, 124–25
contingency, 66
contraceptive, Lysol as, 18, 248, *250*
copper industry, Ghassulian, 236
corn: and rain ceremonialism, 91, 92; symbol visual and written language of, *106–7*, *108–9*

correspondence, 9; in archaeological knowledge, 92–93
cosmology, Chacoan, 85
Coyote, symbolic visual and written language
of, *113*
creation, feathered serpent in, *103, 104–5*
Creekside: An Archaeological Novel (Carmean),
172, 175
Cricket Sings (King), 175
culture change, timescale and, 189–90

Dachau, 238
d'Agata, John: *About a Mountain*, 279, 282–83;
The Lifespan of a Fact, 278–79
Daisey, Mike, *The Agony and Ecstasy of Steve
Jobs*, 279
data, 9, 68; and imagined narratives, 18,
283–84; interpretation and, 127–28
database, Last House on the Hill, 33–36, 37,
42
Database Narrative, 30–32
Dead Women Do Tell Tales (DWdTT),
11–12; micro-histories in, 36–51
Deetz, Jim, as docudrama character, 14, 130,
131–33
demotic, 55, 73; archaeological authorship as,
65–67
desertification, Mediterranean, 72
diachronic violence, 262–63
dialogue, 65, 152; imagined, 15, 129, 130–40
Diamond, Jared, 173; *Guns, Germs, and Steel*,
265
diaries, Holocaust-related, 240
Dido (Çatalhöyük), micro-histories of, 38–40
digital technology, 6, 27, 56, 57; Chimera Web,
29–30
diktat, 8, 12, 55
docudrama, on storytelling, 124, 130–40
documents, 93, 240
Dominguez, Virginia, 172
Dongbei, Lady Hao and, 228
drama, 1, 2. *See also* plays
dualism, Pueblo cosmology, 85
DWdTT. *See* Dead Women Do Tell Tales

eagle, symbolic visual and written language
of, *103–4, 107*
Early Mesoamerican Village, The (Flannery),
251, 257–58

Early Neolithic: Asia, 17, 220, 221, 222–23;
Măgura, 190
Earth's Children (Auel), 172
East Asia, novels about, 16–17
electronic publishing, 2
Eminent Victorians (Strachey), 127
emplotment, 264; modes of, 240–41
Engendering Archaeology (Tringham), 258
English, colonization by, 146–47
environmental issues, Tidewater Maryland,
148–50, 156–63
Escalon, 86, *87*
ethics, 12–13, 69; of invented narratives, 278,
279–80; multivocal representation, 17–18;
text production, 67–68; of using past voices,
83–84
ethnicity, archaeological identification of, 220
ethnic violence, 66
ethnography, 93, 219, 259; Geertz on writing,
173–74
ethnonationalism, 66
Europe, Neolithic households in, 36
European Union, Sicily archaeological parks,
73
events, Holocaust, 244
experimental narratives, 3, 4
expository writing, 18

facilitators, 67; archaeologists as, 12, 59–60
facticity, 10
facts, 279; and fiction, 264–65, 283; of
Holocaust, 244
Fagan, Brian, 3, 220
Fajada Butte, *85*
fascism, in Sicily, 72–73
feasting, Chacoan, 85
feathered serpent, creation of, *103, 104–5*
Feature 634 (Çatalhöyük), micro-histories
of, 38–40
feminist perspectives, 181–82, 258
fertility, and rain ceremonialism, 91, 92
fiction, 1, 2, 172, 217; fact and, 264–65, 283; of
gendered archaeology, 218–19; Holocaust
narratives, 243–45; as informing devise,
101–2; purgative, 19–20
fictionalization, 265
fieldwork, intellectual dispersal of, 57
figurines. *See* Venus figurines
film, 1, 189, 243. *See also by name*

Fingal, Jim, *The Lifespan of a Fact*, 278–79
Flannery, Kent: *The Early Mesoamerican Village*, 251, 257–58; "The Golden Marshalltown," 175
flash fiction, 28
Florentine Codex, 5–6
Foucault, Michel, *The Order of Things*, 263
fragments, 28, 38
Friedlander, Saul: *Nazi Germany and the Jews*, 251; *Probing the Limits of Presentation—Nazism and the "Final Solution,"* 242
frogs: Pueblo water ceremonialism, 91–92; symbolic visual and written language about, 119–*21*

gas chambers, archaeological evidence of, 239–40
Gear, W. Michael and Kathleen O'Neal, *People of the* series, 172
Geertz, Clifford, *Works and Lives,* 170, 173–74
Gemarah, 5, 246
gender, gender theory, 218–19, 220, 229
Georgetown, sedimentation at, 149–50
Göbekli Tepe, 10
"Golden Marshalltown, The" (Flannery), 175
Gottschalk, L. C., sedimentation studies, 148–49, 150, 151
Gradowski, Salman, 240
Gravettian culture, 177
Great Britain, colonialism, 147
Griffin, James B., 218
ground penetrating radar, as novel trope, 225
Guns, Germs, and Steel (Diamond), 265
Guthrie, R. Dale, 180

Hager, Lori, on Feature 634 burial, 39, 40
Hanson, John, in Port Tobacco play, 154–55, 157–59, 161, 162
Hao, Lady: archaeological evidence and novelization of, 220, 221, 226–29; as shaman, 229–30
Henry, Patrick, on sedimentation, 150, 161
hermeneutics, in post-processual archaeology, 258
historical archaeology, 14, 163, 239–40
histories, 20, 58, 69, 264; database narratives and, 30–32; emplotment in, 240–41; global, 265–66; Holocaust, 242–43; landscape, 71,

72–74; micro-, 12, 28; recombinant, 11, 28, 36, 40, 42
historiography, 6–7, 32, 264
Hitler, Ein Film aus Deutschland (film), 243, 252
Hitt, Jack, on Kennewick Man, 173
Holocaust, 17–18; academic study of, 242–43; alternative narratives of, 243–51; archaeology of, 237–40, 262; representation and narration of, 236, 241–42, 251–52, 264
Holocaust deniers, archaeology and, 245
Holtorf, Cornelius, on public context of narratives, 63–64
Honeyman, John, 163
Hongshan culture, 220, 221; at Niuheliang, 223–24; pigs in, 224–25
Hopi, 13, 102; rain ceremonialism, 91, 92; symbolic visual and written language of, *103–21*
Hopitutsqua (Hopi Land), 103
horses: in China, 225, 228, 229
households, Neolithic, 5, 6, 36–37
House of Rain (Childs), 172
houses, Neolithic, 30
human evolution, 219
humor, 124
hyperlinking, 31
hypermedia, 6, 7–8, 13
hypertexts, 1, 5, 30, 93
hypothetico-deductive approach, 145

imagination, 9, 10, 37; in archaeological knowledge, 15, 145–46; and data, 283–84; disciplined, 281, 282; fact vs. fiction in, 19–20
individuals, 60, 266
information, accessibility of, 70
Inner Mongolia, Lady Hao and, 228
Internet, 56, 64
interpretation, 217, 218; and data, 127–28; reconstruction and, 172–73
invention, 278; in archaeology, 9–10, 20; new narrative forms, 284–85
Iraq, 74

Jade Dragon (Nelson), 17, 220, 221; themes and characters in, 223–26
Jade Phoenix, The (Nelson), 17, 220, 221; themes and characters in, 226–30
Jealousy (Robbe-Grillet), 268–69

multimedia projects, 3, 283–84
multivocality, 65, 236, 246; of Holocaust representations, 17–18, 236
Mystery of Chaco Canyon, The (film), 13

narration, 19, 264; chronologically ordered, 267–68
narratives, 6, 18, 27, 66, 73, 74, 75, 217, 278; alternative, 174–83, 241–42, 243–51, 252; archaeological, 265–67; archaeological subjects of, 10–11; database, 30–32; Dead Women Do Tell Tales, 43–50(table); editorial guidelines for, 284–85; historical, 264–65; imagined, 13, 15–16, 83, 86–88, 93–94; interpretive, 127–28; micro-, 12; as micro-histories, 28–29; media and sources of, 43–50(table); public context of, 63–64; standard archaeological, 19–20; true vs. imagined, 283; voice in, 176–77. *See also* vignettes
narrators: omniscient, 176–77, 258–60; subjectivity of, 263
Nazi extermination camps, 10, 17–18, 237; archaeology of, 235, 236, 238–40; fictional narratives of, 243–45; nonfiction narratives of, 245–51
Nazi Germany and the Jews (Friedlander), 251
Nelson, Sarah Milledge: *Jade Dragon*, 17, 220, 221, 223–26; *The Jade Phoenix*, 17, 220, 221, 226–30; *Spirit Bird Journey*, 17, 220–23, 225
Neolithic: Chimera Web, 6, 30; novels about, 17, 221
new pragmatism, 259
Night (Wiesel), 243–44
Niuheliang, 223–24
nonfiction, 279; creative, 1, 2, 3, 18–19, 172–73, 284; Holocaust, 243–44, 245–51
North Carolina, 147
notation systems, choreographic, 16, 191. *See also* Benesh Movement Notation
nouveau roman, 18; concept of, 267–69; past in, 269–70
novels, 1, 3, 16–17, 172, 219; Clara Alden series, 220–30; artifacts used in, 222–23; *The Laughing Spiders*, 103–21; subjects of, 217–18
"Novels of Cahokia" (Whittaker), 172, 174

objectification, objectivism: in archaeology, 217–18, 235–36; in novels, 220
objectivity, 58, 60

objects, 268. *See also* artifacts
open-access, 56
Operation Reinhardt, 237
Opovo project, 6, 36; Chimera Web and, 29–30
oracle bones, Shang Dynasty, 226, 228
oral history, Hopi, 102
Order of Things, The (Foucault), 263
Ordinary Affects (Stewart), 27–28
Ortner, Sherry, 262
Osanni, 223
Other: dialogic, 8; past, 260–63

paintings, 1; Holocaust, 243
palaces, Shang Dynasty, 227–28
paleoporn, 180–81
Papua New Guinea, Jared Diamond on, 173
participants, 59–60
passive voice, use of, 170, 176, 259
past(s), 57, 264; fictionalizing, 269–70; as present, *114–21*
Patuxent River, 163
Pauketat, Timothy, *Chiefdoms and Other Archaeological Delusions*, 175
peasants, Sicilian, 73
Peñasco Blanco, *88–89*
People of the series (Gear and Gear), 172
performance, narrative as, 66
Pergamon Museum, Assurnasirpal II exhibit, 262
phenomenological archaeology, 89; sensory engagement in, 90–92
pigs, in Hongshan culture, 224–25
pilgrimage: to Chaco Canyon, 84, 89; Hopi, *119–21*; imagined, 86–88, 92–93
place, 125, 127
play, 4, 124
plays, 1, 14–15; docudrama, 124, 130–40; Port Tobacco, 153–59
playwriting, 151; methodology in, 152–53, 159–65
plot, for micro-histories, 37–38
Poland, Nazi extermination camps in, 237
politics, 74; archaeology as, 61–62; cultural, 70, 75
polyphony, 246
pornography, Venus figurines as, 180–81
Port Tobacco, 15, 146, 148, 149, 160, 163, 164–65; play about, 153–59